SLAUGHTER
OVER SICILY

SLAUGHTER OVER SICILY

by
Charles Whiting

Pen & Sword
MILITARY

First published in Great Britain in 1992, reprinted in 2006 by
Pen & Sword Military
An imprint of
Pen & Sword Books Ltd
47 Church Street
Barnsley
South Yorkshire
S70 2AS

ISBN 1 84415 342 8

A CIP catalogue record for this book is
available from the British Library

Printed and bound in England
By CPI UK

Pen & Sword Books Ltd incorporates the Imprints of Pen & Sword Aviation,
Pen & Sword Maritime, Pen & Sword Military, Wharncliffe Local history,
Pen & Sword Select, Pen & Sword Military Classics and Leo Cooper.

For a complete list of Pen & Sword titles please contact
PEN & SWORD BOOKS LIMITED
47 Church Street, Barnsley, South Yorkshire, S70 2AS, England
E-mail: enquiries@pen-and-sword.co.uk
Website: www.pen-and-sword.co.uk

CONTENTS

Acknowledgements
Preface

I THE WAR IN THE SHADOWS
1. The Secret Invaders
2. Husky Is Born
3. Operation Mincemeat
4. The Mafia Connection
5. The Führer Swallows The Mincemeat

II THE GREAT PLAN
1. Red Devils And All-Americans
2. 'Enter The Little Fart'
3. Operation Buzzard
4. Countdown

III SLAUGHTER OVER SICILY
1. First Blood
2. Dirty Dancing
3. The Battle Of The Biazza Ridge
4. Slaughter In The Sky

IV END RUN
1. 'A Bridge Too Far'
2. 'Happy Birthday'
3. The Poor Bloody Infantry
4. The Reckoning

Envoi
Bibliography
Index

ACKNOWLEDGEMENTS

I should like to thank a dozen or so newspapers in the United States which helped me with my inquiries. In particular I am indebted to *Buffalo News, Boston Globe, Hartford Courant, WWII Magazine, Syracue Herald American, Albany Times-Union, Rochester Gannett, Philadelphia Inquirer, St Louis Post Dispatch, L.A. Times, Atlanta Journal, Dallas Morning News, Miami Herald, Denver Post, San Francisco Chronicle, Washington Post* and the *New York Times*.

I am also indebted to the many who responded to my 'Author's Inquiry'. Here I would like to single out James Wallace, R. D. Cox, R. D. Miller, Marty Finkelstein, E. H. Wallace, R. Haener, 1st Sgt Howard P Melvin (1st Sgt fifty years ago and his letterhead still bearing the proud motto '*Airborne! All the Way*').

As usual, I cannot express my debt of gratitude to Professor 'Hobie' Morris, Springfield N.Y. and Tom Dickinson and Hy Schoor of New York City, who came up trumps as always. Thanks, all of you.

C.W.
York, 1992.

What they thought or wrote *privately* at the time:
'I do not believe in the airborne division.' General Eisenhower, July, 1943.
'The glider operation on D-Day failed badly.' General Montgomery, July, 1943.
'As far as I can see if anyone is blameable, it must be myself.' General Patton, July, 1943.
'The lessons now learned could have been driven home in no other way... the losses are part of the inevitable price of war in human life.' General Ridgway, commander of 82nd Airborne Division, July, 1943.
'An utter fiasco.' Colonel Chatterton, commander of the British Glider Pilot Regiment.

What they said *publicly*:
'The airborne operation speeded up my drive by seven days.' General Montgomery.
'Despite the original miscarriage, Colonel Gavin's initial parachute assault speeded our ground advance by 48 hours.' General Patton.
'Our losses were inexcusably high... But, in spite of all this, the airborne troops contributed markedly to success in both the American and British sectors.' General Eisenhower.

PREFACE

As they lifted off for that bold plunge into the unknown in February, 1991, the 'Screaming Eagles' of the US 101st Airborne Division knew they had a lot to prove. They had their unit pride in their victories on D-Day in Normandy, the Arnhem drop and the final dash to capture Hitler's lair in the Second World War. They also carried the stigma of the Vietnam defeat nearly twenty years before. As one of them, Texan 1st Sergeant Luftwich, a veteran of that defeat, told the Press, 'This is a chance to put the Vietnam stigma behind me, and my troops will never have to put up with it.' Another member of his company, his sights firmly rooted in the present, told the correspondents waiting for the choppers to lift off, 'We would walk through the gates of hell if we knew we were going home!'

Then the signal flares started to rise above the armada of over 300 helicopters. It was time to go. There was the howl of the starter motors, the first hesitant flutter of the rotors and the sudden ear-splitting burst into full power. One by one, their red lights winking, the airborne armada rose into the sky, twenty-two of them being piloted by women. Their bold dash into the unknown, miles behind Saddam Hussein's huge Iraqi Army, had begun. As the 'Screaming Eagles' spokesman said, adding yet another dubious word to the '100 Hour War's' lexicon, 'This is a bold bodacious action!'

'Bodacious' it was. The plan was for a two-pronged fly-in, covered by Apache attack choppers. One group would land in the desert sixty miles inside Kuwait to set up a massive instant fuel and supply depot. At the same time another 6,000 airborne troopers would land in Iraq itself, some hundred miles within the enemy country.

Naturally the men were nervous. Most of them had never been in action before. Ahead was the dangerous business of abseiling from their choppers while the Iraqis took potshots at them. Then, once they had established themselves deep behind the enemy lines, they would have to withstand all the enemy could throw at them until the ground forces linked up with them. All of them had been schooled in airborne lore. They knew of the tragedy at Arnhem nearly half a century before. Could the same fate overtake them if the link-up with the ground forces didn't reach them before they were attacked by Saddam Hussein's Republican Guards?

To east and west of the 101st Airborne its running mate, the 82nd Airborne Division, was already deep into action. One group had gone with the French armoured brigade, slicing through an entire Iraqi division 'like a knife through butter', as the exuberant French commander General Michel Roquejeoffre described it. In the process they had already taken 3,000 enemy prisoners.

The 82nd Airborne's other group had carried out the traditional role of an airborne outfit. It had dropped by parachute into an area south-west of Occupied Kuwait City itself. Two years before, these same 'All Americans', as the 82nd was nicknamed, had experienced street fighting when they had cleaned out Panama City, locked in combat with General Noriega's paramilitary 'Integrity Battalions'. Now the young paratroopers expected to have to carry out the same task. For Saddam Hussein's troops had reportedly turned the capital into an armed fortress, with armour concealed in the city's houses and anti-aircraft guns positioned on all high-rise buildings.

So these brave young men went into battle just as their grandfathers, the pioneers of airborne warfare, had done nearly half a century before. But, well versed as they were in unit tradition and airborne lore, they were unaware that a mere two years after the US Army had set up its first parachute infantry battalion, a top-level decision had almost been taken in Washington to disband the two airborne divisions. In July, 1943, the Supreme Commander in Europe, General Eisenhower, had written to his boss, General Marshall, in Washington, 'I do not believe in the airborne division'. Shocked by what had happened in America's first campaign on European soil, Eisenhower felt that the US Army's existing four airborne divisions should be broken up. He had powerful support in the nation's capital. General Lesley McNair, the US Army's Commander of Ground Forces, wrote: 'My staff and I have become convinced of the impracticality of handling large airborne units.' He was prepared to 'recommend to the War Department that airborne divisions be abandoned... and that the airborne effort be restricted to parachute units of battalion size or smaller.'

What had happened to bring about this complete re-thinking of official US policy? Why was Washington suddenly thinking of breaking up these highly-trained, all-volunteer parachute divisions, which one day would form that same XVIII Airborne Corps, which half a century later beat the Iraqis in Kuwait? How had the first US Airborne Division, the 82nd, failed in its first battle? What had gone wrong in the airborne invasion of the island of Sicily by the 82nd and its comrades of the British 1st Airborne Division, the same one which had been slaughtered at Arnhem a year later?

Not one of the four airborne operations which took place over the first four days of the invasion of Sicily was a success. Two were downright fiascos, which resulted in great loss of life due to 'friendly fire' and sudden panic, perhaps even cowardice, on the part of the pilots taking the airborne into action. When the planes, bearing the cargoes of dead and dying paratroopers, started arriving back at their bases in North Africa, Brigadier Hackett, 'that broken-down cavalryman', as he always called himself, had to confine the remaining troops and surviving glider pilots of the British 1st Airborne Division to camp in order to avoid a mass 'slugfest' with the US pilots.

Accusations and counter-accusations flew back and forth. The Army blamed the Navy for the tragedy. The Navy blamed the Air Force. The Air Force, in its turn, blamed *both* the Army and the Navy. Montgomery, the British commander, laid the blame fairly and squarely on the American pilots. So did the Divisional Commander of the 1st Airborne, 'Hoppy' Hopkinson. He was killed a month later in Italy, still bitter about what he felt was the cowardice of the American pilots. Ridgway, the commander of the 82nd Airborne, felt the fiasco was caused by faulty airborne planning at Eisenhower's HQ. He saw the chief culprit in General 'Boy' Browning, the elegant ex-guardsman and husband of the romantic novelist Daphne du Maurier, who was the Supreme Commander's senior airborne adviser.

For Colonel Frost, the commander of the 2nd Parachute Battalion, and perhaps the most outstanding parachute commander of World War Two, the valuable talents of his volunteer soldiers had been squandered by incompetent staff officers. As he wrote long afterwards, 'It was yet another humiliating disaster for the airborne forces and almost enough to destroy even the most ardent believer's faith'.

Colonel Gavin of the 82nd Airborne, perhaps Frost's only rival as the outstanding paratroop leader of the War, was so soured and bitter about the whole thing that he wrote to his daughter at the time, 'When this war ends, I think I would like to be a curate in an out-of-the-way pastorate with nothing to do but care for the flowers and meditate on the wickedness of the world.'

Naturally at the time −July, 1943− the airborne assault on Sicily was heralded as a great victory, an outstanding success for this new weapon of war. As the *Daily Telegraph* correspondent, for example, wrote at the time: 'At 10.15 on Friday night, five hours before the assault forces were disembarked on the beaches, gliders filled with troops came down on the

3

Sicilian mainland, and swiftly and silently began their task of disrupting Axis preparation for meeting the invasion. An hour and ten minutes later paratroops were dropped from the skies under cover of darkness.... The enemy seems to have been taken by surprise, for the airborne troops were practically over their Sicilian targets before any flak was encountered. The Allied planes lost in this manoeuvre are officially described as "negligible".' Even as the *Daily Telegraph*'s special correspondent, Ronald Legge, wrote that dispatch, the commander of the British 1st Airborne, General Hopkinson, was swimming for his life in the Mediterranean and Colonel Gavin, commanding the 82nd's first wave of parachutists, was groping his way through a blacked-out Sicily accompanied only by six men out of the three thousand or more 'All Americans' who had been dropped an hour before.

American parachutists were scattered over the whole of Sicily; and not only over Sicily. Some landed in Sardinia, in Malta, and even in the mountains of Southern Italy where their mouldering skeletons were found many years later. Gliders and towing planes were shot down by the score by friendly guns. Gliders were ditched miles out to sea, with over three hundred men drowning even before they had spotted their objective. There was worse to come the following night, with the assistant divisional commander of the 82nd Airborne being shot by his own side and a whole parachute regiment virtually disappearing.

As Colonel Frost wrote years later, 'Although the press at the time was complimentary and made out that many wonderful feats of arms had been achieved, it is doubtful whether this airborne operation had any effect on the success achieved by the initial landing from the sea.' Montgomery was even blunter. In his diary he commented laconically on two of the four airborne ops which were carried out by the 1st Airborne Division. 'The glider operation... failed badly,' he wrote, adding that the parachute operation 'also failed'.

'The big lesson,' he wrote at the time, 'is that we must not be dependent on American transport aircraft, with pilots that are inexperienced in operational flying; our airborne troops are too good and too scarce to be wasted.' For, as Montgomery saw it, 'the [American] pilots... were frightened off their job by the flak.'

Naturally the survivors were proud of their achievements in Sicily. As General Gavin wrote forty years after the event, 'Our young paratroops in combat for the first time stood up to the panzers, fought them to a standstill and drove them from the battlefield.' Undoubtedly British survivors of those early airborne battles would share the same sentiments.

Unfortunately those sentiments were far from the truth. What happened to the Anglo-American airborne in Sicily was military suicide. Hundreds of young men died bravely with few positive results to show for their bravery. In the end it was the 'straight-legs', as the paratroopers of the 82nd called the ordinary footsloggers, who took the paratroopers' objectives or held the main weight of the German counter-attacks: the nameless 'PBI' (Poor Bloody Infantry) of the US 1st Division and the British 5th and 50th Divisions.

The airborne attack on Sicily was a scandal that was hushed up for decades. It taught urgent military lessons that were never learnt, at least by Montgomery. The result, a year later, was Arnhem. But the airborne attack on Sicily placed the whole future of large-scale airborne formations at risk. Only the unlikely intervention of General Douglas MacArthur on the other side of the world, engaged in one of his usual publicity stunts that September of 1943, saved the US airborne divisions from being disbanded.

Today young men of many nations around the world are proud to wear the distinctive red beret of the paratrooper. It is the symbol of the elite, a sign of male boldness and daring, the ultimate macho image. Few of these young men know, however, that fifty years ago the whole concept of airborne forces seemed doomed.

This book tells the story of that first airborne D-Day of World War Two — a great opportunity which turned into a bitter victory.

I

THE WAR IN THE SHADOWS

And many more Destructions played
In this ghastly masquerade.
All disguised, even to the eyes,
Like Bishops, lawyers, peers or spies.

Shelley.

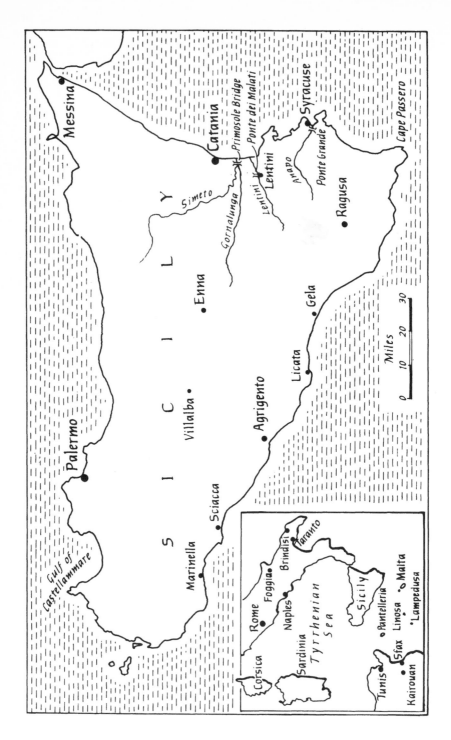

1

THE SECRET INVADERS

The searchlights which had been sweeping the bay for the last fifteen minutes went out abruptly. The plane which had criss-crossed the water at the same time, periodically dropping flares, seemed to have vanished too. Once more the distant shoreline was dead. Nothing stirred. Not a light shone. The Italians, it seemed, had given up on them. It was safe to continue. Lt-Commander Teacher, RN, who had already won the DSO for bravery in action, nodded to his young 'paddler', Lt Cooper, 'All right,' he whispered. 'Let's go'.

Together the two men, clad in outsized rubber suits so that they looked like the Michelin men of the pre-war advertisements of the French tyre company, pushed their canoe from the deck of the submarine into the water. They waited a moment. Then, as the canoe rose on the swell, they jumped in. Almost immediately the submarine which had brought them from Malta began to back away. Within minutes the hum of its dynamos had faded into nothingness. Now the two naval officers were alone on the night sea, paddling steadily towards the enemy coast.

A quarter of an hour later they began to hear the roar of the breaking surf. The swell was becoming nasty. A sudden wind was whipping it up to a white fury. For a while they shipped paddles and concentrated on baling out the canoe with their tin mugs. Within minutes Cooper was panting hard and his teeth had started chattering in the winter cold. But Teacher kept up a cracking pace. Fighting both wind and water, they crept ever closer to the Italian-held shore.

Now they were approaching the surf, a jagged bubbling line of angry water. To their right they could just see the dark outline of the little port of Marinella. No light showed. Not even a dog barked. The natives were fast asleep at this time of the night. But Cooper thought he saw a sentry on the beach. He hissed an urgent warning. Teacher told him his eyes were playing tricks on him. There was no Italian out there. They pushed on.

About a hundred yards from the shore Teacher tapped his young paddler on the shoulder and whispered, 'I'll go in here.'

Cooper nodded. Exerting all his strength, he tried to hold the canoe with its bow to the shore while Teacher pulled on the top half of his rubber suit. Now only the Commander's blackened face was visible. Gently he lowered himself into the water and started to swim for the beach. Cooper strained his eyes to follow Teacher's progress but in a few seconds he had vanished.

Three hours later, at four o'clock that February morning in 1943, the submarine HMS *Unbending* started ploughing its way through a lively sea towards the point of rendezvous with the canoe. On the bridge next to the skipper two ratings operated the brand new secret homing device. While one rating flashed the infra-red light in a wide arc, the other scanned the receiving screen. Green spots on it would indicate the presence of the canoe. Once they were spotted, the other rating could turn his beam in that direction. But the screen remained blank and there was no reply to the transmitter clicking out the canoe's morse signal. The two officers and their canoe seemed to have vanished.

The skipper started to grow worried. Time was running out fast. Dawn came early in the Mediterranean. Aloud he said, 'I'll give them another half an hour. Then we'll go to the outer rendezvous.' He meant a second rendezvous spot about six miles out to sea. The spot had been agreed upon earlier in case the submarine and canoe missed each other at the first rendezvous.

It was about then that one of the ratings operating the infra-red homing device cried, 'I think I've got them, sir! Fine on the port bow.'

The skipper peered through his night glass. Yes, there was something out there. He ordered a change of course. The boat's electric motors rose in pitch as they headed for the spot. Minutes later the canoe hove into sight and the recovery men waited on the submarine's deck to haul the canoe on board. All of them realized how dangerous it was to remain on the surface a moment longer than necessary. 'Christ,' one of them said, as they got their first look at the little craft in the water below, 'there's only *one* of them!'

Exhausted and gasping like a stranded fish, Cooper was taken below and put in the torpedo compartment. Above him the klaxon sounded. The submarine began to dive as the officers rapped out their orders.

Meanwhile the exhausted Cooper had been given half a mug of rum and was able to gasp out what he knew. 'I never saw the old man again,' he panted. 'Not from the moment he left the canoe. Not a sign. I went in as close to the surf as I could. It wasn't any good.'

'Hear anything ashore?' one of the men asked.

Cooper shook his head, 'Not a bloody thing.'

That was that. The most secret unit in the whole of the British Armed Forces had suffered its first casualty in the very first phase of this new undercover campaign.

The Royal Navy's Combined Operations Pilotage Parties (COPPs) – a deliberately misleading designation – had been set up the year before by Lt-Commander Willmott, a regular naval officer. Against a great deal of opposition, he had managed to get the Royal Navy to agree that his COPPs would be very useful in the reconnaissance of enemy beaches prior to a landing. His men were all volunteers, recruited from both navy and army. Each two-man COPP canoe team was made up of an officer, who acted as navigator, and, usually, an other rank commando, who acted as the paddler. All of them, officers and men, had to be first-class fighters, canoeists and swimmers. (They trained by swimming naked in the Solent in winter!)

Carried by submarine to within three or four miles of the enemy coast, they would disembark and paddle their canoe to within reach of the beach they were to reconnoitre. While the paddler kept the canoe in position, the navigator went overboard in a primitive rubber wet suit to scout the shallows and the beach itself.

The COPPs' main function, apart from noting beach defences, was to measure the beach's gradient. This was a vital piece of information needed for the planners to ensure that the assault craft did not lodge on some sand bar out to sea at the mercy of the enemy's guns. The gradient was measured by means of a thin fishing line, leaded at every ten yards. The line was wound round a reel worn on the navigator's waist. By walking and swimming backwards away from the beach, he took the measurements of the gradient, noting the details on a plastic pad carried on his forearm.

It was a slow, nerve-racking and dangerous business, especially as most beaches in Occupied Europe were now guarded and patrolled regularly. But that had not deterred Willmott's volunteers. They had already done sterling work at Rhodes and in scouting beaches in North Africa, prior to the Anglo-American invasion in November, 1942.

But Willmott knew it was vital to keep the presence of his little unit secret from the enemy. Once they learned of the 'secret invaders', as his men liked to call themselves, the enemy would take special measures to be on the lookout for them on any beach they felt was threatened. He knew it was important not to let even fellow servicemen know that such a unit as the COPP existed. He dressed his men up in a mixture of army and naval uniforms. For instance they wore army khaki, but naval epaulettes and caps. It was unorthodox and was frowned upon by the Brass, but it worked.

Used to strange receptions from more orthodox military units, the first

COPP teams, under the command of Lt-Commander Teacher, dispatched to Malta for this new operation, were caught completely by surprise when they landed there. Hardly had their dusty Dakota, flying from North Africa, touched down when a bunch of excited medical orderlies surrounded them and bundled the puzzled COPP men into sealed trucks. In these they were transported to the Island's Rigi Hospital and rushed into the isolation ward. In vain they protested to the surgeon commander in charge. He was adamant. He told them, 'I've had a signal from Algiers. You are all classed as smallpox suspects.' He then told them they would have to stay in isolation until tests had cleared them.

But the surgeon commander did not know the calibre of the men he had imprisoned. To while away the time they organized races with a wheelchair they found in the ward. The idea was to see who could do the fastest lap round the ward. Captain Burbridge, a Canadian, was going all out when the surgeon commander opened the door. Startled, he fell into the Canadian's lap and together they flew through the door and down the corridor to collapse in a heap at the far end. Thereafter the hospital and the smallpox suspects parted company very rapidly.

A few days later Lt-Commander Teacher was ordered to report to the Commander of the 10th Submarine Flotilla at Valletta. The Captain told Teacher, 'We need three of your teams for the next dark period [the period of relatively moonless nights]. Have you everything ready?'

'As ready as it can be, sir,' Teacher answered.

Then the Commander let him into the great secret, one known only to a handful of specially picked men, who bore the codename 'Bigot'. Now that the fighting in North Africa was virtually over, the Allies were planning a return to Europe. 'It's Sicily,' he said. 'The Force Commander wants reports on three sections. They cover a lot of the south coast.'

He went on to explain that three submarines would be placed at the disposal of the COPPs – HMS *United*, *Unrivalled*, and *Unbending*. Another submarine, HMS *Safari*, was on its way from North Africa, bringing another COPP team from there to help them. Teacher was to go back to his base and organize the teams that would be taken out from Malta to Sicily by submarine.

On 27 February, 1943, they had set off for Sicily. Right from the start their mission seemed jinxed. They were spotted by enemy aircraft while they were on the surface. Fishing boats had made their approach more dangerous. Then, when they finally reached the area of operations, they had found that the Italian blackout – they usually worked at night – was lousy. Their targets were too well illuminated for them to make a safe approach. Now their first reconnaissance had ended in tragedy, with Teacher either drowned or a prisoner.

On the night after Teacher's disappearance Captain Burbridge went in to look for him, on the off chance that he might still be alive and at liberty. To no avail. He found no trace and no body. Teacher had to be written off.

But the surveying had to continue. Next day Burbridge and a companion went in again, fighting their way through rough surf to land on an isolated beach and begin their survey. Staking their survey lines to the wet sand and shingle, the two back-paddled into the sea, sounding out the beach gradient until they were two hundred yards from the shore. All the time they kept their eyes fixed anxiously on the stretch of wet sand, for the beach was alive with the dark outlines of sentries. At every seventy-five yards, there was one of the enemy silhouetted against the night sky.

What did it mean, they asked themselves. Had Teacher's body been found? Or had he been captured and made to talk by Italy's feared OVRA, the secret police whose reputation for torture was worse than that of the Gestapo?

But they weren't discovered and next night another team went in. For five nights the COPP teams kept up their nerve-racking work. Then, on 4 March Captain Burbridge, with Lieutenant Cooper, who had been Teacher's paddler on that first ill-fated mission, set off on another survey. The night was windy, but the sea was calm. Their mission that night was to sound out the beach just outside the small Sicilian port of Sciacca. The two young officers said the usual goodbyes and vanished into the night as the submarine backed off and submerged.

Three hours later HMS *Unbending* surfaced at the rendezvous point. No Burbridge or Cooper. For an hour the two ratings with the infra-red homing device searched the surface of the sea. Nothing was revealed. Finally the sub's skipper ordered the craft to make for the outer rendezvous. There the submarine again surfaced and waited.

Then as the sky to the east started to flush the first white of the false dawn, the skipper decided he could risk his vessel on the surface no longer. He gave orders to sail for Malta. The Teacher Number Three COPP team had lost all three officers, and, without the skilled navigators, the paddlers alone were no use. Others would have to continue the work of those first ill-fated secret invaders.

At Allied Headquarters in Algiers the planners, secreted away in a discreet hotel room, were desperate for information about Sicily. Since the first Teacher team had been sent out, fresh beaches had been decided upon. Thus a week later COPP 4 was conveyed to Sicily by HMS *Safari*. Again the deadly game against the elements and the enemy began. The first team twice escaped disaster, but the second one, made up of a Sapper officer, Captain Edward Parsons, and his paddler, Seaman Irvine, didn't. In vain Commander Ben Bryant of the *Safari* tried to raise the team. Then, while lying submerged off the north coast of Sicily, a signal informed the skipper that an enemy message had been picked up reporting a British sub in the Gulf of Castellamare.

'Now how would they know about us?' he asked one of the underwater reconnaissance team.

The man suggested the Italians had picked up the sound of the *Safari's* engines.

Commander Bryant dismissed the suggestion.

The other man then voiced his own doubts. 'Perhaps they've caught Parsons and Irvine?'

'Afraid it looks like it. And Parsons has spun them a cover story about landing from a sub for sabotage.'

Both men hoped he was right. Otherwise the whole operation might be in jeopardy. But they had no time to ponder the matter. At the same instant the lookout at the periscope yelled, 'E-Boat!'

The Skipper sprang to the tube and peered through the circle of calibrated glass.

There it was. A fast German speedboat cut through the waves, a wake of white water hurtling high in the air behind her; and, above, a German flying boat circled, obviously giving the E-boat skipper directions.

'*Dive, dive, dive!*' Bryant yelled, as the klaxons rang. The long game of cat-and-mouse had begun.*

While the *Safari* attempted to elude its pursuers, the losses among the other COPP teams mounted steadily. The submarine *Unrivalled* lost all its COPP teams. Captain John Stevens of the *Unruffled*, a flamboyant character who had been called '*Henri Huit*' because of his bulk, ginger beard and huge appetite when he had served with the French earlier in the war, lost half of his. In the *Safari* only two out of thirteen canoeists returned to Malta. But, with headquarters pressing for ever more information, there were always more brave volunteers ready to carry out this lethal reconnaissance.

Bob Smith, a young naval lieutenant, and his paddler Brand were two such men. Launched by the submarine *United*, they were sounding the area around the fishing village of Gela, one day to be of vital importance to Patton and his Seventh Army, when they ran into a sandbar. They set about charting it with German sentries patrolling the beach so close that sometimes they could hear them calling out to each other in the darkness.

---

* The submarine escaped in the end, but, as Commander Bryant had guessed, both Parsons and Seaman Irvine were captured. Interrogated by the Italians, they 'told more barefaced lies', as one of them said after the war, 'in the next 24 hours than they had told in their whole lives before.'

Their real enemy, however, was not the Germans but the weather, and as the night wore on it began to worsen. By midnight the wind whistling across the sea was whipping up the waves into a fury. Freezing spray lashed the men's faces as they carried out their mission. Time and again their frail craft threatened to overturn as they fought to keep the canoe's bow into the wind.

At last they mapped the sandbank and set out once again for their rendezvous with the *United*. But once out of the relative shelter of the bay, they met the full fury of the gale. Desperately they fought to keep their craft afloat. Finally they reached the rendezvous. Urgently they flashed their signal, as the waves rolled them up and down into the troughs. No answer. In despair they ignited a signal flare. Again no reply. Doggedly they hung on, hoping the sub would spot them soon. Then tragedy struck. There was a loud crack. Brand's paddle had snapped in half. There was no time for finesse now. They couldn't survive long in this kind of sea with one paddle and they knew it. They threw caution to the winds. They flashed a bright beam of white light directly out to sea, praying that they would be spotted this time. But the horizon remained defiantly empty. The *United* had failed to make the rendezvous.

At eight that morning, despondent and very tired, Smith said, 'Either we go inshore and give ourselves up or we bloody well paddle for Malta.' Before the teams set out for Sicily, they had always joked: 'If you don't find your sub, you can always paddle back!' Then it had seemed just like any other piece of gallows humour. Now it seemed to be grim reality, for Smith could see that Brand didn't like the idea of surrendering one bit.

'How far is it?' he asked, wielding his paddle to keep them from overturning.

'About seventy miles,' Smith replied. 'What do you say? Look what she's stood up to already.'

Brand nodded his head. 'All right,' he said firmly. 'Let's have a bash.' He dug in his paddle, while Smith fished out his escape map and started to plot a route.

Smith took a course bearing on the distant cone of Mount Etna, then after a breakfast of biscuit and chocolate, they set off. Taking turns in baling out and paddling, they pushed on, fighting mountainous seas, living from one minute to the next, their whole world the grey sky and the green sea.

Hour after hour they fought the waves. Once they heard the faint hum of a plane. The noise of its motor grew louder. Then it passed overhead and unseen in the grey murk of the sky. They had not been spotted. The Italian patrol plane passed into the distance and they continued the back-breaking work of baling, paddling, steering, both men knowing instinctively that once they stopped and rested they would never start again.

Twenty hours later they were still at it. Smith's arms felt as if they were on fire and Brand had opened up an old hip wound. Again the gale hit them. The waves tossed them up and down, threatening to overturn the flimsy little craft at any moment.

An hour after sunset, fresh tragedy struck. A great wave slammed into the canoe and tore a large rent in the stern canopy. Then, just after midnight, the nightmare started to come to an end. The wind dropped. The howl gave way to a whine and finally to a soft moan. At last the sea was calm and they were able to relax, but somehow they kept on going.

Another dawn flushed the sky to the east. Through narrowed eyes, their faces burned brick-red by the wind and the salt water, their eyelids rimmed with salt, they stared unbelievingly to their front. On the horizon there was a dark smudge. For what seemed an age they could not seem to comprehend what it was until finally Smith croaked, 'Look at that! Will you look at that!'

It was Malta!

All that day they paddled through the calm sea towards the dark smudge. By early afternoon they knew they were saved. In the distance they could see the sleek grey shape of a motor torpedo boat heading straight for them.

Smith lugged out their sole weapon, a Tommy gun, and fired a burst into the sky; then he flashed a signal for help with the Aldis lamp. The torpedo boat replied and hastened towards them.

An hour later they were in Malta. Brand was already a stretcher case and would spend several weeks in hospital recovering from his ordeal. But Smith insisted that he was perfectly fit to row the half-mile across into Sliema Creek to the base of the 10th Submarine Flotilla.

There Captain Phillips, Royal Navy, commander of the Tenth, was waiting for him on the quay.

'Good God, man,' he exclaimed, staring down at the exhausted man in the canoe below, 'what have you done with *United*?'

The *United* never came back, nor did most of the COPP teams. But those gallant young men had done the job they had been asked to do. They had learnt, at great cost, that every beach in Sicily was possessed of a peculiar and thwarting defence. Every beach was protected by a series of sandbars formed about three hundred yards from the shore. They had discovered too that there was just sufficient water above those bars to allow landing craft to cross them, though support and maintenance vessels might have difficulty doing so.

But there was a catch. Slowly the news filtered back to the planners that five men of the COPP teams had been captured in or off Sicily. Lt-Commander Willmott, asked to comment, signalled that his men would certainly not have had time to rid themselves of their telltale sounding reels, their sketch pads or their weird collection of watertight bags for collecting beach samples. Even if the five had not talked, their equipment would tell enemy intelligence officers that these were no ordinary commandos out on a raid.

That Sunday, as Willmott read a prayer at Divisions for his five missing men, he felt a sense of apprehension and despondency. The reason was simple. In his heart of hearts, he knew the great operation to come had been compromised before it had started.

2

HUSKY IS BORN

Just two months before the first COPP team had set out on its fatal mission, a doctor had been alerted for a vital journey at his little cottage at Harefield not far from London. It was nine o'clock on the night of Wednesday 13 January, 1943, when Lord Moran, a veteran of the war in the trenches and now personal doctor to Winston Churchill, received the call telling him the mission was on.

The previous hour he had spent listening to the Brain's Trust on the BBC, a programme in which he had taken part and he had kicked himself mentally 'for things I ought to have said'. Then he'd heard the first part of the nine o'clock news on the Home Service. It had announced that Rommel's *Afrika Korps* was being heavily bombed in Tripolitania. Monty's Eighth Army was going over to the offensive once again.

Outside it was freezing cold and raining heavily, but the Army staff car, as had been promised, was already waiting to take him to Churchill's underground headquarters beneath the Office of Works in London's Storey's Gate. Churchill had spent a lot of time there since his official residence at 10, Downing Street had been partly demolished by a bomb at the start of the new German 'tip-and-run raids', as they were called.

Churchill received his old friend with a smile. He was puffing at one of the big cigars he favoured, despite Moran's warnings that he should cut down on his smoking. Moran found 'the P.M. in high spirits, elated to be on the move once more.' Churchill loved to escape grey, dreary wartime London. He'd go anywhere at the drop of a hat, especially if it was somewhere sunny and hot, and this Wednesday night the Prime Minister was confident that it would be both where they were going.

With the rest of the high-ranking officers who would be accompanying them, they drove to a RAF field near Oxford where the plane which would take them to Africa was waiting. Churchill told Moran that it wouldn't be long now before the war in North Africa was over. The Germans were running and there would be no second Dunkirk for Rommel's men; the Royal Navy would see to that. Just like Field Marshal Paulus's German Sixth Army trapped near Stalingrad in Russia, there would have to be a mass surrender of the Italo-German forces in Africa.

Now the time had come to discuss plans for the future, in particular where the Anglo-American armies would attack continental Europe. That was why Churchill and his staff were flying to Africa. At Casablanca he would meet Roosevelt, who would fly five thousand miles from the United States, his first trip outside North America since Pearl Harbor in 1941.

Roosevelt would travel in luxury. Churchill, for his part, would fly in an unheated bomber for fourteen hours at 7,000 feet, with only a 'piss bucket' for sanitation and two mattresses thrown in the back for Churchill and Moran to sleep on.

That night sleeping on the mattresses was not a success. As the rest snored in their seats, Moran awoke to find Churchill, who was naked save for a skimpy silk vest, crawling about the plane because his toes had connected with something red-hot in the fuselage. He explained that his toes were burning. 'We shall have the petrol fumes bursting into flames. There'll be an explosion soon.'

That problem was solved, but an hour later Moran awoke again to find the half-naked Premier struggling to keep the draught out with a blanket. As Moran recalled after the war, 'On his hands and knees he cut a quaint figure with his big, bare, white bottom.'

Three hours later everything was transformed. The gloom and rain of a rationed, wintry England had vanished. Instead Winston and Moran breakfasted 'in a bungalow outside Casablanca, with the sun streaming in from a blue sky and oranges on our plates.'

The next day President Roosevelt arrived. Although the US President was a decade younger than Churchill, he was an invalid who might die at any moment. Crippled by polio since 1921 and confined to a wheelchair, his lower body was wasted away and useless. He had difficulty in breathing, was afflicted by severe trembling of the hands and had to drink from an outsize mug so that he didn't spill anything; had heart trouble and would often go into slack-mouthed trances. But his personal doctor, Admiral McIntire, took it upon himself to keep this knowledge from the world. No one, not even Roosevelt's estranged wife Eleanor, knew just how sick the President really was.

Now these two sick old men (Churchill himself was soon to suffer a severe illness) would decide the fate of Western Europe. For the Casablanca Conference of January, 1943, had been called specifically to decide where the Anglo-Americans would go after the successful conclusion of the fighting in Africa. Warming their old bones in the

African sun, they would make the decisions that eventually would not only beat the Germans, but also shape the future of Europe for the next half-century. 'Commodore Frankland', as Churchill was code-named, and 'Admiral Q', Roosevelt's code-name, wanted their chiefs-of-staff to agree here in Casablanca where the might of the Allied armies would make their first strike in Europe. Dunkirk was nearly three years ago. Now the Allies were going back!

The British had come to Casablanca well prepared to press their own case. Before they left Britain, Churchill had told his service chiefs to concentrate on further action in the Mediterranean, but they were 'not to force the Americans', but to take plenty of time to make them see the British point-of-view. 'The process,' he said, 'was going to be the dropping of water on stone'. To this end they had brought with them a 6,000-ton freighter, converted into a reference library. In the freighter were all the essential files pertaining to further action in the Mediterranean area, together with a complete staff of War Office clerks. In essence, the ship was a floating filing cabinet.

It was Churchill's aim to involve the Americans in a new strategy which would place the emphasis on invading Europe in 1943 somewhere along the Mediterranean seaboard. He did not think the Anglo-Americans were strong enough for a cross-Channel attack. For him the purpose of the conference was to convince the Americans they should invade Europe through what he called 'the soft underbelly' of the continent. (One day that 'soft underbelly' would become 'the tough old gut' but by then many young men would have lost their lives to give the lie to Churchill's theory.)

Roosevelt's key military advisers, General Marshall, the US Chief-of-Staff, and Admiral King, Commander-in-Chief of the US Atlantic Fleet (a renowned Anglophobe of whom Eisenhower once observed that the Allied war effort would have gone a lot more smoothly if they had shot him at the start of the war) thought otherwise. Both Marshall and King wanted a cross-Channel invasion of France in 1943. King held the view that the British would only invade France when there was no resistance left and they could 'march in behind a Scottish bagpipe band'.

The site of the historic meeting was at the Hotel Anfa in the suburbs of Casablanca. General Patton was made responsible for security and he ensured that not only the Hotel but the whole hilltop on which the Hotel was located was surrounded by rings of barbed wire and gun emplacements. Whenever the President came into the Hotel he was surrounded by bodyguards toting sub-machine guns, whom the future British Premier Harold Macmillan thought were really Chicago gangsters released to guard the President.

But Patton's main worry was to conceal the presence of so many VIPs from local spies and enemy agents, of whom there were many. Only the week before the conference started he had found a hidden microphone in his own office and suspected it had been planted there by one of the rival French factions in the city or perhaps by a German spy.

But Patton could not stop his superiors venturing outside the compound while waiting for the conference to begin. All of them wanted to see the notorious Casablanca *boushir* − the red light quarter. Here, enclosed in a complete walled city, were hundreds of whores plying their trade. Of them it was said that there were only three ways of ever leaving the *boushir* − by marriage, by purchase or by death!

Even the austere General Marshall, whom the President himself dared not call by his first name, went along to have a look, surrounded by a platoon of heavily armed MPs. Here he bumped into a British party led by the Chief of Combined Operations, Lord Louis Mountbatten, who commented breezily, 'Good show! Scenically the finest I have ever visited, except of course Bhamawaddy in Upper Burma.'

'Quite,' another very British voice agreed. 'For sheer purity of line nothing can touch good old Bhamawaddy, what!'

Thereupon their guide told the two parties that the VD rate in the *boushir* was one hundred per cent. Hastily they did an about-turn and fled, all thoughts of 'purity of line' forgotten.

That hard, moralistic Ulsterman, Alan Brooke, the Chief of the Imperial General Staff, had no time for jaunts into the red light district. Back in 1939 he had threatened to sack Montgomery, then one of his divisional commanders in France, because the latter had suggested opening brothels to stop his soldiers contracting VD. His idea of recreation wasn't sex, but bird-watching. In his off-duty hours he tried to identify local bird species and noted once in his diary, 'Spent a really peaceful afternoon in the lovely garden... and found some very interesting specimens.'

Not that he had much time for bird-watching in Casablanca that January. He had come to North Africa with a very definite plan of strategy for the allied forces in Europe. In accordance with Churchill's views and his own, he wanted the Anglo-American forces to be used in the Mediterranean and not in North-West Europe. He agreed with Churchill's point-of-view that the Russian 'ally' should be kept as far to the east as possible. By driving up through the centre of Europe, the Russians, once they started to advance, would be prevented from entering Western Europe proper, for by then, with luck, the Anglo-Americans would already be there. His opposite number, General Marshall, thought differently. He had no time for political considerations, just military ones. In his opinion, the best way to beat Germany was to cross the Channel in force and head straight for Berlin.

21

Brooke made his position quite clear. On the first day of the discussions on future strategy in the West he told Marshall: 'We are not strong enough for such an ambitious venture [a cross-Channel attack as proposed by the Americans]. It would only result in disaster if we tried.' He backed up his statement by reference to the terrible slaughter inflicted on the Canadians at Dieppe the year before and the fact the US Army was virtually green, with only a few of their troops having had combat experience in North Africa.

Marshall observed, 'I think the Mediterranean is a kind of dark hole into which one enters at one's peril.' But Brooke could see that the American was weakening. After all, the British had been fighting the war for nearly four years now. Presumably they knew better than the relatively new and inexperienced Americans. Marshall conceded that; 'But under the present circumstances I'll support operations against Southern Europe,' he added, 'and I'm opposed as much as ever to interminable operations in the Mediterranean.' He did not want a repetition of the British campaign in North Africa which had nearly taken three years to complete. All the same, Marshall had given way to the British; the latter had won. As General Wedemeyer, the US official observer at the conference, summed up the American position bitterly afterwards, 'We came, we listened and we were conquered!'

Now the talks turned to exactly where in the Mediterranean area Europe should be invaded. There was some discussion of Sardinia as a likely spot. Greece followed. But in the end both countries were turned down by the British. The reason was simple. Churchill already had a pet plan of his own, which dated back to the spring of 1940. This was for the invasion of the island of Sicily off the tip of the Italian boot.

Churchill and Brooke reasoned that if Sicily fell to the Western Allies, it would bring down the dictatorship of the Italian *Duce*, Benito Mussolini. Owing to Italian losses in North Africa and Russia, where several of Italy's best divisions had fought in support of Hitler's *Wehrmacht*, Mussolini's rule was already shaky. In Churchill's opinion, a successful Allied campaign in Italy proper would do the rest. His own people would topple the *Duce*.

Once Mussolini was gone, Churchill knew from his contacts with Italian diplomats in neutral countries, Italy would undoubtedly sue for peace. This would leave the country wide open for a rapid Allied drive right up Italy. In a matter of weeks perhaps, the whole military situation on the Continent could be transformed in favour of the Allies. Eisenhower, the new Allied Supreme Commander, favoured this plan and so Sicily was decided upon.

It all seemed too easy. But General Wedemeyer, for one, was not convinced. Of all the Brass present, General Wedemeyer was the only one who had attended the German *Kriegsschule*, between 1936 and 1939. He felt he knew something of the mettle of the *Wehrmacht* and its generals. German officers were always quicker off the mark than their Allied equivalents. At this very moment somewhere in the vaults of the German High Command in Berlin there would already be a contingency plan drawn up for the eventuality that Italy broke away from the Reich. (Wedemeyer was right; there was.) Sicily, he believed, would lead nowhere. He characterized it, correctly as it turned out, as 'a side show... and it may cost lives'. It certainly would.

But the decision had been made. As soon as the conference had broken up immediate moves were made to implement the decision to attack Sicily once the fighting in North Africa had ceased. A planning committee was set up. It would be in charge of the planning of what would become the largest Allied invasion of the war, even bigger than D-Day. It began, however, modestly enough in Room 141 of the St Georges Hotel in Algiers, after which the top-secret planning committee was named 'Force 141'.

Chief-of-Staff of Force 141 was Major-General Charles Gairdner. The forty-five-year-old British General was better known for his pre-war polo playing activities than his wartime generalship, though he had briefly commanded 6th Armoured Division in the desert.

Under Gairdner's leadership a swift succession of plans for the invasion of Sicily, code-named 'Husky', was produced. But each, in turn, was rejected as unsatisfactory on one ground or another. By April, 1943, the frustrated planners had reached 'Husky Eight', which seemed at last to find approval from the top brass involved – Eisenhower, Air Chief Marshal Tedder and Admiral Cunningham, the commander of the British Mediterranean Fleet. But the top brass had not reckoned with Montgomery, whom an exasperated General Patton was now calling the 'little limey fart'.

The commander of the now victorious Eighth Army didn't think much of Gairdner or his Force 141. He felt that Gairdner was 'not up to it; he doesn't know the battle repercussions; he is a bundle of nerves; he inspires no confidence; the whole atmosphere is far removed from war; and the work they produce has no relation to the practical realities of battle'. It was obvious, at least to the victor of El Alamein, that 'Husky Eight' just wouldn't do.

While the weary planners went back to their drawing-boards once more and with only three months to go before the invasion of Sicily began, Force 141's Intelligence officers had problems of their own. By now, thanks to the bravery of the secret invaders, they knew a great deal about the topography of the island's beaches. They knew something, too, of Sicily's beach defences. But what of the morale of the men manning those defences?

From the censored letters of Sicilian POWs in Allied hands in North Africa and the replies of their loved ones back on the island, the Intelligence experts had learned that Sicily seemed to be defended mainly by Italian troops, many of them native Sicilians. But little was known of the morale and fighting spirit of these troops. Naturally all letters coming from Sicily to North Africa were censored. The question still remained wide-open: *would the Eyeties fight*?

As US Admiral Pye admitted frankly that year to a class of Naval Intelligence officer students at America's Naval War College: 'Gentlemen, you are working in a field of naval service which was sadly neglected in peacetime and which now, even after two years of war, is still in the primary stages of development, especially in North Africa and Italy.'

The Admiral's statement typified the situation on the other side of the Mediterranean. Intelligence was groping in the dark over there. Even the newly formed American OSS (the forerunner of the CIA) had been unable to infiltrate agents into the Italian peninsula. The organization had plenty of Italo-Americans who had family connections with the 'Old Country' and spoke Italian fluently, but that didn't help much in Sicily. There the closely knit family ties and the general insularity of the people, who spoke a dialect which was virtually unintelligible to Northern Italians, laced as it was with Arabic, Spanish, French, even German words, meant that Sicilians only really trusted their own kind.

Britain, for its part, had maintained a secret service operation in Italy since 1929. It had been run by the redoubtable Captain Claude Dansey of the SIS, of whom Professor Hugh Trevor-Roper had written, he 'was an utter shit, corrupt, incompetent but with a certain low cunning'. But by the time Italy entered the war on Germany's side in May, 1940, that organization was in tatters. If it had any agents still working for it, then they certainly weren't in Sicily. So where was the vital intelligence they needed to come from?

There was another problem that spring which worried the Intelligence staff of Force 141. By now, of course, they knew that at least five of the secret invaders had been captured in Sicily. They also knew something of the methods of the Italian OVRA; its use of rubber truncheons, electric shocks, homosexual rape and its noxious 'castor oil treatment'. They reasoned that those five young men, brave as they were, would undoubtedly have talked by now.

They knew too that there was constant traffic between North Africa and the European mainland. There were those French 'Vichyites' who refused to serve under the Anglo-Americans and were repatriated. There were hundreds of Tunisian fishermen of Sicilian extraction who regularly went to sea, sometimes calling on their native island. And there were scores of German POWs who had managed to escape from the great sprawling POW camps in North Africa. (After all nearly 400,000 of them had surrendered and there were not enough men to spare to guard them all.) All of these people, Force 141 Intelligence reasoned, would be questioned by Italo-German Intelligence on the other side of the Mediterranean. Any one of them could blab the great secret. The gigantic build-up which German reconnaissance planes had spotted all over North Africa was not intended for Greece or Sardinia, but for Sicily.

Was there any way of fooling the enemy as to their real intentions? The Allied Intelligence officers of Force 141 well knew that, if Hitler learned that Sicily was to be invaded, he would immediately send fresh German troops to the island to bolster up the Italian garrison. The Führer knew, just as the Allies did, that any further Italian defeats might well mean the end of Mussolini. Hitler had to maintain the 'Pact of Steel' between them at any cost. With a life-or-death struggle being waged in Russia, Hitler simply could not afford a breakdown of his southern flank at this crucial stage of the war.

So, in Algiers and faraway in London, in secret offices dotted all over the capital, men of all professions and backgrounds who made up Britain's wartime Intelligence establishment racked their brains to come up with a solution. They were mostly conceited, opinionated men, products of the great public schools and privileged backgrounds. They thought highly of themselves and little of the rigidity of the regimented German mind. Yet they were astute enough to know that Hitler took little heed of the advice of his experts. He relied on his own intuition. In essence, they knew that any deception plan they dreamed up would have to fool the Führer and not just the officers of the German Secret Service, *die Abwehr*. How could it be done?

Back in 1917 Colonel Meinertzhagen, an Intelligence officer on the staff of General Sir Edmund Allenby, had used an elaborate dodge to fool the German-Turkish forces facing Allenby's men as to where the next British attack in the Sinai desert would take place. On 10 October, 1917, Meinertzhagen had ridden out into the desert looking for a Turkish patrol. It was not something that senior Intelligence officers did normally. But Colonel Meinertzhagen had with him a bloodstained haversack, containing dispatches etc, which purported to show when and where the next attack by Allenby's army would take place.

Meinertzhagen did not search long for his Turkish patrol. As soon as the Turks spotted the lone rider and opened fire, the brave Colonel wheeled his horse around and began to ride back the way he had come, flat out. He wanted the Turks to think that he had panicked and was riding for his life. First he dropped the bloodstained haversack. That was followed by his rifle, water bottle and finally his binoculars, with his name engraved on the base of the leather case. (He knew that the Turks knew he was one of Allenby's senior staff officers.) Then he was gone, leaving the Turks to pick up his bits and pieces, hoping that they might find something of value.

The haversack was soon at German HQ. Now Meinertzhagen played his second card. He assumed the Germans would use the code the haversack also contained to intercept and decipher British wireless traffic coming from a radio station near Giza. This they did, and Meinertzhagen used the station to feed the enemy with false information about the coming British offensive.

Finally, as Allenby's cavalry secretly moved up to their new assault positions, the cunning Colonel had an RAF plane drop 120,000 packets of cigarettes over the Turkish lines opposite. The Turkish infantry were chronically short of cigarettes and they did not question why the *Inglezi* were dropping them the precious cigarettes. They seized upon the packets greedily and puffed their heads off.

Hours later, when Allenby's cavalry launched their surprise attack at a spot completely unknown to the Turks and their German allies, they found the frontline trenches filled with sleeping Turkish infantrymen, out to the world behind their Maxim machine guns. The cigarettes which had fallen from heaven were not the manna the Turks had supposed. They had been heavily spiked with opium. Two months later Allenby marched in triumph into Jerusalem and the campaign in the desert was over.

'The Meinertzhagen ploy', as it was often called in professional British Intelligence circles, had always been regarded in the British Army as one of the most successful Intelligence coups of all times and those engaged in 1943 in the attempt to fool Hitler as to the whereabouts of the first Allied assault in Europe wondered if a similar ploy would succeed in a more sophisticated age. Would a bloodstained haversack do the job twenty-odd years later? They thought not. The idea was still excellent, but this time the vehicle for the plant would have to be authentic.

Thus, while in New York another strange project which would have repercussions right into our time was being initiated in order to discover what was going on in Sicily, in London the men of Intelligence began refining the 'Meinertzhagen ploy'. Once more the old trick, dressed in new trappings, was to be trotted out to fool the Hun.

3

OPERATION MINCEMEAT

The great deception had started innocently enough in the Junior Carlton Club, in the heart of London's clubland. There a young naval officer listened respectfully to the measured words of a wing-collared, white-haired pathologist who was probably the world's leading specialist in his field.

In his long career in criminal pathology and forensic science, Sir Bernard Spilsbury, who one day would die by his own hand, had come across many curious and eerie examples of man's ingenuity in doing away with his fellow human beings. But on this icy day, over coffee and port, he little realized he was becoming involved in the most amazing case in his long career.

The young lieutenant-commander, Ewen Montagu, of Naval Intelligence, the son of a lord and a product of Harvard and Trinity, already a King's Counsel, patiently and methodically fed his questions to the old man. Privately he wished Spilsbury would not talk to him as if he were addressing a jury at the Old Bailey. Still the old man knew his stuff and he wanted to be able to present a watertight case to the highly critical Twenty Committee.*

While the ancient waiters flitted back and forth Commander Montagu persisted with his questions: 'What would be the specific characteristics of a body which remained in the water several days after a plane crash? How would they be recognized? What might be recorded as the cause of death, providing the person in question had not died on impact?'

Sir Bernard's professional interest was aroused by the young K.C.'s skilful questioning. He said, 'Death would probably result from a

---

* Ewen Montagu and Squadron Leader Sir Archibald Cholmondley of Air Intelligence have always been regarded as the fathers of the great deception. But there is some evidence that General Macfarlane, while Governor of Gibraltar, suggested a similar scheme to 'C', head of the British Secret Service, before them.

lowering of the person's temperature, especially if the man in question were to float by means of a life-belt. First he would fall unconscious. Death would occur several hours later.' Sir Bernard's voice droned on and on.

Then Montagu posed the all-important question. 'Would there be any outward signs of how the man had met his death?'

Sir Bernard considered for a moment. Obviously he wasn't given to answering such questions lightly. After all, the answers he had often given to bewigged judges in the Old Bailey, not far from where they now sat, had meant the difference between life and death for some unfortunate clutching the rail of the prisoner's box. 'No,' he said, 'in my opinion there would be no outward characteristics of the manner of death.'

Commander Montagu's heart gave a jump. It was the answer he had been hoping for. Now he was sure he could convince the Twenty Committee that 'Operation Mincemeat' was a viable proposition.

Montagu's suggestion that, to mislead the enemy about the Allies' next move, a body would be ditched in the sea as if it had come from a crashed plane, carrying with it important documents indicating that the Allies' objective was elsewhere than Sicily, went not only to the Twenty Committee of Intelligence experts but right up to Churchill himself, and then from Churchill to Eisenhower and from him to the US Combined Chiefs-of-Staff in Washington. It was a long process, involving many meetings, but finally it was approved and Montagu could go ahead. There was the risk that the Germans might not be taken in by the deception and establish the truth, i.e. that Sicily *was* the target, by reading the evidence presented to them in reverse. But that was a risk the plotters were prepared to take.

Now Montagu needed a body. As a KC, he knew how to cut his way through red tape. If he needed a body urgently, the best way to find it was through the office of the City of London Coroner, Mr Bentley Purchase. Surprisingly enough, despite the fact that it was wartime, a corpse was not easy to find. As Bentley Purchase told the young naval officer, 'You can't get bodies just for the asking. Even with bodies all over the place, each one has to be accounted for.'

Montagu persisted and eventually he, together with Sir Bernard and the Coroner, visited the mortuary at Horseferry Road, London. Here there were bodies aplenty in the icy vaults of the Victorian Mortuary: bodies of men killed in the blackout, bodies of men torn to pieces by bombs, bodies that were of no earthly use to Montagu. Finally a suitable body was found, which Montagu described: 'The body was that of a young man in his early thirties. He had not been very physically fit for some years before his death, but we would accept that, for, as I said to a senior officer who queried the point, he does not have to look like an officer – only a staff officer.'*

Montagu waited anxiously while Sir Bernard went to work on the corpse, tapping it here and there, paying particular attention to the corpse's chest. He concluded that there was liquid in the man's lungs which would probably lead to any enemy doctor who examined the corpse believing that he has died by drowning, though a careful post-mortem would tell him otherwise.

It was the answer Montagu had been waiting for. As he confessed after the war, 'At one time we feared we might have to do a body snatch, but we did not like that idea if we could avoid it.'

Now they prepared to transfer the body to the offices of the Twenty Committee above those of a music publisher in Regent Street. But there was a problem. They had to dress the corpse and put a pair of boots on his feet, *but the feet were frozen solid*! The old coroner, however, was up to the problem. After all he had been hardened in the rough-tough school of police surgery in which the body was slit by one stroke of a scalpel from throat to pubes so that the organs needed for examination could be examined easily. Police surgeons were paid on a 'body' basis and had no time to waste. He sent off one of Montagu's men to bring down his electric fire from his own office.

When he returned, Bentley Purchase plugged it in and held the single bar beneath the dead man's feet. 'We'll thaw the feet out,' he said, 'and as soon as the boots are on, we'll pop him back in the refrigerator and refreeze him.'

Steam soon began to rise and there was the sound of dripping water.

On 4 February, 1943, the Twenty Committee met at their weekly Monday conference and confirmed the arrangements. In cold officialese, the minutes of that meeting ran as follows: PLAN MINCEMEAT. The plan is the same as PLAN TROJAN HORSE. The details of the plan were put forward by Commander Montagu and F/Lt Chomondeley. It was reported that a body had been procured and it was explained that this would have to be used within three months and that various points of detail would have to be decided before the Plan could be put into operation.

'It was decided that Air Ministry representatives on the Twenty Committee should make the necessary arrangements for the flight during which the body will be dropped; that the Admiralty representatives should

---

* Fifty years later there is still controversy about who the man really was. Even as I write, a correspondent in a daily paper maintains he has discovered the identity of the 'Man Who Never Was'. The secret will probably never be disclosed.

find out a suitable place off the Spanish coast where the body can be dropped; that the War Office representative should go into the question of providing the body with a name, necessary papers etc. It was agreed that the N.A. [Naval Attaché] Madrid should be informed of the plan so that he will be able to cope with any unforeseen repercussions which may come his way.'

'Operation Mincemeat' had been approved and the 'Man Who Never Was' had been born.

That spring, while the date of the invasion of Sicily grew ever closer, Montagu tackled his first problem — how to create a realistic cover story for Major Martin of the Royal Marines, as the body had now become. For days on end he and his colleagues at Naval Intelligence (they included the future creator of 'James Bond', Commander Ian Fleming) talked the problem over. What would a Major of Marines normally carry about on his person? Money, theatre tickets, bills, letters would be the obvious things. But how could the letters, for example, contribute to establishing the corpse's genuineness? Under normal circumstances letters were usually trivial.

In the end the planners decided that Major Martin had just become engaged. Accordingly, he was to carry on his body two 'passionate' letters from his fiancée, one mentioning a 'posting overseas'. Montagu pushed the matter a little further. A man who gets engaged usually buys a ring. But a ring might put him in the red. So Major Martin would carry the bill for the ring and a discreet letter from his bank manager mentioning his new overdraft. Parents sometimes don't like their children to marry, so Montagu invented a Victorian-type father for Martin who wrote to his son that he did not like 'wartime engagements' one bit. However, if his son was prepared to go ahead, then he must 'forthwith' have his last will and testament drawn up 'just in case'. The bogus identity was beginning to take shape.

The next step was to prepare the 'ploy'. As Montagu recalled after the war: 'We drew up a private letter from the Deputy Chief of Staff to General Alexander who commanded our armies in North Africa. This private letter enabled him...to mention small transparent details...which would make the enemy believe that we were going to land troops in both Greece and Sardinia.'

Lord Louis Mountbatten was convinced he should allow his name to be affixed to another letter to Admiral Cunningham. It read:

'Dear Admiral of the Fleet,

I promised V.C.I.G.S. that Major Martin would arrange with you for the onward transmission of a letter he has with him for General Alexander. It is very urgent and very 'hot' and there are some remarks in it that could not be seen by others in the War Office. It could not go by signal. I feel sure that you will see that it goes on safely and without delay.

I think you will find Martin the man you want. He is quiet and shy at first but he really knows his stuff. He was more accurate than some of us about the probable run of events at Dieppe and he has been well in on the experiments with the latest barges and equipment which took place in Scotland.

Let me have him back please as soon as the assault is over. He might bring some sardines with him — they are 'on points' here.

Yours sincerely
Louis Mountbatten.'

The letter obviously built Martin up as an expert on assault landings; the references to Dieppe and the latest experiments with barges in Scotland made that quite clear. But the real sting was in the last sentence of the letter. It was the reference to rationed sardines. An enterprising *Abwehr* specialist poring over the message would surely get it eventually. In translation into German it worked even better. 'Sardines' become '*Sardinen*' and '*Sardinen*' is very close to the German place name '*Sardinien*', which is Sardinia.

Natürlich, he would congratulate himself on his smartness. *Der Herr Admiral* Mountbatten was allowing himself a little joke. *The Allies were going to invade Sardinia.*

On 18 April, 1943, Operation Mincemeat was ready to go into action. Major Martin's body, carefully packed in dry ice in a container labelled 'optical instruments', was loaded into the Royal Naval submarine HMS *Seraph* at the Scottish port of Holy Loch. Commander N.L. Jewell was no newcomer to clandestine operations; he had landed General Clarke in North Africa before the US invasion, where the General had lost his trousers. The skipper solemnly receipted the 'optical instruments' and told his Number Two privately to tell the crew that the container held an automatic weather station.

Then Jewell went down to his tiny cabin where, behind a drawn curtain, he exchanged a few words with Montagu and Cholmondeley, the fathers of the great deception. The conspirators shook hands and the two Intelligence officers went ashore. Then they turned away and walked back to the Humber staff car. Their job was over. They had worked seven months on the task. Now it was up to Jewell — and the Germans.

Everything went all right on the first and the second day. They were passing through 'U-boat alley', the corridor that led from the German-held French ports into the Atlantic. Here anything that moved below or above the surface was bombed automatically by Coastal Command because the Admiralty had decreed that everything in this area was enemy. But Jewell felt safe. All Allied aircraft had been ordered to be on the lookout for a British sub on a special mission.

The third day of the voyage passed peacefully enough too. There was plenty of enemy shipping about, mostly French and Belgian fishing boats under German control, but no one spotted them. On the fourth day Jewell received a message from London ordering him to change course. He was to tackle a group of enemy ships moving in the general direction of the Spanish ports along the Bay of Biscay. The Admiralty thought this would be a good cover, in case the Germans had picked up the British submarine in these waters.

Jewell set off at twelve knots, occasionally coming up to periscope height to survey the sea to his front. On the fourth occasion a trio of twin-engined Hudsons of Coastal Command fell out of the sky and headed straight for the submarine, dropping depth charges as they came. Jewell hit the alarm klaxon. His Second shouted, 'Dive, dive, dive,' and they started going down. The depth charges began to fall behind them. While the submarine's crew held their breath, Jewell took them even further away from the scene of danger. Once out of danger Jewell concentrated on the funeral of Major Martin.

On the next day HMS *Seraph* surfaced off the mouth of the Rio Huelva. It was still daylight and, although Spain was officially a neutral country, Jewell knew that there would be coast-watchers in German pay.

As soon as it was dusk he cautiously approached the coast, running his diesels at half-speed so the sound was kept down to a minimum. Again he ran into trouble. Out of nowhere a swarm of Spanish fishing boats appeared, the carbide lights on their boats spreading bright incandescent circles on the water. Jewell submerged fast and decided to cancel the operation for that night, but after a while he changed his mind. He tried once more, but again luck was against him. There was yet another fleet of Spanish boats fishing for *sardinas*. This time he dived under the boats and groped his way slowly through the murky water until the submarine came to rest just off the Punta de Umbria. He was ready to discharge his strange cargo.

Jewell now moved fast, for he knew he had not much time before dawn. He ordered all the ratings and petty officers below, leaving only the submarine's officers on deck. The ratings clattered down the ladder, leaving the officers, clad in dirty overalls, duffle coats and corduroy pants staring at the skipper in bewilderment. Hurriedly Jewell filled his officers in on their strange mission.

Now followed an eerie scene, as they checked out the body of Major Martin, ensuring that the vital briefcase with the letters to the high-ranking officers in the Mediterranean was firmly attached to his wrist by the chain. Finally they fitted the corpse with a yellow 'Mae West'.

But the strange nocturnal ceremony was not over yet. Devotedly the skipper lowered his head and folded his hands. His officers knew what that meant. They lowered their heads and followed suit. In a few simple words, he murmured the committal ceremony for the body lying thawed and dripping on the deck. It must have been one of the most bizarre 'burials' in the history of the Christian church.

The little ceremony over, the body was slipped into the water. Jewell's voice rose a couple of levels as he started to rap out his orders. Once more he was the typical young Royal Navy submarine skipper. The diesels started to chug as the boat moved away back to sea. The ripples grew to waves. The waves became higher and higher and the body of 'Major Martin' was forced ever closer to the shore. As a final move, the container which had brought him all the way from Regent Street to this remote place off the Spanish coast was destroyed with a burst of machine-gun fire. HMS *Seraph* started to sink beneath the surface. Her part in the great deception operation was over.

Just after dawn that day, April 30, 1943, the body, with the briefcase still attached, was discovered by a Spanish fisherman. The fishermen hereabouts were used to finding the dead bodies of Allied airmen, shot down while crossing the Bay of Biscay or running into trouble as their planes made the dangerous approach to Gibraltar. They knew the British always paid for the return of the bodies of their men, so the fisherman hauled the body aboard and headed for the shore. There, at the little port of Huelga, the fisherman handed over the corpse to the Spanish Navy.

While the Spanish authorities informed the British Vice-Consul at Huelga, who knew nothing of the plot, that the body of a British serviceman had been found in the sea off the port, the local doctor, Fernandez Contioso, carried out the post-mortem. His findings were that the unknown soldier had been in the water up to five or six days and had died of drowning. This checked with items found in his pockets — theatre tickets dated 27 April and his bill from the Army and Navy Club, which gave the 24th as the date of his departure from the club. All the time, the local *Abwehr* agent was busily photocopying the documents found in the briefcase, ready for dispatch to Berlin.

The Vice-Consul reported the finding of the body to the British Embassy in Madrid. There the Minister, Sir Samuel Hoare, known from his years in the Chamberlain cabinet as 'Slippery Sam', asked the Spanish authorities that the body of 'Major Martin' should be released at once. The Spanish Navy Minister, Senor Salvador Moreno-Fernandez, refused politely but firmly. His excuse was that the authorities wanted to check the dead man's papers. In reality he wanted to give the German agents of the *Abwehr* as much time as possible.

Back in London Montagu and the rest of the Twenty Committee rubbed their hands with glee. The delay meant that the Germans and their Spanish friends were beginning to bite.

Meanwhile Montagu had put Martin's name on a casualty list published in *The Times* for 4 June. By chance the list contained the name of two officers who actually had lost their lives in air crashes in the same area. Major Martin was buried with full naval honours at Huelva (his grave is still there).* His broken-hearted fiancée sent a wreath and the Vice-Consul sent his distraught family photographs of the grave; the Spanish naval party fired a volley over the grave.

Finally the Spanish handed the briefcase attached to the body back to the British Embassy in Madrid. A few hours later the briefcase was on its way to Gibraltar. From thence it was flown directly to London, where the experts went to work on it at once. Tests revealed within a day that the documents it contained had been tampered with and that the envelopes had been carefully resealed. Now London knew that the Spaniards, and presumably the *Abwehr*, had read the fake documents. This was confirmed some time later by Ultra. Signals between the *Abwehr* office in the German Embassy in Madrid and Admiral Canaris' HQ in Berlin's Tirpitzstrasse increased threefold. At that time Ultra was unable to read all the messages encoded in the *Abwehr* cipher, but the three hundred per cent increase between Madrid and Berlin was evidence enough. The Germans had fallen for 'Mincemeat'. Now there remained one overwhelming question: *Would Hitler fall for it, too?*

* The gravestone reads: 'William Martin, Born 29th March 1907. Beloved son of John Glyndwyr Martin and the late Antonia Martin of Cardiff, Wales. *Dulce et decorum es per patria mori*. R.I.P.'

4

THE MAFIA CONNECTION

In the same month that the *Seraph* set sail with its strange cargo, General Sir Alan Brooke, the Chief of the Imperial Staff, drove over from the War Office in Whitehall to Number 21, Queen Anne's Gate, a tall elegant 18th Century house. Here he was ushered into the office of General Stewart Menzies. There, standing behind the desk reputed to have belonged to Nelson, stood the master of the house, the head of the secret organization whose *official* existence has only recently been acknowledged.

Menzies, a product of Eton and the Life Guards, with influence at Court, had been head of Britain's Secret Intelligence Service since 1939. In that year he had suffered the bitter blow of having his Continental spy networks destroyed by the Germans after the 'Venlo Incident'.* But he had rescued his own reputation and that of his organization by the success of the Ultra decoding operation.

The Chief of the Imperial Staff had come to see the head of the SIS to discover what 'C', as he was codenamed, and his organization knew about Sicily. Brooke knew that he had been in the intelligence game since he had been wounded in France in 1914 and had, thereafter, gone on the Intelligence staff at GHQ. If any one knew what was going on in Sicily, it would be he.

'C' was not very encouraging. Ultra, he explained, was providing virtually nothing on the Italians. They did not use the Enigma coding machines employed by the Germans, which provided Ultra with its rich booty of intelligence on all the Germans' moves. Brooke asked about spies. Both the Allies and the Axis used scores of spies in the Middle East; Cairo, for instance, was still swarming with them, as was Istanbul in Turkey. Again 'C' had to disappoint him. He said that the geography and provincialism of the island made it exceedingly difficult to infiltrate agents

* See Leo Kessler: *Betrayal at Venlo*, Pen & Sword, London, 1991.

into Sicily. The local police and the dreaded OVRA, Mussolini's secret police, well trained in nearly two decades of operations against the Mafia, soon spotted any newcomer to Sicily. As for the locals, still dominated by Mafia terror (though Mussolini had gone a long way since 1922 in breaking the power of that sinister organization) they kept strictly to themselves, having little to do even with their fellow Italians. For them only Sicily and Sicilians counted.

Gloomily Brooke drove back to his office. That night in his diary he recorded that the SIS had concluded: 'Sicily must be so closely guarded, also the islands [off the coast of Sicily], that it would be wasteful to expend.... trained agents on such a hot target.'

What Brooke did not know was that for nearly half a year now another Allied Intelligence organization had been actively engaged in trying to establish agents and spies in Sicily. It had all started in April, 1942, when Menzies' own Ultra Intelligence had warned the US Navy that the German Navy was dispatching long-range U-boats to the American eastern seaboard to attack the US convoys leaving New York, Boston and other ports on that coast. They would strike the US ships almost immediately they had left port and set sail into the open sea.

Admiral King, the head of the US Atlantic Fleet, anglophobe that he was, had pooh-poohed the British warnings. He took no advice from the British. What followed was a massacre worse than the disaster at Pearl Harbor, which had brought America into the war. In a period of six months four hundred tankers alone were torpedoed and sunk by the German 'sea wolves' of Admiral Doenitz's submarine fleet.

A spy mania erupted along the eastern seaboard and as far back as Washington. The German U-boat commanders seemed to know everything that was going on at the US ports of embarkation. They knew the dates of sailing and the cargoes of virtually every ship that set off to cross the Atlantic. Twice troopships carrying the first US soldiers bound for Belfast and Liverpool had narrowly escaped being torpedoed. Then the great French luxury liner, the *Normandie*, capable of carrying a whole US division to Europe, had burned out and sunk at her Manhattan pier under mysterious circumstances. Sabotage, German-inspired, was suspected.*

In Washington, a pretty young married woman, Inga Fejos, who had been Miss Denmark in 1931 and who had been Hitler's guest at the 1936 Olympics, became a primary suspect. She was having an affair with a

* The discovery of a German U-boat off Point Pleasant, N.J. in November, 1991, prompted US naval historian Harry Cooper to observe to the *Buffalo News*: 'These U-boats penetrated every single one of our harbors on the East Coast. There's one captain who sat right off Coney Island, watching the swimmers thru his periscope!'

young naval officer working for the Office of Naval Intelligence in Washington, who had important political connections and a multi-millionaire father, who until recently had been the US Ambassador in London, J. F. Kennedy. Was this beautiful young woman just after Kennedy's money, or did his weekends with 'Inga-Binga', as Kennedy called her, serve some more sinister purpose?

Naval Intelligence and the F.B.I. thought the latter. Her apartment was searched and many damning documents found, including deposits from international arms merchants and receipts for telegram messages to Berlin. 'Inga-Binga' was not arrested. As always, the Kennedys protected their own and Lieutenant John Kennedy was shipped off to a PT boat squadron in the Pacific to gain his hero's reputation.

Meanwhile, in New York, the 3rd Naval Intelligence District operatives were reasoning that Nazi U-boat skippers had a whole host of potential spies and informers in the many Italian-Americans who worked the city's waterfront. The men who ran the ports in the area and the East Coast fishing and canning industries were predominantly Italian-Americans or of Italian heritage. They spoke Italian among themselves, were proud of their heritage and lived mostly in Italian ghettos. For the Naval Intelligence operatives these men and women were primary suspects because Mussolini was still Hitler's loyal ally. Possibly, they reasoned, the 'wops' and 'guineas', as they were contemptuously called, felt their first loyalty not to the USA but the 'Old Country'.

There was, however, one group of these Italian-Americans who felt nothing but hatred for Mussolini; he had hounded and persecuted their families for years. These were those Italo-Americans, many of them union leaders and racketeers, who held allegiance to what they called *la costa nostra*, known to the world as the Mafia.

It was a big, bluff, ex-publicity man and former World War One petty officer, now a middle-aged lieutenant in Naval Intelligence (soon to be Lt.-Commander), Charles Haffenden, who first decided that the Mafia could be used to check if there were Italo-Americans spying on Allied shipping leaving the East coast ports for the Germans. Haffenden, a flamboyant underworld buff, who liked to show off and at the same time cultivate an air of mystery, set to work to make his first contact with the 'syndicate', as it was called in the USA in those days, from his offices in New York's Astor Hotel. He knew exactly where to go from his pre-war associations. He went to Joseph 'Socks' Lanza, a 41-year old union boss, who played a big role in the crime organization which dominated New York's underworld in the '40s.

'Socks' Lanza controlled the city's major fish market, the Fulton Fish Market, where, dressed in a grease-stained fish apron, he ruled with a rod of iron. Without a kickback in the shape of a regular payment from a man's weekly wage, no worker could get a job at the market.

But there was more to 'Socks' Lanza than just a traditional union boss on the take. In 1939, after being released from a two-year prison sentence to take up his new job with the United Seafood Workers union, he purchased a summer home for himself and his mistress on Long Beach next to the house owned by one Charles Luciano, the brother of the infamous 'Lucky' Luciano.

'Lucky' Luciano had been born near Palermo, Sicily, in 1897. In 1904 his parents had emigrated to the States and settled in on the east side of Manhattan. Never a US citizen, Luciano had first been arrested at the age of 19. Thereafter he had made his living from crime. He had clawed his way upwards in the organized rackets of the time, making his money from drugs, booze, even at one time from pimping. On 16 October, 1929, he was imprisoned in a warehouse by a gang of rival narcotic dealers. They tied him by his thumbs to a beam. The racketeers tortured him all night long until his thumbs jerked from the rope as he writhed and turned under the agony of their beating and he fell to the floor apparently dead. Thereupon the torturers fled. Somehow Luciano managed to crawl away and was picked up by the police. 'Don't know who did it,' he told the Staten Island police, adding threateningly, '*I'll* take care of myself'. This survival, after 'being taken for a ride', was thought so miraculous by his fellow mobsters that thereafter he was always known as 'Lucky' Luciano.

By the mid-thirties he was the leading boss of the Mafia in New York. As one of the crime reporters of the time wrote, 'He was wily, rapacious. He was savagely cruel. For years, like some deadly King Cobra, this droopy-eyed thug coiled himself about the Eastern underworld and squeezed it implacably of its minted gold. He was the bookmakers' joy, a Dracula masquerading as Good Time Charlie'. The purple prose did not do full justice to Lucky Luciano. He had a power concept ahead of his time. He felt that organized crime should appear to be legitimate, as it appears today. He thought that narcotics, extortion, prostitution etc. should be organized into 'chain stores like A & P'.

But by the mid-thirties Luciano had a powerful enemy gunning for him — Thomas Dewey, a young US attorney with political ambition. As United States Attorney for the Southern District of New York, he had twenty young District Attorneys working for him, who started a systematic and successful campaign against gangsters and organized crime. One by one they were sentenced to prison until, finally, on 18 June, 1936, Dewey succeeded in convicting Luciano of 'compulsory prostitution'. He received a sentence of 'thirty years minimum, fifty years maximum'.

This was the man, now completing his sixth year in Dannemora high security prison in upstate New York, whom Haffenden wanted to contact through 'Socks' Lanza and 'Little Man' Lansky, one of the few non-Italian/Sicilian gangsters of the period. He reasoned that if Luciano agreed to help US Intelligence, the other gangster bosses would fall in line. For a start he wanted the underworld bosses to use their connections to ascertain if there was any spying going on in the Fulton Fish Market and other such places. The mainly Italian fishing boat captains who supplied the market might well be the ones who were taking out supplies and information to the German U-boats lurking off the eastern seaboard.

Both Lanza and Lansky agreed to help arrange the contact with Luciano. However, there was one condition. Luciano had to be removed from the strict régime of Dannemora to the easier atmosphere of Great Meadows Prison near Albany, the capital of New York State.

Naval Intelligence agreed and in May, 1942, Luciano was transferred to Great Meadows with eight other convicts who were used as cover. A week or so later Lanza and Lansky went to visit Luciano to enlist his aid. Several visits followed in June and Luciano was reported to have stated, 'This is a good cause'. He ordered his visitors to make contact with two other Mafia overlords, Frank Costello, who acted as the Mafia's fixer and political spokesman, and Joe Adonis, the ruler of Brooklyn. Although unaware of the full extent of the unholy alliance between the Mafia and Naval Intelligence, the New York State legal authorities allowed it to go ahead in the cause of national security.

Thus it was that, with Luciano's approval, Haffenden was able to infiltrate his agents into the docks, fish markets and Mafia-run unions. As Lanza explained after the war, 'We'd hang around that vicinity where all the fishermen hang out. In some cases, I'd go down myself and have a drink with the agent that Haffenden would designate and I would go down with him and introduce him, "This is John or Henry," or whatever.... Sometimes we would get an agent to work in one of the packing places. That was my union too. I would get him a card.'

In other cases Haffenden's agents would be planted in the boats that fished the east coast to spot for submarines or any suspicious activities on the part of the fishing crews.

Gradually the unholy alliance between the Mafia and Naval Intelligence spread right along the coast of New England and as far south as North Carolina. By the end of 1942, when it appeared that the Allies were beginning to win the Battle of the Atlantic, Naval Intelligence had a vast network of agents and contacts thanks to that sinister figure in Great Meadows Prison. For the head of the Third Naval District had warned Haffenden that the Mafia connection had to be kept a close secret: 'When you sleep with dogs, you wake up with fleas'. As few people as possible needed to know, he told Haffenden, that most of Naval Intelligence's success was due to Luciano.

By the spring of 1943 the Third Naval Intelligence District was also busy collecting strategic intelligence about the Mediterranean theatre of operations. It had taken upon itself the task of finding Italo-Americans with connections and families in Sicily. This project was helped considerably by Joe Adonis, who ruled Brooklyn and seemed to know everything in that crooked kingdom.

Haffenden, who had now been promoted and given command of the new 'F' section which dealt with Sicily, then suggested that attempts should be made to contact ex-Mafia criminals who had been sent back to the island after serving prison sentences in the USA. Haffenden reasoned that the Mafia still dominated Sicily, despite Mussolini's attempts to crush it. If these Mafia men who had once lived in the States could be induced to support the USA, they could rally the populace against the military garrison once the Allies had landed. This would greatly speed up the conquest of the island.

In particular, Haffenden suggested that the unofficial head of the Sicilian Mafia, the grandly styled Don Calogero Vizzini, would be the best man to rally the Sicilians. He had his men in virtually every town and village throughout the island. He would be the key figure in any Mafia-led revolt.

But who would risk his life being smuggled into the island to meet Don Calogero Vizzini, Haffenden was asked. The Commander had his answer ready: Lucky Luciano. The latter had already suggested to Haffenden that the Allies invade the island west of Palermo along the Gulf of Castellammare. (Surprisingly enough, although Luciano could not have known this, an invasion in that very spot had been one of the original options considered by the Husky planners.)

As Haffenden's superior, Captain MacFall, told a secret court of inquiry into the affair after the war, 'Commander Haffenden stated to me that Luciano would naturally have to be released from prison and be given proper papers in order to proceed to Sicily via a neutral country, such as Portugal. In order to effectuate such release, according to Haffenden, he said he could arrange for the Governor of New York, Governor Dewey, to pardon or release Luciano'.

Captain MacFall was horrified. The thought of Haffenden, backed by the US Navy, appealing to the man who had sentenced Luciano to jail back in 1936 to have him released appalled him. All the same, he passed Haffenden's request on to his superiors, but someone in Washington turned the scheme down. Luciano would not be going to Sicily to rouse the native population on the Allies' behalf.

But that was not the end of the Mafia connection. In Washington it was suddenly realized that the American task force had no officers who spoke fluent Italian and who were used to liaising with the native population. Where could they find such men – and quickly? Commander Robert Thayer, a former member of the New York District Attorney's office, now of Naval Intelligence, came up with the answer. Why not use the Naval Intelligence officers currently working with the Mafia in New York City?

In May, 1943, he went to New York, reported to the Third Naval District and spoke with those officers who had worked with the Mafia. He told them that he needed a team of volunteers for special duty within the next two hours. Four young naval lieutenants, all speaking fluent Italian and all, save one, with Mafia contacts, volunteered on the spot, although they knew nothing of the proposed mission. A day later they were flown to North Africa to prepare for the invasion.

The four volunteers now realized that it was not only their knowledge of the Italian language they would be putting to good use once they had landed in Sicily, but also their experience with the Mafia in New York. As one of them, former Naval Lieutenant Paul Alfieri, testified after the war, 'One of the most important plans was to contact persons who had been deported for any crime from the United States to their homeland in Sicily, and one of my first successes after landing at Licata was in connection with this, where I made beneficial contact with numerous persons who had been deported. They were extremely cooperative and helpful.'

Asked if these friendly 'natives' were formal members of the Mafia, Alfieri, reluctant to disclose his contacts, answered, 'Well, they would never admit such, but, from my investigative experiences in New York City, I knew that they were.'

In the end, even with the assistance of the Mafia, US Intelligence failed just as the SIS had in placing agents in Sicily, but the attempt was to prove disastrous for Sicily, post-war Italy and ultimately for the world. The Mafia connection and the use of these connections with the Sicilian Mafia during the campaign in that island and the subsequent Allied military government of Sicily rehabilitated the criminal organization. With Allied help, sometimes unwitting, sometimes through the corruption of Allied officers, the Mafia cornered the black market, put their own people in positions of authority, not only in Sicily, but later in Italy proper. Don Vizzini came into his own again as head of the Sicilian black market. In the years to come the overweight, bespectacled Sicilian only needed to snap his fingers to bring mayors, politicians, generals, even cardinals, running to his modest home in the tiny town of Villalba in Central Sicily. After the war his rejuvenated and revitalized Mafia would turn away from the black market into more profitable activities, such as drug-running to the United States and other countries, a plague which is still with us.

The Allies were returning to Europe with the aim of toppling the Fascist tyranny of Mussolini and Hitler. They would do so, only to replace it — unwittingly — with a new one, the Mafia.

5

THE FÜHRER SWALLOWS THE MINCEMEAT

When Churchill had first been informed of 'Operation Mincemeat', he had been told it might be difficult to make the body of Major Martin float towards the Spanish shore. Quick-witted as always, he had growled, 'Then we must make him swim again.' Now it appeared that there would be no need for a second Major Martin. The Germans appeared to be swallowing the bait.

By 7 May, 1943, German High Command staff officers were beginning to change their initially cautious approach to the documents found on the body. At the beginning the diary of the High Command had noted 'No judgement can be passed at present on the authenticity of the document [General Nye's letter to General Alexander]'. Four days later the diary recorded that Hitler had been visited by the new Head of the German Navy, Grand Admiral Doenitz, who was told of the captured documents. Hitler was reported to have told the Grand Admiral that he would hold Sardinia with all available forces and that an invasion of Sicily, originally the High Command's prime target for the invasion of Southern Europe, was considered less likely.

Meanwhile, as the Germans deliberated the '*Martin-Dokumente*', as they were called, a host of new deceptions had been launched in the Middle East to reinforce the belief that the Allies would not land in Sicily.

Under the command of Brigadier Dudley Clarke, a force of British officers, using double agents with codenames such as 'Crude', 'Smooth', 'Funny' and 'Pessimist', tried to give the impression that Allied forces in the Mediterranean had been increased by 50 per cent. This was followed by a series of raids and photo-reconnaissance operations in the Balkans. Both these operations, code-named 'Cascade' and 'Animals', were designed to strengthen German belief that the Balkans was the Allies' next target.

Clarke reasoned that, 'The best way to mislead the Germans is to decide what they themselves would like to believe, and then feed it to them.' He thought, as one of his staff officers expressed it, that Hitler's generals would go for the Balkan option, for this would 'enable us to protect them, not to mention their oil, from the Russians whilst they let us re-occupy the West unopposed. The Nazis also hope for the Balkans. They think, probably rightly, that they can more easily keep their people united against the Russians and against us in a joint attack than if we appear as an alternative and more civilised enemy to whom a surrender could be made without a complete annihilation.'

Brigadier Clarke's analysis of the German mentality was remarkably shrewd. But what he didn't − couldn't − know was that neither generals nor Nazis decided German operational policies. Those decisions were made exclusively by Adolf Hitler and the man he depended upon almost totally to guide him through the intricate and complex world of the war in the shadows, that shadowy figure known by his subordinates behind his back as 'Father Christmas'. In that late spring of 1943 it would be, above all, 'Father Christmas' who would make up the Führer's mind for him.

Nearly fifty years after his death − strangled with a length of chicken wire in a concentration camp in the last weeks of the war at Hitler's express order − historians of the Third Reich have still not been able to make up their minds about Admiral Wilhelm Canaris, known on account of his shock of white hair and benign manner as 'Father Christmas', the head of the German *Abwehr*. A loyal monarchist in World War One, he immediately set about trying to undermine the Weimar Republic after the Kaiser's downfall. He welcomed Hitler and then tried to unseat him after 1933. Yet, after being party to one of the first attempts to assassinate Hitler before 1939, he threw his considerable energy and skill into helping Germany to win the war once it had begun. Yet, during that war there were three well-documented instances of Canaris trying to warn his country's enemies that Germany was about to invade their lands. In 1943 he made an offer through his many friends in Spain to meet 'C' for secret talks in that country. With memories of the Venlo Incident in mind, when the *Abwehr* successfully kidnapped the two heads of the SIS in Europe, Anthony Eden, the British Foreign Secretary, vetoed the meeting. But the request seemed genuine enough. As American journalist, William Shirer, a longtime observer of the pre-war German scene, once summed Canaris up, 'He was so shadowy a figure that no two writers agree as to what kind of a man he was, or what he believed in, if anything much.'

In March, 1943, Canaris had maintained confidently that he agreed with Mussolini. Once the African Campaign had ended in the Allies' favour, they would next invade Sicily or Sardinia. Now, after perusal of the photocopies of Major Martin's documents, he concluded that Greece would be the target. This was the advice he gave to Hitler. So, on 12 May, Hitler issued a directive stating that in the Mediterranean Sicily would be downgraded as the Allies' primary target. Instead, he ordered that 'measures regarding Sardinia and the Peloponnese take precedence over everything else'.

The German High Command started making immediate redeployments. The 1st Panzer Division was sent to Greece and in due course no less a person than Field-Marshal Rommel, recently defeated by Montgomery, would follow. More German divisions were switched from Russia to that country. Sardinia was reinforced, while German planes were taken away from Sicily and sent to Greece.

By 13 May the diary of the German High Command noted: 'It can be gathered from [Nye's letter] that a landing operation on a large scale is to take place in the Western Mediterranean in the course of which Sicily is to be attacked as a mock objective... The main landings will take place... apparently on Sardinia... In the judgement of the Army General Staff the documents are, without a doubt, authentic.'

Canaris's *Abwehr* congratulated itself that it had deceived the British. The British, the opined, believed Major Martin's briefcase had not been tampered with. It was stated in a signal which Ultra picked up: 'The Armed Forces High Command Intelligence Division has furnished an exact report on the way in which the British documents fell into Spanish hands and, following their perusal, the documents were treated with special care in a manner which made it impossible to recognize that the papers had been opened. The papers were returned to the British via the Spanish Ministry of Foreign Affairs in the original case.'

All these self-congratulatory messages and new directives on the disposition of German forces in the Mediterranean area must have been music to the ears of the British plotters. They appeared to have pulled it off.

In the end, however, British Intelligence had to conclude that the Major Martin documents had reached as far as the German High Command and that the Germans *seemed* to have accepted them as genuine. But British Intelligence had no real evidence that the enemy had been fooled. What if *they* were carrying out some kind of deception game? Had Hitler *really* relegated Sicily to a secondary Allied target after Sardinia and Greece?

Churchill exhibited no doubts. He demanded to know the outcome of 'Operation Mincemeat'. His demand forced the planners to make up their minds. So in mid-May they cabled the Premier, who was attending a conference in Washington, '*Mincemeat swallowed whole*'.

Straight from that conference, Churchill flew the Atlantic in a Clipper to land in the harbour at Gibraltar. Here he was collected by the

Governor's ADC, ex-actor Anthony Quayle. The year before, acting for the governor, Quayle had picked up the body and briefcase of one Captain J. Turner, whose plane had crashed into the Mediterranean.

Turner's body had been washed up on the shore of Spain, carrying with him a letter in plain language, giving details of the coming Allied landings in North Africa. The recovery of Turner's body and that all-important letter had been the inspiration of 'Operation Mincemeat'. Quayle could hardly have visualized that the great man next to him in the Governor's car had actually ordered a great deception plan, based on the Turner affair, to be put into operation.

Naturally Churchill did not inform his escort what had been done. Instead he said, 'Young man, are you prepared to sell your life dearly? You know that this old Rock is going to become the centre of dramatic events.'

Quayle, who had been trying to see some action ever since he had volunteered for the Army in 1939, mumbled something appropriate and got on with his job of being a polite, attentive ADC.* Later he took Churchill back to the harbour from whence he flew to Algiers to attend yet another conference.

The arrival there of a small, plump, balding gentleman in his late sixties did not go unnoticed, despite the alias he was using – Alfred Chenfalls. The skinny-legged Arabs who lounged about the airport were not fooled by the cover name. Even in North Africa, 'Mr Schurchill' was well known. The news of the British Prime Minister's arrival was soon known to Admiral Canaris's local *Abwehr* resident.

Thus, while Churchill and his military leaders conferred on what to do after the invasion of Sicily, and later toured the recent battlefields of the successful North African campaign, Canaris was busy preparing a little surprise.

On the afternoon of 4 June the Churchill party assembled at Maison Blanche airport just outside Algiers. From there they would fly to Gibraltar, where Churchill would rest and then continue his journey to London. Again the British party was observed by the local *Abwehr* agents as it started to file aboard the aircraft at three-thirty that afternoon.

An hour later the plane arrived at Gibraltar. Here Churchill was told that he couldn't fly on to Britain; the weather was too bad. Impotent, Churchill allowed himself to be invited to dinner by the Governor,

---

* It would be another six months before Quayle finally saw action. He jumped with an SOE team into Albania to help the partisans. There his brave actions were strangely paralleled in the film *The Guns of Navarone* in which he starred seventeen years later.

General Mason MacFarlane. After dinner, however, the PM was informed that the weather had begun to improve. If he wished, his plane could take off at ten that night.

While a mad scramble took place in Gibraltar to get the Prime Minister ready for the night flight, a British commercial plane was waiting to take off for London not far away at the Portuguese capital, Lisbon. On board there were thirteen passengers, including the international film star, Leslie Howard, the epitome of the British gentleman, although he had been born an Hungarian. But it wasn't Leslie Howard who caught the attention of the lounging *Abwehr* agent at the airport. It was the portly gentleman puffing a big cigar as he waited for the take-off: one Alfred Chenfalls, who had given his occupation to Portuguese immigration as that of chartered accountant. The *Abwehr* man didn't believe it. This was the same man who had been spotted in Algiers with the Churchill party. This was indeed Churchill himself!

The German Legation in Lisbon was alerted immediately. For some reason known only to the English, Churchill was present in Lisbon. Soon he would board a British Overseas Airways flight for London. It was a startling development.

The *Abwehr* head of station at the Legation sent an immediate signal to Berlin for the attention of Admiral Canaris personally. He read that Churchill would be flying on BOAC Flight 777a in an all-metal DC3, piloted by a Dutch captain, Quirinius Tepas. The passengers were a mixed bag, but they did include three women and two children, plus Leslie Howard, who had earned the hatred of the Nazis on account of his portrayal of an Englishman who smuggled Jews out of Germany in the movie *Pimpernel Smith*. He also read that the plane was unarmed and would fly over the Bay of Biscay without an escort.

It must have all seemed very strange to Canaris. The Führer never travelled without carloads of security men, all heavily armed. Nor did he fly without at least a squadron of escorting fighter planes. Yet, he must have reasoned, Churchill habitually took only one Scotland Yard detective, Inspector Thompson, with him as protection on his worldwide travels. Whatever his thoughts, he did give out the order alerting *Luftwaffe* bases in south-west France to be on the lookout for the plump political pigeon who would soon be flying within range of their planes.

So it came about that, not long after, Oberleutnant Bellstedt, piloting a twin-engined Junkers 88 from *Kampfgruppe 40*, based at Kerhouin-Bastard *Fliegerhorst* near Lorient on the coast, spotted the DC3 over the Bay of Biscay. It was an easy kill. Bellstedt, who was later killed in combat in Russia, described afterwards how he made two passes at the unarmed plane, blazing away with his 20mm cannon until it burst into flames and hurtled into the sea, taking with it its doomed passengers. The fact that one of those passengers was Leslie Howard made headline news around the world and the *Luftwaffe* was forced by public opinion, shocked by his death and those of the women and children, to hold a public inquiry. But otherwise there was no mention made of that obscure accountant who bore so strong a resemblance to Churchill.*

Alfred Chenfalls, accountant and amateur violinist, had been in the wrong place at the wrong time − twice. It had cost him his life and that of Leslie Howard. But why had Admiral Canaris ordered the attempted murder of Winston Churchill in the first place? Since 1939 there had been an unwritten agreement between Britain and Germany *not* to shoot down civilian planes, which in wartime usually carried neutrals, diplomats and women and children. It could only have been Canaris who had sufficient power to give that order. In the rush of events that first of June, Canaris would not have had time to consult anyone else of importance about the decision to assassinate the most important politician in the British Empire. The Führer himself was far away at his Eastern Front Headquarters.

Why had he ordered the assassination attempt? Could it have been that he had not really been fooled by 'Operation Mincemeat', plus all the other deception schemes carried out by Brigadier Dudley Clarke's double agents? Did Canaris know that Sicily was the Allies' first objective all along? Did he reason that the intended invasion of Sicily had been one of Churchill's pet projects ever since 1940, but that the Americans objected to it? If Churchill were eliminated, did he think, then 'Husky' might not be launched? It followed that the Americans would then have their way. They would promote their own favourite scheme − a cross-Channel invasion into France. But that could not be launched in 1943. Thus Hitler's '*Festung-Europa*' might be saved for another year. By then the whole political-military scene in Europe could have changed and the Fatherland might well be able to negotiate a more favourable peace with the Western Allies than the shameful 'unconditional surrender' which President Roosevelt had demanded in January, 1943. Although at times Canaris had been actively disloyal to Hitler, his loyalty to the Fatherland had never wavered since, as a 14-year old naval cadet, he had sworn his oath of allegiance to Kaiser Wilhelm II.

Ever since the humiliating defeat at Stalingrad in the early months of 1943, the belief had been growing that the only way to victory over Russia was to come to some sort of agreement with the Western Allies so that

* Surprisingly enough, Chenfalls turned out to have been a personal friend of the Chief of the Imperial Staff, Sir Alan Brooke, for over a quarter of a century. In what capacity Brooke never explained.

Germany could be left to cope with the war in the East. Some high-ranking Party officials and members of the General Staff believed Goebbels' propaganda lies that the Western Allies had slowly begun to see the light; that they saw in communism a greater menace than that of Hitler's 'New Order'. One day, as Goebbels said in Berlin, the Western Allies might well be fighting the '*roter untermensch*' at Germany's side. Canaris did not fall for Goebbel's lies. Russia could only be beaten by keeping the 'Second Front' from starting in Europe as long as possible; and he was prepared to go to any lengths to do just that.

Back in 1939 Canaris had declared roundly that his *Abwehr* was made up of 'gentlemen' and not a bunch of 'SS murderers'. By 1943 Canaris had realized that the kid-gloves were off. Espionage was no longer a gentleman's game. In 1943, which might well decide the fate of his beloved Germany, there was no time for the subtle, long-term methods which had characterized his service at the beginning of the war. Now it was necessary to strike hard, fast and brutally, with the maximum immediate effect. Political assassination was in!

Already Hitler had asked him to parachute Russian renegades into Russia in an attempt to assassinate Stalin. Bodies dressed in British uniforms had been dropped into Yugoslavia in the territory controlled by the partisan leader Tito. On the bodies were letters personally addressed to Marshal Tito. It had been planned that, when he opened them, the high explosive they contained would blow him to pieces.

When Hitler learned of the planned meeting of the Big Three (Stalin, Roosevelt and Churchill) in Teheran – the Germans had tapped transatlantic telephone calls between the latter two – a long-range team was parachuted into Iran with orders to kill all three Allied leaders.

In fact, it seems that not only Canaris, but the whole of the Axis top brass, were *not* fooled by the Allied deception plan. In June General Alfredo Guzzoni, who commanded all Axis forces in Sicily, ordered his naval commanders to be on the lookout for the first Allied convoys from North Africa heading for the invasion of the island. For the 66-year old General, brought out of retirement to defend Sicily, was firmly convinced it would be the Allies' first target. Forty-eight hours before the invasion fleet started landing its troops Italian naval fliers confirmed his predictions when they spotted the first Allied ships off Malta heading for Sicily.

Field-Marshal Kesselring, the overall German commander in the Italian theatre, also thought Sicily would be the Allies' first objective. As he wrote afterwards, 'Eisenhower was wrongly informed when he claimed the invasion of Sicily was unexpected. The Axis powers were clear about it, except for the exact location of the assault area.'

In the end it was Ultra, as usual, which came up with the conclusive evidence that, although Hitler might have been fooled by the Allied deception ploys, his generals were not. Some time in mid-June, Enigma signal traffic revealed to the 'boffins of Bletchley' that the Germans had moved two divisions to the island — the formidable Hermann Goering Panzer Division, which had fought bravely and well in Russia, and a new mobile division, the 15th Panzer Grenadier Division. Six months of costly and cunning attempts to deceive the enemy as to where the landings might come had failed. It was just the first of the many failures of the greatest airborne and seaborne assault of the Second World War.

Just how ineffective was the whole war in the shadows, which had engaged the talents and energies of so many people from Cairo to London and New York City, was revealed five days before the invasion of Sicily. On that day, Monday 5 July, 1943, General Patton, Commander of the US 7th Army, which would invade the Island together with Montgomery's Eighth Army, surreptitiously sneaked aboard the brand new US transport *SS Monrovia*, the ship which would serve as his headquarters during the first hours of the assault. Up to this moment he had been firmly convinced that the tight security blanket thrown about 'Operation Husky' since its inception the previous January had been totally watertight. He was in for a big surprise.

He had been prepared to reveal the Army's objective to his men aboard once the *Monrovia* had sailed. To his dismay he found that every single GI aboard the ship already knew where she was going! The day before, it developed, while the transports taking the invading force to Sicily had still been berthed in Algiers and Oran harbours — both places were infested with enemy spies — the solicitous US Special Services organization had distributed pamphlets to the GIs entitled *A Soldier's Guide to Sicily.*

But it went deeper than that. As the *Monrovia* edged its way out of the inner harbour and the French pilot, his job done, prepared to go over the ladder to the pilot boat waiting down below, he turned to the ship's skipper, Commander T.B. Brittain, and said with a knowing smile, '*Bon voyage, mon commandant, pour Sicile.*'

II

THE GREAT PLAN

'A camel is a horse planned by a committee.'

1

RED DEVILS AND ALL-AMERICANS

On the afternoon of Monday 10 February, 1941, eight already obsolete British Whitley bombers lumbered into the air over Malta and set course for Southern Italy. Back home on the previous day Mr Churchill had broadcast his famous message to President Roosevelt: 'Give us the tools and we will finish the job'. But all the people of Britain, now alone and without allies, saw of the war was constant bombing of their major cities. The night before it had been London's turn again. Tonight it would be the turn of Swansea. Otherwise the only battles in which the British Army was engaged were against the Italians in remote campaigns such as that currently being fought in Eritrea and Libya, where two days before the British had captured Benghazi. In essence, the phoney war between Germany and Britain had been resumed.

But on this day the Imperial General Staff was out to show the world, and the enemy, that the British Army could, and would, return to the Continent from which it had been ejected so ignominiously eight months before. It was going to be a 'small show', as the generals phrased it, using the outdated slang of the 'old war', but it would define the British Army's determination to return to Europe.

Two twin-engined bombers were to attack the railway yards at the Italian city of Foggia; this would be the diversion. The other six were laden with thirty-three parachutists, members of the newest branch of the British Army, 'X' Troop of Colonel C.I.A. Jackson's 11th Special Air Service Battalion. The mission of these thirty-three volunteers was to parachute into southern Italy where their objective was to destroy the aqueduct which carried the main water supply for the Province of Apulia over a small stream called the Tragino.

The planners hoped that, if the mission were successful, it would cut off the main water supply to the towns of Taranto, Brindisi, Bari and several other small towns of the region. They reasoned that the cutting off of the

Italian civilians' water might spread a mood of alarm and despondency. They hoped that this bold attack on their homeland might have a direct effect on the morale of Italian troops currently fighting in Albania and Africa. Above all, it would demonstrate that the British Army *could* fight back on the Continent.

Eight months before, on the very day that France surrendered to a triumphant Germany, 22 June, 1940, Winston Churchill had ordered the formation of a 'five-thousand-strong parachute corps'. 'Operation Colossus' would be the first action to be carried out by this new corps. The Germans had already shown in Poland, Norway, Holland, Belgium and Greece just how effective their own 'Hunters from the Sky', as they called their paras, could be. Now it was the turn of the British.

The Whitleys flew over the Italian coast in excellent weather, unhindered by flak or the fast Italian Fiat fighters. Ahead of the little formation of bombers, they could already see their objective – the aqueduct clearly outlined in the bright winter moonlight. Inside the bombers the red warning lights winked on as the parachutists grouped round the hole in the fuselage of the Whitleys, feet dangling in space. All were volunteers for the 11th Special Air Service Battalion and all were volunteers for this mission. All were uncertain, too. Not about the drop but about what might happen afterwards. How would they escape after they had completed their mission? What would happen if they were captured? Would the Eyeties shoot them as saboteurs?

In the lead plane, a young signals officer, Lieutenant Anthony Deane-Drummond looked around his companions who would be the first parachutists ever to go into action. Afterwards he recorded, 'They looked cheerful, but pale, and they, too, were looking round at their companions.' Suddenly the green light flashed. The time for contemplation was over. Now all was action.

One after another they fell out of the hole, feet tightly clasped together, hands held rigidly to their sides, as the drill prescribed. One... two... three... till all eight had dropped in a tight stick, dropping from four hundred feet to land some two hundred yards from their objective. They hit the hard ground, the first few of the many who would follow them in the glorious history of the British Parachute Regiment. Others were not so fortunate. They landed well away from the objective. But Deane-Drummond's party had no time to worry about them. They rushed their objective and immediately set about the vital task of preparing it for demolition. A dozen gawping Italian farm labourers who turned up out of nowhere were pressed into service with cigarettes and threats. Cheerfully enough, they started to bring in the supplies that these strange invaders from the heavens had brought with them.

1. Commander Charles Haffenden, "a flamboyant underworld buff" (p.37).

2. The 'Husky' Cs-in-C at Casablanca (see pp. 18-23). *Left to right* Eisenhower, Tedder, Alexander and Cunningham. Behind is Harold Macmillan, with Bedell Smith on his left.

3. Looking south towards Gela, focal point of "Patton's Seventh Army landing on the south coast" (p.64).

4. Men of the US 1st Infantry Division, 'The Big Red One', landing at Gela on D-Day, 10 July, 1943.

5. "The key Primosole Bridge, the gateway to the plain of Catania and beyond" (p.84).

6. General Bradley, Commander of US 2nd Corps, with General Patton, Commander of US 7th Army.

7. "The Hermann Goering's most feared weapon, the Tiger tank, a metal monster that was virtually unstoppable" (p. 121).

8. "The American ammunition ship *Robert Rowan* had sunk after taking a direct hit, but her bow was still exposed and from it poured a thick pall of black smoke" (p. 125).

Thirty minutes after midnight on that February Tuesday the aqueduct was ready for demolition. A warning shot was fired. The weary paras withdrew to a safe distance. In a minute the blast of the explosion would come whirling down the valley. Nothing happened! Major Pritchard, in charge of the operation, decided to go and check. As he recalled after the war: 'When we had covered one hundred and fifty yards there was what I can only describe as the Father and Mother of an explosion as the thousand pounds of gun-cotton charges were detonated with the usual accompaniment of flashes, concussion and shower of debris.'

When the smoke cleared, the paras could see they had done it. The aqueduct was in ruins. They had carried out their first mission successfully! Now they had to escape, and the whole of southern Italy must have been roused by that tremendous explosion.

Leaving behind a young signaller who had injured his ankle in the drop* with some kindly Italian peasants, the paras broke up into three parties. These parties would make their way individually to the mouth of the River Sele. Now for the first time their officers told the other ranks the rest of the plan. At the mouth of the river a British submarine would be waiting to take them off. It says much for the courage of those ordinary soldiers and NCOs that they had all volunteered, not knowing that an attempt would be made to get them out of Italy. All of them had believed up to now that they had been sent on a one-way mission. Their spirits picked up immediately.

Dumping all their weapons, save for their Colt pistols, they set off cheerfully, each man carrying a pack containing thirty pounds in weight of food and water, sufficient to last them for five days. They reckoned that, by rationing themselves carefully, they would not need to have any contact with the civilian populace on their way to the mouth of the River Sele. Thus they could avoid populated areas.

Unfortunately they ran into difficulties right from the start. When crossing fields they met knee-deep mud which sucked at their boots and made every step a test of endurance. Then there were the farm dogs. In Italy, it seemed, every peasant hovel had a shaggy underfed dog, whose sole duty it was to bark its head off and alarm the whole neighbourhood. Sweating in spite of the February cold, they slogged their way through the mud, desperate to reach the coast before the Italian military caught up with them. But their luck was running out. One party was trapped on a

* Nearly fifty years later that same young signaller told the author that he had been 'volunteered' for the mission by a friend, who, in the event, didn't go. But he had gone willingly enough because he was bored by training and wanted action. Surprisingly enough he has now retired to that same part of Italy where he first landed with every man's hand against him in 1941.

mountain ridge. Under the command of Major Pritchard, the weary paras formed a perimeter and, lying in the snow, prepared to defend themselves as the long line of Italian *carabinieri* came ever closer. But that wasn't to be. The Italian para-military police were not going to risk their hides unnecessarily. They began their last 'assault' by driving a crowd of men, women and children in front of them, shielding themselves behind the civilians. Pritchard ordered his men not to open fire. What was he to do? He realized that, if he did order his men to start shooting, he'd kill innocent civilians. With a sinking heart he rose to his feet, dropped his pistol and ordered his men to raise their arms in surrender.

Another party, under the command of Lieutenant Daly, tried to bluff their way out. They pretended they were a party of Germans on special duty. Their rimless helmets and camouflaged smocks made them look roughly like German soldiers he thought, as he told local people they were under orders to report to Naples on special duty by two o'clock that afternoon. For a while it seemed their bluff might work. But one local mayor grew suspicious and detained them while he called for the *carabinieri*. They entered Naples all right that afternoon, but it was in rusty chains to which great cannonballs had been attached.

So it all ended in tragedy, with those first paras, the forerunners of thousands to come, going into the bag until the end of the war, though both the radio operator with the broken ankle who was left behind and his CO, Lt Deane-Drummond, succeeded in escaping to serve again*.

The *Daily Telegraph* reported that day, 'British parachutists – appearing in the war for the first time – were dropped over Southern Italy. Rome claimed that they were all captured before they could do damage'. That about summed it up. It was a raid that went badly wrong . But 'Operation Colossus', as it was grandly named, had given the new British paras the boost they needed. The fledgling force had been in action for the first time and had successfully carried out the first part of its mission.

Rapidly the force started to expand from a battalion to a brigade. An ex-guardsman, Brigadier 'Boy' Browning, was given command. The name 'special air landing battalions' vanished to be replaced by 'parachute regiment'. Browning, tall, slim and elegant, brought with him the traditional spit and polish – bullshit the troops preferred to call it – of the Brigade of Guards. He also decided that these new paras should have a distinctive headdress. Accordingly a number of different-coloured berets were modelled in front of Field-Marshal Sir Alan Brooke for his decision. He hesitated between blue and maroon red. Finally the great man turned

* Deane-Drummond was captured again at Arnhem and succeeded once more in escaping after hiding in a cupboard in a German HQ for nearly two weeks.

to the orderly who was modelling the headgear and asked his opinion. The private soldier said, 'Well, sir, I really like the red beret as the blue reminds me of some labour corps.' Thus the anonymous private made the decision that the British para would be distinguished by his red beret, the red beret which had since been adopted by airborne forces round the world. This would be the beret that Browning's First Parachute Brigade would wear when it went into action in North Africa in November, 1942.

While this had been going on, another group of soldiers who one day would also wear the proud red beret of the airborne warrior had been establishing themselves. These were soldiers who would not drop out of the sky by parachute to go into battle, but who would fly in by glider – the men of the air-landing squadrons and those who flew them in, the pilots of the Glider Pilot Regiment.

The future Colonel Chatterton was the power behind the Glider Pilot Regiment, which he helped to form and for which he designed its tactics right from the start. Chatterton had been a naval cadet, but had transferred to the RAF and gained his wings to become a member of the RAF's aerobatic team. Unfortunately, he had a bad crash and was invalided out of the service. At his routine annual medical examination as a reserve officer in 1938 he had been told he was to be classified as Category C. This meant that in any future conflict, if he were ever called up, he would be confined to ground duties. That did it for Chatterton, who had a temper which he sometimes found difficult to control. In a fit of pique he joined the Territorial Army.

When war broke out in 1939 he went to France with the British Expeditionary Force in the 5th Queen's Royal Regiment, returning in the summer of 1940 as a major. The winter that followed found him utterly bored and desperate for any kind of active service. When volunteers were invited for a newly formed glider unit, he was one of the first officers to go. Shortly thereafter he was given command of the 1st Glider Pilot Regiment.

Unlike most RAF fighter pilots, which he had once been, Chatterton was very strict about dress, drill and discipline. Whereas most RAF pilots abhorred 'bull', Chatterton insisted upon it. He brought in two ex-Guards sergeant-majors to drill his newly fledged glider pilots. They were drilled relentlessly, as if they were being prepared to troop the colour before King George VI instead of fighting the controls of a flimsy wood-and-canvas glider taking troops into action.

But the men didn't hold it against Chatterton. He had style and an engaging way with his pilots, who were all NCOs. As one of his officers recalled long afterwards, 'He could stand up in front of men and enthral them with words.' For the two years that followed until his pilots finally went into action he would need all the eloquence he could muster. For Chatterton had to start right from scratch.

Back in 1931 a would-be romantic novelist and two young RAF officers designed a glider capable of carrying cargo, which would be towed by a powered plane. On 20 June the first glider, named after the novelist, Barbara Cartland, was air-towed from Manston to Reading where it delivered its cargo of mail. Later that year the 'Barbara Cartland' raced an express train from London to Blackpool and won the race easily. But the authorities soon heard of the project and decreed that air-towed gliders were dangerous. They banned them and Barbara Cartland went back to writing novels in which the heroine remained virginal right up to altar.

So when Chatterton started looking around for glider types suitable for training his budding pilots, he found that only four were available and three of those were pre-war German models. Rapidly, however, new all-British models were evolved, one following another until British industry came up with the Horsa, the most advanced model of its time, capable of carrying men, or (unlike the American Waco glider) both a gun and the jeep to tow it.

But the gliders themselves were not Chatterton's only problem. There remained the question of evolving a new kind of battle tactic involving gliders. The Germans had twice used gliders operationally — in the capture of Eben Emael in Belgium in 1940 and of Crete a year later. Understandably they had not revealed all the details of their use of gliders. So Chatterton had to make up his own tactics.

Right from the start he insisted that his glider pilots would not merely fly the gliderborne troops into action, but that, once they had landed, the pilots would take their place in the firing line. Thus his pilots were trained to be first-class infantrymen. Thereafter he had instituted a whole series of new ideas on how the landing sites for gliderborne troops should be controlled and organized during a fly-in; how the gliders should be landed, at what height and under what weather conditions; how gliders could be retrieved for future operations, etc, etc.

By the time Colonel Chatterton, as he now was, arrived in Africa in the spring of 1943 his expertise was badly needed. For a whole air landing brigade was on its way from Egypt to take part in the first British mass gliderborne attack. They were not alone. The whole of the 1st British Airborne Division was assembling in North Africa: three parachute brigades under the command of General 'Hoppy' Hopkinson who had just succeeded 'Boy' Browning, the Division's first commander.

At last a whole British airborne division, four brigades strong, was going into action. The real test of the 'Red Devils', as the German

Afrika Korps had called the Division's 1st Parachute Brigade during the fighting in North Africa, was about to begin.

During that same June when Churchill had ordered the creation of a British parachute formation a Major William Lee of the US Army was told by the War Department in Washington to form a 'parachute test platoon'. Like Churchill, the Americans had been impressed by the use of German parachute troops in Belgium and Holland, where the 'Hunters from the sky' had virtually conquered the latter single-handed in five days.

Lee's brief was to experiment 'on ways of delivering soldiers to the battlefield from airplanes'. A tough, forceful regular, Major Lee asked for and got 48 volunteers from the 29th Infantry Regiment stationed at Fort Benning, Georgia. Although in years to come Fort Benning would become known as the cradle of the United States parachute troops, those first forty-eight 'bent legs'* were trained far from the Fort.

Lee took his fledgling paras to the site of the 1939 World Fair just outside New York. There he introduced his novices to the 'Tower'. This was the parachute tower built the year before by the 'Safe Parachute Company'. It was a grand fairground stunt which had attracted a great deal of attention during the Fair. For a dollar, the visitor could make a controlled descent by parachute, which ran to the ground on wire guides.

'There were four arms to the Tower,' one of those early parachutists, Casper Schwarzkopf, recalled years later, 'so that four of us, all dressed up in flying helmets and sometimes goggles, could descend at one go. The idea was good, because you were not going down by yourselves. There were three other guys going through it together.' Indeed the Tower, with its four arms, proved so good in initiating the budding parachutist that it became standard training equipment for the four US parachute divisions which followed.

Partially trained on the Tower, Major Lee now took his first volunteers back to Fort Benning where his platoon made its first drop from a plane on 16 August, 1940. Now as 1940 gave way to 1941, more and more volunteers were coming forward for this new exciting arm of the US service – one which offered the ordinary enlisted man fifty dollars a month more in 'jump pay', a lot of money in the early forties. By the spring of 1941 a whole parachute battalion had been formed, the 501st Parachute Infantry. More battalions were to follow soon.

One of the first Regular Army volunteers for this new formation was elegant Captain 'Slim Jim' Gavin. Born to a poor family, Gavin had enlisted in the Army as soon as he was old enough. Unlike most of his

---

* 'Bent legs' were paras, 'straight legs' were ordinary infantry, in the jargon of the parachutist.

contemporaries at West Point, Gavin did not gain his appointment to the Academy through a nomination by a senator, but by a stiff competitive examination. In the thirties he went through the usual infantry appointments for a junior officer, but in 1941 he found himself back at West Point as a tactical officer. In this capacity he had been mainly concerned with tactics and the discipline of the cadets. Gavin was fascinated by the revolutionary use by the Germans of paratroops and gliderborne infantry in the early years of the war. Thus, as soon as the USA started its own parachute corps, he grabbed the first opportunity to volunteer.

Just as the British airborne pioneers had been faced. with a host of perplexing problems, ranging from what kind of boots a parachutist should wear to how and from what position a para should drop from the plane, Gavin, now Plans and Training Officer under Brigadier-General Lee, was confronted with similar problems. There was the question of boots for instance. The Germans had rejected the traditional *Wehrmacht* jackboot for their fledgling paras back in '36. These had been replaced by a short leather boot with a thick sole which gave more support to the ankles. The British had stuck to the traditional 'ammunition boot', but had reinforced the sole. Gavin's staff decided on the German model and gave their men the laced boot which reached nearly half-way up the calf.

Gavin also discovered, as he wrote himself, that 'they had to discard drill in an effort... to train the paratroopers in the highest peak of individual pride and skill. It was at this time that the use of the nameplates was adopted, the purpose being to emphasize the importance of an individual's personality and reputation'. Just like the British para's red beret, the US paratrooper's name above his breast pocket was adopted, not only by the whole of the US Army, but by armies all around the world.

Young Captain Gavin was very much concerned with making a reputation with this new outfit. He had struggled into West Point as a private of no particular education or background, but since then he had had his defeats. Ten years before he had been washed out of pilot training, something which had stung for a long time. Then, when he had volunteered from West Point for this new arm of the service, his superior had written in his efficiency report that, 'he does not seem particularly fitted to be a paratrooper'. As the months went by and the USA finally got into the war, Gavin was determined to show his former superior just how good a paratrooper he was, in the end becoming the most outstanding US paratroop commander of them all.

In the spring of 1942 Brigadier-General Lee went to Washington with Gavin to discuss the creation of the first US Airborne Division. The British already had one. Why not America? The War Department was sceptical at first, but in the end they agreed. But they had certain stipulations. The future airborne division had to be one which had already completed its basic training. In addition, the division could not be from the Regular Army or the National Guard. The War Department thought the States would not agree to one of their divisions becoming airborne. Further, the War Department insisted, the division selected would be one based where flying weather was generally good and close to an air base.

Only one division met all these requirements. This was the 82nd Infantry Division, stationed at Camp Claiborne in Louisiana. The old 82nd Division had fought in France in the First World War where it gained a fine reputation and the nickname of 'All American' because there were Americans from every state in the Union serving in its ranks. On 25 April, 1942, under the command of Brigadier-General Omar Bradley, while all over the States the movie houses were showing Gary Cooper starring as 'Sergeant York', who in the old 82nd had broken up a whole German battalion single-handed and had won the Congressional Medal of Honor, the Division was reactivated. Before the war was over, the new 82nd would win a large number of that coveted medal.

Now, under the command of General Matt Ridgway, the 82nd was rapidly turned into an airborne division by adding two parachute regiments to it and making one of its infantry regiments gliderborne. All heavy equipment was replaced by lighter material, capable of being carried by glider or dropped by parachute.

The two parachute regiments to be allotted to the new airborne divisions were the 504th and 505th Parachute Infantry Regiments. The latter was activated at Fort Benning in early July, 1942, and Gavin was honoured to learn that he had been recommended to command the new regiment. But it turned out to be a tough assignment. Not only had he to turn his raw volunteers into tough paratroopers at a very smart pace, but he also had to curb their youthful exuberance. His men were always getting into fights with the men of Patton's 2nd Armored Division stationed nearby or with local civilians who they thought had taken one of their number for a ride. Once Gavin was informed by his worried adjutant that one of his troopers had been arrested for having 'intercourse with a young lady on the lawn of the courthouse in Phoenix City'. Gavin's reaction was: 'Well, in view of the fact that that young man will be asked to give his life for the country in the next few months, I suggest we give him a medal.'

While all this was going on, visitors, including Churchill and 'Boy' Browning, the father of the 1st Airborne Division, came and went. But one visitor from Britain, in particular, disconcerted Colonel Gavin. As he recalled: 'After he inspected a 505th Honor Guard, he looked directly into my eyes, grasped my hand and said with a slight touch of emotion, "Good luck". As fleeting as the moment was, I have never known another exactly like it. He knew something that I didn't know and it scared me just a bit and made the moment one I would never forget.' The visitor was the British Foreign Secretary, Anthony Eden. Two months later Gavin would find out just what Eden knew that he didn't. By then the 82nd Airborne Division was camped in a sea of pup tents just outside the Tunisian town of Oujda in North Africa. On 24 May, 1943, Gavin was called to the headquarters of his divisional commander, General Matthew Ridgway. Ridgway was the son of a colonel of English descent, though he never particularly liked the English. He had been in the Army since 1917 and looked like a tough, fighting soldier, though in fact he had never fired a shot in anger. Soon, however, his time would come.

Asking Gavin to sit down, he said he was going to tell him something top secret: 'I've been notified,' he said, 'by Seventh Army that we're going to parachute into Sicily... the night of 9 July.' He went on, 'There are not enough C-47s to drop the entire parachute element in the initial assault. So I have decided to give the mission to your 505th as regimental combat team.' Ridgway explained that this combat team would include not only Gavin's 505th but also the Third Battalion of Colonel Tucker's 504th Parachute Infantry Regiment, plus the 456th Parachute Artillery and B Company of the 307th Airborne Engineers. In all, 'Slim Jim' would have over '3,000 men under his command when the drop was made around midnight at full moon on 9 July.

'I don't have to remind you that you and your men will be the first armed Americans to set foot on Hitler's Europe and that you will be making history by participating in the first night-time mass parachute drop.'

Gavin nodded his understanding. With unusual formality the two senior officers, neither of whom had been in combat before, shook hands. This is what their whole life had been about — West Point, the stamp of marching feet on gravel, the daily routine of army posts, dealing with drunken soldiers, the endless drills, the same old boring faces at the Officer's Club year in, year out. Now at last they were really going to earn their pay.

That night as he walked alone in the desert, digesting the news, Gavin stared at the African moon. 'I have always remembered looking at the moon as it rose,' he wrote afterwards, 'knowing that the second time it

2

'ENTER THE LITTLE FART'

By May, 1943, there had been Husky One, Two, Three, Four, Five, Six, etc. As soon as Montgomery, 'the little Fart', as Patton was now calling him, realized that he was to play a major part in the invasion of Sicily he routinely turned down plan after plan. He felt that these plans, drawn up by staff officers with no battle experience under 'slack' leadership, going right up to the overall ground commander Field-Marshal Alexander (both Montgomery and Patton agreed that he was a 'fence-sitter'), were not realistic enough. The fact that he had just emerged as the victor in North Africa after three years of war allowed Montgomery to throw his weight about mightily and effectively.

One of the initial problems had been what part the Americans would take in the coming invasion. At first it had been thought that they would form a corps under the command of Montgomery's Eighth Army. Montgomery felt there should be just one overall commander in Sicily — he, himself, naturally, but by this time he was beginning to get the measure of the Yanks. He didn't think that they had performed too well in what little fighting they had seen in North Africa, but he did know they were proud and jealous of their independence and doubted if they would accept the junior role in his own army.

Now, with only two months to go before the invasion and still no agreed-upon plan, Montgomery decided it was time to reach agreement at last. As he wrote in his diary at the time, 'I am going to Algiers tomorrow 7 May to have the whole thing out with the Chief of Staff to Eisenhower and try to get something settled. He is a firm ally of mine and I hope to get a move on. I very much doubt if Eisenhower will allow 2 US Corps to be in Eighth Army... There is no doubt that Allies are very difficult people to fight with, especially when political considerations are allowed to override all sound military common sense. I shall see tomorrow what the answer is. But some answer one must have!'

So on Wednesday, 7 May, Montgomery descended upon Eisenhower's headquarters in the Hotel St Georges in Algiers like Christ come to cleanse the Temple. As he had already suspected, Eisenhower's Chief-of-Staff, fiery-tempered Bedell Smith, would not buy the use of the US 2nd Corps under Montgomery's command. Unknown to Montgomery, Patton had already protested to Eisenhower about the proposed use of the 2nd Corps. Eisenhower had agreed with him, although later Patton felt a great deal of bitterness towards him for not having stopped the proposed measure right from the start. 'Ike,' he wrote in his diary, 'is more British than the British and is putty in their hands... God damn all British and so-called Americans.'

So Montgomery was not particularly surprised when Bedell Smith informed him that there were going to be two separate invasions: Patton's Seventh Army landing on the south coast around Gela, with Montgomery's Eighth landing to the east not far from Syracuse. Montgomery accepted the fact that he would no longer be in overall charge. As he jotted down in his diary, 'It was something to get that clear as the organization for command and control could now be worked out.' What was needed in the light of that decision was some sort of coordination between those two separate invasions.

Later Montgomery cornered Bedell Smith in the lavatory and told him, 'The Eighth Army and the Seventh Army (must) land side by side, giving cohesion to the whole invasion.'

Bedell Smith agreed. As Montgomery wrote in his memoirs, 'I remember asking Ike, to his great amusement, if he had ever been told that the final plan for Sicily had been put forward in an Algerian lavatory.' In the event, the whole sorry Sicilian campaign, costing thirty thousand casualties, certainly seemed to have to been cobbled together in just such a setting.

We have already seen that in May the 'All Americans' had been given their airborne assignment. But what of the British 1st Airborne Division, also in North Africa, busy collecting its component units of three parachute brigades and one air-landing brigade? What was going to be its role in the new plan?

Browning had now relinquished command of the Division to become Eisenhower's senior airborne adviser. His place had been taken by General 'Hoppy' Hopkinson, who until two months before had been commanding the Air Landing Brigade. Hopkinson had been an amateur pilot and a pre-war glider enthusiast. He lived and breathed gliderborne warfare.

Now that a final decision had been made in Algiers, Hopkinson went to Montgomery's headquarters to plead for a role for his new division, in particular for the Air Landing Brigade which he had so recently commanded. Hopkinson wanted a mass glider landing of the whole brigade, some 1,200 men, at night, to kick off his divisional attack.

Later code-named 'Operation Ladbroke', this would be the first part of the two-division airborne assault on Europe. Brigadier 'Pip' Hicks' men of the Air Landing Brigade would land outside the port of Syracuse and capture and hold the vital Ponte Grande Bridge over the River Anapo until the seaborne troops of the 5th Infantry Division linked up with them the following day and pushed on to Syracuse.

Montgomery, who had no previous experience of airborne landings, gave his agreement without contacting Browning, and a jubilant Hopkinson was able to return to his HQ with a plum role for his division in his pocket, totally unconcerned that there was not a single British glider in the whole of North Africa to take his troops into battle.

Colonel George Chatterton was one of the first to be let into the secret. He listened with mounting horror and disbelief as Hoppy revealed his great plan. A night landing on unknown terrain, carried out by glider pilots who had not flown for three months and who had virtually no training in night flying? And where were the tugs and the gliders to come from?

Hoppy was completely unperturbed. 'We'll soon put that right,' he snapped confidently. 'The US air force are going to supply tugs and gliders.'

That did it as far as Chatterton was concerned. The pilots of his two Glider Pilot Regiments, one of which was still back in England training, had little enough experience flying the British Horsa glider. Now they were expected to fly the totally unknown American Waco glider – *at night*! He expressed his objections very strongly.

Hoppy's manner changed dramatically. He knew that Chatterton's Regiment was only attached to the 1st Airborne and not directly under his command. All the same he said sternly, 'Now look here, Colonel Chatterton, I'm going to leave you for half an hour and in that time you can study the photographs [of the proposed landing sites]. If, at the end of that time, you still feel that this is too difficult for you, you can consider yourself relieved of your command.' And with that he stalked out.

Chatterton considered the situation. Technically Hopkinson couldn't relieve him, but he *could* make life unpleasant for him in North Africa and after all Hopkinson was the senior man. Rank hath its privileges, as the old Army saying had it. One way or another Hopkinson would manage to get him sent back to the UK in disgrace.

Angry at the dilemma in which he had been placed, the Colonel stared at the first of the aerial photographs. What he saw appalled him. The proposed landing site for the gliders was a number of rock-strewn fields sloping down sharply from the side of a mountain. A worse landing site for inexperienced pilots, flying at night in unfamiliar gliders, could not have been imagined. He realized that he was faced with a brutal choice. Whether he liked it or not, the landing would take place. Hoppy was determined to get his division into action and Montgomery *had* sanctioned the plan of the glider-borne landing. If he refused to take command of the flight-in, then Hoppy would find someone else to do so. That someone might well be very inexperienced. The result would be an even greater loss of life in his Glider Pilot Regiment and he had not been training his young NCOs for over two years to throw away their lives just like that.

The half-hour passed leadenly. Finally Hoppy stalked in and looked down at the glum Colonel. Chatterton rose to his feet, but said nothing. 'This terrible operation,' as Chatterton later called it, was on, and Hoppy knew it. He continued his briefing, while Chatterton listened moodily. Hoppy, however, as Chatterton wrote afterwards, 'was like a little boy. He was *so* pleased!'

Ridgway, Hoppy's opposite number commanding the 82nd Airborne, was not at all pleased with the way that Hopkinson had gained approval for his daring plan, going behind Browning's back to do so. He felt he had problems enough with his own Division; and now this.

There was his assistant divisional commander, Brigadier 'Bull' Keenens, for instance. In his youth 'Bull' had been a dare-devil motorbike rider, given to outstanding feats of courage. But over the long boring years of peace he had become a heavy drinker. As Gavin recalled years later: 'He came across [to North Africa] in a different ship than Ridgway's. He was senior officer aboard. He was drunk most of the time. He'd have us do crazy things... It just drove you bananas.' Now Keenens, a non-parachutist, spent most of his time drawing up orders, hardly ever visiting the troops in the field, something which irritated Ridgway greatly. Should he relieve Keenens before or after the great operation? In the end Mars would make that decision for him.

'Bull' Keenens was not only the senior officer in the 82nd who was causing headaches for the hook-nosed divisional commander. There was Colonel Lewis, commander of his 325 Gliderborne Infantry. The bespectacled Colonel's glidermen were an unhappy lot. They had not volunteered to be gliderborne like the paratroopers, nor did they wear the glamorous jump boots or metal parachute wings of the latter. More importantly, they did not receive the fifty dollars jump pay of the paratrooper, despite the fact that their job was just as dangerous, crashing down on to the battlefield in a flimsy glider made of wood and canvas. All that denoted they went into battle by air was the title 'AIRBORNE' on their shoulders.

Harry Lewis, Ridgway felt, did little to raise the morale of his disgruntled men. Just before the Division had left the States, for example, he had asked his officers to submit lists of their fellow officers whom they felt would turn yellow or become unreliable in combat.

Then, when they had reached Africa and had completed their first training exercise, an extraordinary scene took place. As one of Lewis's officers described it afterwards: 'At the critique [of the just completed exercise] all the officers of the Regiment were present, seated on the ground, hot, dirty, tired and sleepy, having been up all night. Normally these critiques would be where "junior officers" caught hell.' This time it was different.

Colonel Lewis, who affected a clipped moustache of the style favoured by Hitler, suddenly went into a tirade about the lack of leadership and mistakes he believed he had seen. At the height of his condemnation of the divisional leadership he stopped, totally losing his composure. In a breaking voice he said, 'And, gentlemen, combat is only two weeks away.' Then he turned and walked away, visibly sobbing. As the officer witness recalled later, 'We felt leaderless, and *this* was the man who was going to lead us into combat.'

Then there was Colonel Ruff, commander of the 509th Parachute Battalion, which had been attached to Ridgway's 82nd for the Sicily operation. Ruff's Battalion had made three combat jumps in North Africa and had fought for a while under the command of the British 1st Parachute Brigade in some very hard fighting. They were very proud of their association with the Red Devils. Indeed, many of them, illegally, wore the red beret, including the battalion surgeon, who sported pistols and grenades instead of the usual medical bag. Nicknamed 'Little Caesar', Ruff and his men did not take kindly to these 'greenhorns' from the States who had never heard a shot fired in anger. The men of the 509th were a constant source of trouble, always involved in brawls with the newcomers of the 82nd.

Now, in addition to all his troubles with his own soldiers, Ridgway saw his division being milked of equipment, in particular aircraft, in order to support the British glider operation. For not only did the British not possess gliders, they were also lacking the planes to tow those non-existent gliders. Where were the gliders and planes to come from? Naturally from the Americans, which would mean his own operations would be curtailed. By May, when Ridgway had informed Gavin that he would be leading the 82nd's airborne assault into Europe, Ridgway already knew that he would receive on account of British needs, planes enough for just one initial combat jump on a regimental scale. His second regiment, Colonel Tucker's 504th Infantry, would have to go in as a second wave on the following day. As for Colonel Lewis's 325th Glider Infantry, there was no provision for sufficient gliders or tugs to take them into action by air. They would have to travel to Sicily by sea.

Ridgway put the blame for all this, not on Hopkinson, but on Browning. He felt that Browning had a patronizing attitude to the 82nd and favoured the British as being more combat-experienced.

Ridgway, who had first met Browning when he had visited the 82nd in the States, remembered him, as 'an exceedingly capable officer, both professionally and intellectually. Very keen mind, a man of great gallantry and initiative, the sparkplug of the British airborne effort.' Still, they could not hit it off, especially now they were working closely together in Africa.

On one occasion Browning appeared at Ridgway's Command Post to discuss the airborne component of Operation Husky. His reception was frosty, for, as Ridgway wrote afterwards to General Keyes, Patton's deputy, Browning 'had drawn up a plan which would put him "in command status" of all airborne operations'. He thought that Browning wanted to be in charge of all the planes allotted to the airborne operation and this meant, in Ridgway's opinion, that the British 1st Airborne would get the lion's share of them. At the meeting Browning asked Ridgway if he had a plan and could he see it. Ridgway hedged. 'I don't have a plan. Not until General Patton, my army commander, has approved... do I have a plan.' On that note the meeting ended.

A few days later Browning rubbed Ridgway up the wrong way yet again. Browning wrote directly to Colonel Doyle Yardley, the new commander of the unruly 509th Infantry (Ridgway had had Ruff sent home), and asked permission to inspect the battalion. A year earlier it had fought under Browning's command and it was he who had awarded the 509th the honour of wearing the red beret if they wished. Now he wrote to Yardley stating that he considered the 509th was 'one of us'.

Ridgway wouldn't tolerate that. All requests to inspect his battalions had to go through the proper channels, i.e. through his HQ. He wrote Browning a nasty letter refusing the inspection. Wiser heads on his staff convinced Ridgway not to send it, but he managed to convey his displeasure by other means. Browning never inspected the 509th Parachute Infantry.

The open quarrel between the two airborne commanders now came to Eisenhower's notice and he summoned Ridgway to his Algiers Headquarters. Eisenhower tolerated no animosity between his British and American officers; he knew it was vital for the success of the coming battle that they worked together on a team basis. As he was fond of quoting to anyone who would listen, 'You can call the other guy a son-of-a-bitch. But if you call him a British s.o.b., then pack your bags and go.'

Now he put Ridgway through the mill on account of his attitude to Browning. Ridgway lost his temper and began defending his stand on the basis that he was trying to defend the prestige of the US Army. Now Eisenhower lost *his* temper. He hauled Ridgway over the coals, concluding with the statement that Ridgway 'might as well start packing up for he was going home.' In the end Ridgway appealed to Patton, the commander of the Seventh Army, and the latter managed to appease Eisenhower. Ridgway was allowed to stay. His career, which would take him to the highest echelons of command, Commander-in-Chief of the US 8th Army in Korea, head of Nato, etc, was saved.

Meanwhile the rest of the US Army was working hard to ensure that Hopkinson got his gliders in time for the great airborne division. The US Waco gliders sent over from the States for the operation had been lost, among a vast amount of other equipment, somewhere in Africa. Eventually they were tracked down to the French port of Oran, two hundred miles to the west of where the 1st Airborne Division was assembling.

Speedily the Americans assembled a team of hundreds of Air Corps mechanics, taking them off such vital work as repairing bombers used on softening-up missions for the coming invasion, and set them to work assembling the Wacos. Chatterton and his glider pilots joined in, knowing that time was of the essence.

They had never even *seen* a Waco glider before, but, by using the handbooks that came with the crated bits and pieces of the gliders, they set about assembling them under the fierce African heat, living in the wooden crates as they emptied them.

Within three weeks the combined efforts of the American mechanics and Chatterton's glider pilots had resulted in 350 Waco gliders being assembled. On 14 June, the day after that tremendous feat had been completed and with only three weeks to go before the start of 'Husky', the US 51st Troop Carrier Wing, under the command of Colonel Ray Dunn, carried out its first training exercise with the Wacos. It wasn't a great success. As already stated, the Waco could not carry both a jeep and a gun. Chatterton had tried to solve the problem by having two Wacos flying in tandem, one carrying a jeep, the other carrying the gun. If they both landed safely and together, then the combination would work. Unfortunately this first training exercise showed that that would not be the case. Most of the guns landed that day were immobilized before the towing vehicles reached them; the jeeps were too far away.

In addition, too many of the Wacos had suffered damage during the landing on the stony African earth. Two days after the exercise, every single Waco was grounded for repairs. Chatterton fumed. He needed

Horsas, but he had been informed that it was impossible to bring them out from England. Transport was too scarce and flying them out was too risky. The accepted maximum range for a Halifax bomber towing a Horsa glider was 1,000 miles, but the distance from the closest point in Southern England to the closest in Africa was 1,300 miles — three hundred miles too many. But how could he operate with only the Wacos flown by inexperienced pilots?*

In the end he decided to do what his divisional commander, Hopkinson, had done: call upon the Americans for help once more. Perhaps they would provide the experienced Waco pilots he needed so vitally if he was going to deliver Hicks's Air Landing Brigade safely to their three landing zones.

The American glider pilots who had just appeared in Africa seemed to have arrived there only by chance. Behind them they had had a long and puzzling odyssey. On leaving the States they had sailed to the Argentine. From there they had sailed to Australia. When within sight of Sydney Harbour their ship had been re-routed and they had sailed for India. But they had been switched once more, arriving first at Aden and then in Egypt, where they were finally disembarked, after a voyage which had taken them half way around the world.

Now they spent their time training the British glider pilots on the Waco until, one day, as one of them recalled, there was 'a notice on the squadron bulletin board for five volunteers for detached service with the British. Nothing was said about flying into Sicily'.

The fourth name on the volunteer list was that of Flight Officer Bob Wilson. He was greeted, with the twenty-odd other volunteers (they came from all the US squadrons), by Colonel Chatterton personally. 'He gathered us together,' Wilson remembered, 'and thanked us for volunteering for the invasion of Sicily. That's about as close to being scared to death as I have ever felt.' But the US volunteers, equipped with the red berets of the British Airborne and armed with the unlikely British sten gun, manufactured at a price of six shillings and eight pence and distributed about the pilot's person in three pieces, were going to perform just as heroically as their British comrades in the battle to come.

But the problems for the airborne, both British and American, continued to mount. Ridgway, having just escaped from being fired by Eisenhower, thanks to Patton, now locked horns with another Britisher. This time he was a much more formidable figure than Browning. Indeed

---

* Chatterton felt that his pilots should receive 100 hours instruction in the Waco for the Sicily operation. In the end they received a grand total of 4.5 hours, with only 1.2 hours of night-flying in the glider.

he was no less a person than the Commander-in-Chief of the British Mediterranean Fleet, crusty old Admiral A.B. Cunningham. The 60-year-old Admiral had started his naval career commanding one of the first oil-fuelled ships in the Royal Navy, a torpedo boat. Thereafter he had skippered a destroyer in the Dardanelles campaign in the First World War and had gone on steadily up the ladder of promotion until he had retired as a vice-admiral in 1937. On the outbreak of war he had been recalled and made C-in-C of the Mediterranean Fleet. In May, 1940, when Italy entered the war on Germany's side, the Mediterranean Fleet leapt into prominence as Cunningham went straight into action in true Nelson fashion. In 1940 he sank half the Italian fleet in an aerial action at the port of Taranto, a bold stroke which became the model for the Japanese attack on Pearl Harbor a year later. In March, 1941, he succeeded in driving off what was left of the Italian Fleet at the Battle of Matapan, in which three Italian heavy cruisers were sunk. That about put the end to the Italian naval presence in what Mussolini had once proudly boasted was 'mare nostrum'.

Cunningham, who after Matapan had destroyed Rommel's supply shipping and successfully helped Malta and Tobruk to withstand protracted sieges, was now regarded as the most experienced Allied naval officer in the whole of the Mediterranean. But he liked to do things his own way. In addition, he was not particularly impressed by the Americans.

Thus, when Ridgway made an urgent request to him to ensure that when the 82nd Airborne's aerial assault crossed the Allied convoys heading for Sicily, as they would, the ships below wouldn't open fire at the planes, Cunningham did nothing. Ridgway asked for joint exercises of ships and planes. Again nothing. As Ridgway lamented, 'We were informed that the Navy would give no assurance that fire would not be delivered upon aircraft approaching within range of the vessels at night.'

Ridgway's anxiety rose even further when he received that signal from naval headquarters in Malta. He knew that his second wave of paratroopers, Colonel Tucker's 504th Regimental Combat Team, flying in a day after the actual landings, would not only fly over the invasion fleet but also over thirty-five miles of active battle front along the invasion beaches. There was no time left to re-route his two regiments. He had to persist in his demands for assurances from the Navy. Therefore he signalled that 'unless satisfactory assurances are obtained from the Navy, I would recommend against the dispatch of airborne troop movements.' It was a bold move for a major-general who had already been threatened with dismissal by the Supreme Commander to make. In essence he was saying he would refuse to order his division into combat.

But the threat worked. On 7 July, two days before Gavin's Regiment was scheduled to jump, kicking off the 82nd Division's mission in Sicily, Ridgway received an assurance from Seventh Army that the Navy was prepared to withhold fire. But there were certain stipulations. The Navy demanded that the troop carriers should not deviate from certain specific routes and that the planes should not come closer than seven miles from the naval convoys, etc.

Ridgway, who agreed to the Navy's stipulations, was relieved by the decision, but what he didn't know was that the Navy had no real means of passing down instructions on what was going on to its subordinate units. Either because of secrecy or lack of appropriate channels, most of the naval vessels and those of the Merchant Marine about to set sail with the invasion troops knew nothing of the airborne invasion to come.

Admiral Hewitt, in charge of the US fleet carrying Patton's Seventh Army to the invasion beaches around Gela, was not to learn of the airborne assault until twenty-four hours before it took place. By then it was too late for him to inform his naval gunners and those of the merchant ships, which formed the bulk of the invasion fleet, not to fire on *all* aircraft which came within sight of the invasion armada.

Years later, in his book *Crusade in Europe*, General Eisenhower wrote of the Navy's role in the invasion of Sicily that 'the Navy, in its escorting, supporting and maintenance function, performed miracles and always in exact coordination with the needs and supports of the other arms.' The statement was a pious fiction. The reality was terribly different.

On that hot July day in Africa when Ridgway received his assurance that his airborne troops would not be fired upon by naval anti-aircraft gunners below in the invasion fleet heading for Sicily, that assurance wasn't worth the paper it was written on.

3

OPERATION BUZZARD

In 1940 Gordon Jenks had been a trumpeter in the Highland Light Infantry's dance band. Now he was a staff-sergeant in the Ist Glider Pilot Regiment and the proud possessor of the red beret and the upturned blue wings of a glider pilot. On this particular spring day he was spruced up with his silver cap badge and his boots gleaming. For Staff Sergeant Jenks was about to depart on a well-earned thirty-six hour pass to London.

But it wasn't to be. While he waited for the truck which would take him to the nearby station, he watched one of the Halifaxes, which towed the Regiment's Horsa gliders, start to take off. On board the converted four-engined bomber were two of his fellow glider pilots, bound on a secret mission. Suddenly black smoke started to billow from one of the port engines. The big bomber seemed to falter in midair. The smoke grew thicker. Then suddenly the whole plane erupted in smoke and flame. The Halifax simply disintegrated. All the startled Jenks could see were pieces of falling debris. His two glider pilot comrades and the crew of the plane had perished.

Later Jenks attended the funeral of the RAF crew and the two glider pilots. Using his precious trumpet which he had with him at all times, he blew the sweet, sad notes of the 'Last Post', following it with 'Reveille'. As he recalled afterwards, 'They fired three volleys and I started to play. Never had I played with so much feeling as at that moment.' For the first time since he had joined Chatterton's glider pilots he realized just what a strong bond existed between the RAF and the men of the Glider Pilot Regiment.

What Jenks did not know that day (though he'd soon find out to his cost) was where those two dead glider pilots had been going. For their mission had been very secret.

Out in Africa, despairing of the Waco glider and feeling the urgent need for Horsas — even a dozen of the bigger gliders, Chatterton reasoned, might swing the balance in favour of the Air Landing Brigade — he had sent an urgent signal back to the UK. Could nothing be done to ship out Horsas, even if there was no shipping space available to send them by sea?

At the War Office it was considered impossible to send Horsas by the air route. The distance was too great for a tug-glider combination to make it from England to North Africa. Besides, the Germans in France regularly patrolled the air space off the French coast right down to the Bay of Biscay. What chance did a clumsy slow-moving tug-glider combination have against a German fighter?

Squadron-Leader Wilkinson, a long-time friend of the Glider Pilot Regiment, set out to prove that the distance, at least, could be covered by a Halifax-Horsa combination. Wilkinson, who the previous year had survived 'Operation Freshman', a gliderborne attempt to knock out the Norwegian plant supplying Germany with heavy water for the production of an atomic bomb, first had his Halifax fitted with extra fuel tanks. Then he decided that the Horsa he would tow would drop its undercarriage after take-off, thus reducing the drag factor. Then Squadron-Leader Wilkinson set off on his self-imposed experimental mission. For a whole day he cruised back and forth over England, towing a Horsa, keeping close to base in case anything went wrong. By that evening he had broken the 1,000-mile ceiling which the experts had set for a Halifax-Horsa combination, clocking up 1,300 miles and landing with a small amount of fuel left in the Halifax's tanks. The long haul to North Africa could be done.

Wilkinson's experiment convinced the authorities that they should start a large-scale operation, code-named 'Operation Buzzard', which would ferry the Horsas that Chatterton needed so desperately between the closest point in Britain, Portreath in Cornwall, and Salé in North Africa, a distance of 1,400 miles. During the first hours of the long flight the Halifax-Horsa combinations would be escorted by twin-engined Beaufighters until they reached the Bay of Biscay where the fighters would have to turn back. In order to avoid being picked up by German radar in France, the RAF insisted that the combinations fly at 500 feet. Because of the dangers and difficulties of the long flight, plus the problems of flying so close to the sea, each Horsa would be allotted three glider pilots who would man the controls for certain specific times.

It was going to be a tough assignment. Everyone involved knew that. For the Halifax crews there would be long hours towing a defenceless, engineless plane, close to enemy territory. The Halifaxes would also be laden with extra fuel. In the event of a crash landing, the plane would probably disintegrate in a ball of flame. For technical reasons the combinations could only fly during daylight hours, with German fighters only a hundred miles away at their fields in Brittany. Even if enemy radar did not spot them, there was still the chance that visual contact might be made. There was also the problem that the Beaufighters could accompany them for only three hours; thereafter they would have to fly unprotected for six hours until they were picked up again by Allied fighters based in North Africa.

As for the Horsa pilots, they knew that, in case of an attack, they had only two options: stay with the tow and chance being riddled with bullets and set on fire or slip the tow and crash into the sea below and risk the chance of being drowned. The glider pilots' choice was literally that of being 'between the devil and the deep blue sea'.

The hazardous long-distance flight to Africa was inaugurated by Major Alisdair Cooper, who had come to the Ist Glider Pilot Regiment as adjutant. Behind him as he sailed above the cliffs at Portreath came three other gliders, one of them piloted by trumpet-player Staff Sergeant Jenks, together with two pals, Sergeant Percy Atwood and a cockney, Sergeant Harry Flynn.

Jenks' glider was the first of the four to run into trouble. As the glider crossed the clifftops there was a violent crash. The Horsa started to swing from side to side three hundred yards behind the Halifax. The pilots soon found out what had happened. Part of the undercarriage which they had jettisoned on take-off had shot upwards and lodged in the starboard wing. By dint of much effort and muscle power they jammed the controls to port and in this manner, the only way to control the crazy swaying of the glider, they set off on their long journey to Africa.

The weather worsened. It was too much for one combination. The Halifax signalled it was turning back. Now there were just three of them, with Jenks' team fighting to keep their plane in the air. The strain on their shoulder muscles was almost impossible to bear and, in spite of the cold, they were lathered in sweat. So they settled for thirty-minute spells at the controls, with Jenks, when off-duty, trying to keep their spirits up by playing swing music on his trumpet.

The pilot of the third glider, Sergeant Nigel Brown, now ran into trouble. He seemed to have lost his Halifax towing plane. As he recalled afterwards, 'The tug simply disappeared. I could just about make out the V of the towrope, but where the Halifax was I couldn't tell. I didn't think we could get far. Any moment I expected the line to snap or be shredded on the tug's propeller blades. It was terribly quiet in the cockpit. Suddenly the radio silence was broken to say that one of the gliders was going down.'

It was that of Major Cooper, the team leader. He was fighting his glider through thick cloud, praying he wouldn't hit the water without warning, for the flimsy craft would simply break up under the impact. Suddenly he broke through the cloud and below him, only a hundred yards away, he could see the angry green swell. He shouted a warning. Next to him Sergeants Hall and Antonopoulos braced themselves for the crash. The Horsa slapped into the water. There was a rending of canvas and a splintering of perspex as the nose caved in and the icy water came flooding into the fuselage.

The pilots scrambled on top of the sinking glider and inflated their rubber dinghy, each praying that the other gliders or their tugs had radioed their last position back to Air-Sea Rescue.

Now there were only two combinations still flying: Brown and Jenks. The former had suddenly emerged from the cloud into a clear sky – and a shock. Brown now realized why he had been unable to see the Halifax towing his Horsa. He was flying parallel to it and above it! Gingerly he began to ease the glider back to its correct position, some three hundred feet behind the Halifax.

Jenks had now passed the danger zone around the Bay of Biscay. While Flynn took over the controls, he got out of his khaki serge and slipped into the cooler khaki drill of the desert. Lisbon came into view. The sun blazed. The controls seemed easier now and the pilots relaxed in the perspex-lined cockpit. They took off their shirts and sat in their braces, wearing dark glasses to cut out the glare. They had been flying for ten hours.

As, far to the rear, a Norwegian corvette picked up Major Cooper and his co-pilots, Brown's crew spotted Rabat in North Africa. They had nearly done it; they had virtually carried out what some people had thought was a suicide mission; at least, two of them had. Beyond lay Salé Airstrip, Morocco, where they would land.

Jenks' damaged Horsa went in first. As the Halifax released the tug Flynn was at the controls, while Jenks stood at the door watching the white sands below flash by. They had been released at 600 feet. Flynn made a slow, gentle turn to reduce speed. They had no flaps to control their speed. He would have to chance his luck, hoping that by raising the nose at the very last minute he might be able to slow the crippled glider down. There was a sharp crack. The undercarriage chute had been forced open. It flew underneath the plane and caught the tailfin. Watched by a gawping crowd of Americans and Arabs, the glider came in at a tremendous rate. It hit the deck with a bump. Sand whirled into the air. The glider shuddered, as if it might fall apart at any moment. It hurtled forward, tearing at the mesh below until, finally, in a cloud of sand and dust, it swung round in a ninety-degree turn and shuddered to a halt. The three NCOs emerged just as Sergeant Nigel Brown came in to make a less spectacular, but perfect, three-point landing.

Now that it had been proved that it could be done, more and more Halifax-Horsa combinations set out from England. One glider was shot down over the Bay of Biscay by a Junkers 88. Another Halifax aborted its mission when one of its engines failed. It turned round and nursed itself and the glider three hundred miles back to Cornwall, just reaching the coast before another engine failed. Two Halifaxes reached Africa and released their Horsas over the desert. They sailed away into the distance never to be seen again.

But the determined pilots carried on, knowing their odyssey was not over when they reached the African landing strip at Salé. In front of them lay another 350 miles to the Air Landing Regiment's base at Kairouan in Tunisia. This entailed flying at 7,000 feet to cross the snow-tipped Atlas Mountains.

Still they kept coming out from England. A week after he had ditched with Major Conway, Sergeant Antonopoulos was at the controls, with Major Conway and Sergeant Hall as his reliefs, when the flight of the gliders was attacked by two Focke-Wulfs over the Bay of Biscay. While Conway opened fire on their attackers with a rifle stuck through one of the ports, Antonopoulos took violent evasive action. He remembered 'following the tug through some very steep turns. Finally the towplane pilot spoke over the intercom and said, "It's no good. Would you please pull off?" I pulled the rope release lever and the Halifax quickly climbed into the clouds and disappeared.'

The sergeant pilot was now all alone. He decided that attack was the best defence; he had no alternative. 'One Focke-Wulf was just below me and I dove at him. I don't know what was in my mind, but I thought, I'll get the bastard. It must have worried him because he stopped firing and at the last second we both turned away.'

Now he was alone in the sky, with the two German planes rapidly winging their way back to their French bases. He had to ditch. 'There was no problem about landing. I was the greatest ditcher of all time and had written the definitive report on how to do it. We went out of the hatch, inflated the dinghy and got in. We tied the dinghy to the nose of the glider which would be much easier to spot from the air, but the waves kept lifting the glider bodily and smacking it down again. The dinghy was drifting under one wing and I could see us being hammered into the water. We cut the rope and drifted away.'

The first day wasn't too bad. They huddled together, lashed by spray, cocking their ears to the wind in an attempt to catch the sound of plane engines, reasoning that the Halifax would have signalled where it had ditched them. But large waves were swamping the frail craft, the salt water spoiling most of their food. Not that it mattered much, for they were all seasick, vomiting constantly.

'Until the second day,' Sergeant Antonopoulos recalled, 'we weren't too worried. We had our rations, a flare pistol and some rum in a hip flask that my mother had given me, but as the days passed and nothing came we started to get despondent. Once a Halifax with a Horsa in tow flew over but failed to see our flares. We saw ships several times but they failed to see us. At first we were too proud to give ourselves up to a German ship.'

But steadily things grew worse. 'On the fourth day we were turned over by a huge wave and we lost our food, our flare pistol – almost everything. That changed the whole complexion of things. From then on we were really depressed. We had no means of attracting attention or feeding ourselves and we started getting thin and weak. Paddy Conway got sunstroke and started telling us the story of his life. He kept offering to go over the side and leave us all the rations, which we had lost anyway, but we talked him out of it.'

By the sixth day they were almost at the end of their tether, drifting in a leaking dinghy on a seemingly endless sea. Their bodies were now covered in salt sores and their tongues were thick and coated. It took them ages to swallow their only surviving food, Ovaltine tablets, but their mouths were parched and they could not salivate.

Most of their remaining strength now went on baling out the seawater from the dinghy, which was losing air. In between bouts of delirium, they tried to clear the water from the bottom of the dinghy three or four times a day, pumping away at the bellows. But it was a difficult and painfully slow process. Sergeant Antonopoulos remembered, 'My heart would pound and my ears felt as if they were going to burst.' By the end of his session on the bellows he would be shaking and trembling all over and unable to focus his eyes. At night he started seeing six moons instead of one.

On the morning of the eleventh day the three living skeletons, tongues furred and feeling like leather, awoke to find themselves sailing through a thick fog. 'Suddenly,' Antonopoulos recalled, 'we heard the sound of an engine, a sort of chug-chug-chug sound. Out of the mist came this little fishing trawler. We had whistles and I started blowing mine. We hadn't much strength and although I thought I was blowing hard, I wasn't. There was a fellow leaning on the tail of the boat and I remember the look of surprise on his face when he spotted us. Soon they were alongside and pulling us aboard. They were Spaniards and all I could do was to remember some long-forgotten Latin and say "aqua". One of the men corrected me, but they gave us water.' A week later Sergeant Antonopoulos was back in England. Sympathetic comrades encouraged him with, 'Keep trying, Harry. You'll make North Africa yet.'

But there was no need for the Sergeant to attempt another flight to North Africa. For time was running out for Colonel Chatterton. The first Horsa glider had arrived at the Air Landing Brigade's base at Kairouan on 28 June, twelve days before the invasion was due to start. Chatterton would have to be satisfied with the eighteen other gliders which followed. There was no more time to bring others across.

In the meantime Chatterton had followed Colonel Gavin's example and had flown from Malta over the target area in Sicily in a Beaufighter. Standing between the pilot and navigator, he had flown up and down the coastline at a mere fifty feet, trying to assess the terrain where the gliderborne troops would land, but the countryside merged into a green blur strewn with brown rocks. Like Gavin, Chatterton was discouraged. He had flown back to Africa in an apprehensive mood.

The Colonel had good reason. As one of his subordinates wrote at that time, 'Practically none of the glider pilots have sufficient training and it is too late now to rectify the mission.'

His pilots' lack of training and their unfamiliarity with the Wacos they would be flying were not Chatterton's only problems. He was also worried about Colonel Dunn's US 51st Troop Carrier Wing. The American C-47s, which would make up the majority of the planes which towed his gliders, were slow and vulnerable. They were unarmed and unarmoured, lacking self-sealing petrol tanks.

Because of these defects and the fact that his pilots feared for their own safety, Colonel Dunn planned to have his C-47s release their tows 3,000 yards out to sea to avoid the Italian coastal flak. This meant that the undefended gliders would have a two-mile approach over water in the darkness. But Chatterton's pilots had absolutely no training in this kind of approach. How would they recognize their landing sites?

Fortunately two companies of the South Staffordshire Regiment with the Air Landing Brigade flying in Horsas would be towed in by RAF Halifaxes, which were armed and not as vulnerable as the American C-47s. They would go right over the coast and land in the fields near the bridge at Ponte Grande over the Anapo Canal. With luck they would seize the key bridge by a *coup de main*. The rest of Hicks' Air Landing Brigade would then follow.

The diarist of the Ist Airborne Brigade, under Hopkinson's command, was making optimistic promises about the chances of the rest of the Air Landing Brigade which was to be launched into the assault 3,000 yards out to sea: 'The landing of gliders by moonlight is a perfectly feasible operation and the casualties from crash landings are unlikely to be excessive. The glider pilots will have little difficulty in locating the landing area.'

Chatterton was not so sanguine. He had accepted Dunn's decision to slip the tows so far out to sea, but that decision had created fresh problems for him. At what height should his gliders come in? To dodge under the Italian radar screens they had to come in fairly low. But if they came in too low they faced the possibility of crashing into the sea prematurely. Flying over water at night, he knew, was difficult enough for the pilot of a plane *with* an engine. There was also the problem of the Italian flak. If the Italian gunners spotted the gliders and the latter were too low the glider pilots stood little chance of taking evasive action.

Chatterton agonized on what he should do: at what height should he order his pilots to go in? As he wrote after the war, 'I was perplexed to know what height I should give to the gliders to cast off for landing. I felt desperately alone in trying to make my decision and I left it to the last moment.' In the end Colonel Chatterton was unable to make that overwhelming decision. 'I have to admit', he wrote, 'I could not decide whether to instruct the tug pilots to go much higher or to keep to the lower height of 2,000 feet.'

Ridgway and Gavin were also running into final difficulties. The practice jumps over Africa with the air alive with thermals and the ground below as hard as concrete were causing many problems. On 5 June, for instance, when two battalions jumped in a mass formation, the wind was howling across the desert at 30 mph, ten more than the safety limit. Of the 1,100 men who jumped that day two were killed and fifty-three suffered fractured limbs.

On another occasion, when Bob Hope was scheduled to come to entertain the division that night, another battalion jumped, and, as one of Colonel Tucker's 504th Parachute Infantry wrote after the war, 'Two of the new boys making parachute jumps landed in giant cactus trees, which held them suspended and screaming there from the terrible agony of being made into human pincushions. They died an awful death before we could get to them. The spines being too numerous to pull out, they were buried with them sticking into their bodies.'

So many of the 82nd's key men were injured in these practice jumps that Ridgway decided to curtail their training programme severely. As Ridgway wrote in his memoirs, 'To reduce injuries it was decided that only one or two men would actually jump from each plane during training exercises.' So it was that whole sticks would still be carried in each C-47, but only one man in the stick would jump. It was an absurd situation.

While Ridgway still postponed his decision whether or not he should sack his assistant divisional commander, 'Bull' Keenens, Gavin was actively relieving officers he felt were unsuitable for the battle to come. One of his key officers was the commander of his Second Battalion, James Gray. Gavin accused him of having gone absent without leave. Gray protested that he had gone by plane to Tunisia 'to inspect the area' from which the airborne assault would soon be launched. His excuse was not accepted. As he wrote later, 'Gavin advised I was relieved of command since he had to report to Division that he didn't know where I was.' Perhaps Gavin simply used the AWOL charge to get rid of him because 'he was a nice, personable, genial man, who liked to play poker, but he didn't belong in airborne.' In the battle to come, Gavin was to learn that he had not been severe enough in weeding out unsatisfactory battalion commanders. It was a lesson he learned at bitter cost.

On 18 June the training of the 82nd Airborne Division ended. That day General Eisenhower arrived for a final review. This time there would not be the customary demonstration jump. For 'visiting firemen', as they were called by the Army, always seemed to demand a jump. Ridgway feared more casualties and he turned down the request for a demonstration.

As one of the 'All Americans' wrote later, 'There was no cheering, no waving handkerchiefs, just the Division almost lost in an empty expanse. It was our greatest moment. Sometimes I think that the men who marched there for the last time that day are the real winners, with this, their brief bitter-sweet moment of glory.' Against Ridgway's repeated protests, these hastily trained divisions would attack at night. In the British case the Ist Airborne's assault would be led by a gliderborne attack in gliders piloted by partly trained pilots flying unfamiliar planes. They would be towed to their objective in a plane unsuitable for the operation and be released two miles out to sea by pilots who had never practised this sort of operation.

The Americans, who had virtually no night-jumping experience, (in the British Army in order to obtain the blue wings of a parachutist, the trainee had to do at least one night jump) would be transported to battle by pilots who had had little combat flying experience and had had no training to speak of in night flying and personal navigation. Most of them were pre-war civilian airline pilots who had not needed to know how to navigate because they had flown on fixed routes, being directed by radio beams from a tower.

These pilots would also be flying over the great invasion armada heading for Sicily. Although Ridgway thought the problem of 'friendly fire' had been resolved, it had not. As he would soon find out to his cost, subordinate units of both allies, down to individual ships and anti-aircraft batteries, had not been warned to expect friendly aircraft flying overhead.

The veterans of the British Ist and 8th Armies had always opened up at any aircraft which had come too close in the desert; all too often they had been caught out by tip-and-run raids. The less experienced Americans were understandably a little trigger-happy and tended to do so the same. Ridgway, if he had known the situation, would rightly have been highly apprehensive.

Back in August, 1941, Hitler had ordered the 'Conqueror of Crete' to attend his headquarters to discuss the recent capture of that island by General Student and his paratroopers. Despite the fact that every fourth paratrooper dropped on the island had been killed and another 3,400 wounded, Hitler was friendliness itself. Although Student expected criticism and had prepared his arguments – the high speed of the wind, the inexperience of the pilots who had taken his paras to battle, the surprise appearance of British armour – Hitler made no reference to the appalling number of casualties his division had suffered.

Later Hitler simply said, 'General Student, I believe the days of the paratrooper are over.' And that was that. From then onwards, with a few exceptions, Germany's paras fought as ordinary infantry. For Hitler had spotted the fundamental weaknesses of the airborne attack on Crete – the many imponderables involved in any large-scale airborne operation. In his opinion, the only reason that Student had achieved his final success was because the British had been surprised by the attack from the air. (In fact they hadn't, for Ultra had already warned General Freyberg, the British commander in Crete, that paratroopers were on the way.)

Now, two years later, Allied airborne planners were repeating all the same mistakes, only on a much larger scale. It was a recipe for disaster.

4

COUNTDOWN

On 21 June, 1943, the airborne troopers started to move into the sealed-off staging camps around Kairouan, Tunisia, the closest point in North Africa to their objective, Sicily. Here Army engineers had constructed eighteen crude strips in the middle of the desert. These were six thousand feet long and three hundred feet wide. Six of these crude strips were intended for Hopkinson's 1st Airborne Division, plus Colonel Dunn's 51st Air Transport Wing, which would be supported by the British 38th Air Group. The remaining twelve would be used by Ridgway's 82nd Airborne and Colonel Hal Clark's 52nd Wing, who would fly in Colonel Gavin's and, later, Colonel Tucker's regiments.

By now the last details of the plan had been worked out. They called for four separate airborne strikes, all of them by night. The British 1st Air Landing Brigade would kick off the two-division assault. Under the command of Brigadier 'Pip' Hicks, the oldest of the airborne commanders and a veteran of the First World War, the glidermen would fly into action in 144 Waco and Horsa gliders towed by the 51st C-47s and a handful of Halifax bombers and Albemarles of the RAF's 38th Group. This operation was code-named 'Ladbroke'. It entailed Hicks' Brigade seizing the vital Ponte Grande Bridge and holding it until the Eighth Army's forward troops linked up with the defenders.

This would be followed by the jump of Gavin's Regimental Team. They would be carried into action by 266 C-47s and jump over four drop zones north of Gela. It would be Gavin's job to prevent any counter-attack on Patton's Seventh Army coming across the beaches. Again it would be the 82nd paratroopers' task to hold on until a link-up was achieved by the seaborne force.

On the following night the C-47s would bring in the rest of Colonel Tucker's 505th and supply elements as reinforcements. They would land on a drop-zone west of Gela, already secured by their comrades of the

504th. As Ridgway was too old for parachuting and would come in by sea to take over overall command, 'Bull' Keenens, the assistant divisional commander, would fly in with Tucker as an observer. But he wouldn't jump. He would return to Africa to take over what remained of the 82nd.

The final airborne assault would be carried out by the most experienced airborne formation of the whole two divisions. This was the 1st Parachute Brigade, commanded by Brigadier Lathbury, a tall, horse-faced regular officer who had been in the Army for nearly twenty years. Lathbury had formerly commanded the 3rd Parachute Battalion and was an aggressive advocate of airborne warfare. His Brigade had fought and dropped throughout the 1st Army's North African campaign and, despite having suffered grievous losses, it remained a very tough outfit indeed.

Typical of the calibre of Lathbury's men was his Sergeant Major, John Lord, an impressive figure formerly of the Grenadier Guards. Lord was wont to welcome all new drafts to the 1st Parachute Brigade with 'My name is Lord − Regimental Sergeant Major − my initials are J.C. But don't let that fool you, for *I'll* have no mercy on you.' Later, after his capture at Arnhem, he had his fellow airborne prisoners at Fallingbostel prisoner-of-war camp blanco their equipment white, high polish their boots and gleam their cap badges. When the 8th Hussars finally liberated the camp in April, 1945, they found Lord's Red Berets guarding the gates in spick-and-span order, as if they were on duty at Buckingham Palace! Lord exemplified the spirit of the 1st Brigade.

The Brigade was expected to capture the key Primosole Bridge which was the gateway to the plain of Catania beyond. Montgomery had placed vital stress on this operation. Lathbury's men, he had emphasized to Hopkinson more than once, together with gliderborne troops, must hold the bridge until the ground forces linked up with them, probably on the morning after the drop. Once the bridge was seized, Montgomery's armour could then break out across the plain and head for the campaign's ultimate objective, the port of Messina. This port, at the island's northernmost tip, was Sicily's link with the mainland. If it were captured in time, Axis forces in Sicily would be trapped. Montgomery envisaged that then there would be the same mass surrenders in the island as those which had crowned his recent campaign in North Africa. But that was *before* the airborne landings took place.

So the paratroopers and the glidermen settled into their tented camps in the stifling July heat, waiting for the call to arms. At times the wind took the temperature up to 130 degrees. As Ridgway wrote after the war, the wind was like 'the breath of hell'. Water was strictly rationed and the men of the 82nd Airborne, less used than the veterans of the 1st Airborne to a strict water discipline, customary in the British Army, neglected washing and shaving, preferring to use their water ration for drinking.

The 82nd's food supply service broke down. For a while the paratroopers existed on a stomach-churning diet of spam and marmalade. Morale slumped. The paratroopers had been told to expect steaks and ice cream to fatten them up for the coming mission. Instead it was fried spam for breakfast, midday and evening meal, followed by a spoonful of jam or marmalade, washed down with sugarless black coffee. In the end Ridgway had to draw a thousand dollars from the Division's welfare fund to lay on a beef dinner 'with all the trimmings' washed down with one bottle of warm beer per man.

There were flies everywhere. As one of the paratroopers, Lt Kenneth Shaker, recalled, 'We usually had our meals while sitting on the ground. Blasts of hot air blew sand into our mess tins and into our food. It was futile to try to pick out the specks, so we ate it, sand and all. When we drank coffee we learned to clench our teeth to strain out the dead flies and then we would spit them out.'

The flies brought with them the dysentery which was now rampant. Hundreds of paratroopers, laden down with equipment and clad in overalls, dropped over Sicily, carrying more in their pants than spare ammunition.

It was not only the wind and the flies which plagued them. As the historian of the 504th wrote, 'Kairouan, the second most holy city for the members of the Mohammedan religion, was the site of one of the largest burial grounds in the world. Bodies were interred only two feet below the surface of the ground and each tomb featured an air-conditioning vent that was to serve as an escape hatch for evil spirits that might have inhabited the bodies of the faithful. Unfortunately, and much to the discomfort of those nearby, evil spirits were not the only elements to escape through the vents and the air constantly reeked with the odour of departed Moslems.'

Plagued by the heat, the poor rations and the flies, with lots of time on their hands after their training, the men were, as Ridgway put it, 'so lean and tough, so mean and mad, that they would have jumped into the fires of torment just to get out of Africa'. But they were also very short-fused, ready to start a fight at one wrong word, imagined or otherwise. As the Battalion Surgeon of the 509th Parachute Infantry Battalion, D. Carlos Alden, recalled, 'Each morning I made a routine call to the encampment's infirmary, I could always tell which side — the 509th or the 82nd — had won the previous night's brawls by counting the number of black eyes and broken noses.'   The British took the period of waiting in a more sanguine manner. In particular the 1st Parachute Brigade, which had suffered two thousand casualties in the North African campaign, the equivalent of the full strength of the Brigade, had long grown accustomed to the hard living conditions of the desert. Unlike the Americans, their officers kept them training almost to the last day. The 1st Brigade commanders didn't want their men to grow stale or apprehensive about the coming battle. Each day they worked and trained from four-thirty in the morning until midday. Then they lounged in their tents, trying to get some sleep in the oppressive heat which was alleviated by the cool of the evening.

But even the veterans were not altogether proof against the harshness and loneliness of this remote place. As one of them remembered, 'We sat and sweated and became irritable at the slightest cause, while depression hung heavily on our shoulders. After a hard campaign, this arid plain was purgatory to battle-weary men and all our thoughts were of a cool, green land a thousand miles away.'

For commanding officers like Colonel John Frost of the 2nd Parachute Battalion there was no time for thoughts of home, though he, like so many of his officers, was only recently married. The tough, no-nonsense veteran, whose first experience of combat as an airborne soldier went back to the raid on Bruneval in France to capture a top-secret German radar device, was concerned not to make the same mistakes his battalion had made in their last combat jump. Previously, like the other two battalions in the Brigade, his Second Battalion had jumped armed only with pistols and sten guns tucked away in the parachute harness. The rest of their weapons had been dropped in containers either before the stick had jumped or in the middle of the drop. Thus, before his paras could become effective, the men had to find the containers. This time the 1st Parachute Brigade was dropping in darkness, which would complicate the matter even further. Frost was now working on a new method of jumping, with the men's heavy weapons attached to their legs by parachute harness or in a kitbag connected by a toggle rope to the man's foot. This meant they could go into action at once.*

Another problem facing Frost was the weather. In this region — and Frost assumed it would be little different in Sicily — the heat created thermals which kept the men aloft much longer than normal. Indeed, during practice jumps men, instead of coming down, had been forced upwards again by the thermals.

Another veteran of the 1st Brigade, Alastair Pearson, the commander of Lathbury's First Battalion, also had his problems. His men got on well with the American pilots of Dunn's 51st Troop Carrier Wing, but he was not so happy about them. As he said after the war, 'The British had little

* Eventually this method was generally adopted by British paratroopers.

confidence in the pilots' navigational abilities. The Americans had only one navigator to five aircraft so they flew in a V formation, following the leading aircraft. If the leading plane got lost or shot down, the rest of the group had a major problem'. Again it was a problem that remain unsolved; and in the event Pearson's assessment of the American pilots' abilities proved tragically correct.

But whatever the doubts of Lathbury's battalion commanders about the coming battle, their junior officers and the rank-and-file were very confident. Lieutenant Peter Stainforth of the Airborne Engineers, for instance, was 'greatly impressed' when he and his men were finally let into the great secret and were shown into the briefing hut to see their objective.

'The wealth of information presented, particularly by two enormous air photographs, each six foot by four, which nearly covered one wall,' made a great impression on the young sapper officer. As for the detail they included − pillboxes, barbed-wire fences, trenches, etc − 'it was obvious that in this operation nothing had been left to chance.'

But Stainforth was wrong − a great deal *had* been left to chance. In particular, the rank-and-file had not been informed of the strength of the German opposition on the island. Most of them, especially the Americans of the 82nd Airborne, believed that their presence in Sicily was limited to a 'few German technicians'.

As we already know, Ultra had picked up the information about the two main German formations in Sicily − the 15th Panzer Grenadier Division and the Hermann Goering Division, named after the head of the *Luftwaffe*. In the case of the latter formation, it was currently stationed just where the 82nd Airborne's drop zones were located, ready to counter-attack any invader coming ashore around Gela. This, of course, was exactly where Patton's Seventh US Army would be coming in to land.

Naturally both Montgomery and Patton knew from Ultra intelligence of the presence of these two German units, but it was seemingly up to Eisenhower, as Supreme Commander, to decide whether subordinate divisional commanders should be informed of their presence.

In May, at about the time that Ultra had revealed the presence of the Germans, Eisenhower had received a top-secret letter from General Marshall in Washington reiterating the need for the most stringent security precautions in respect of Ultra. After the Axis defeat in North Africa it had been feared that Ultra intelligence would dry up. It was thought that, instead of using the compromised Enigma machine for passing on signals, the Germans would resort to landlines. But, to the delight of Allied senior commanders privy to the Ultra secret, the Germans continued to use Ultra. Therefore *nothing* should be done which might compromise Ultra. After all, in all the long centuries of warfare, what commander had been blessed with the ability to know what the enemy's next move was going to be as soon as he had decided upon it?

But what if the paratroopers of the two airborne divisions now to be employed in 'Husky' were told to expect to meet German formations immediately they landed? In the mass confusion of a paradrop, with troops scattered over miles of the countryside, as they usually were, some of them would definitely be captured. What if these para captives told the German interrogation officers that they had been briefed before take-off to expect to meet this or that German outfit? The Germans would very soon come to the conclusion that their precious Enigma coding machine, which they had always thought was infallible, had been compromised. Immediately they would change their method of sending signals and that would mean that the Allies would be without that tremendous advantage when they eventually invaded France.

By now Patton's Intelligence staff, under the redoubtable Colonel Koch, had been informed of the presence of the two German divisions on Sicily. As he told General Patton on 1 July, five days before the Seventh Army Commander embarked on the *Monrovia* for the invasion, 'We estimate the German garrison in Sicily consists of 60,000 men. The Italians have six static divisions stretched out along 500 miles of coastline and four field divisions in reserve further inland. The coast defense divisions are understrength, underequipped and of low combat quality. The field divisions may be better, but they are short on equipment. What is more, only one of them is posted in our assault area.'

He went on to say, 'As far as the Germans are concerned, they have two divisions, one of them panzer. They are strictly hot mustard, but short on tanks. However, they are both pointed towards the invasion area, the Hermann Goering Division just above Gela.'

That information must have worried Patton greatly. He counted on the 82nd to hold the high ground beyond Gela until the seaborne forces linked up with them and the beaches were secured. Gavin's paratroopers would land with no heavy weapons to speak of and their only anti-tank weapons were their bazookas, which had already proved highly unsuccessful against German tanks in the North African campaign, their projectiles bouncing off German armour like ping-pong balls.

What should he do? In his diaries Patton makes no mention of the dilemma. Eisenhower had ordered that, in order to protect Ultra, the knowledge of the presence of the two German divisions in Sicily should go no lower than Army Headquarters. Dare he disobey that order and tell Ridgway what might be waiting for him in Sicily? Or should he let the 82nd Airborne go blindly into the attack, knowing as he did that the lightly armed paratroopers might well be overrun by German tanks?

Patton, in the future, became well known for his tendency to disobey orders from his superiors, even when they were given by the Supreme Commander himself. Among other breaches of discipline, he captured the German city of Trier without permission, ordered the disastrous raid on Hammelburg POW camp in order to rescue his son-in-law and finally brought about his dismissal as governor of Bavaria on account of his stand on the employment of ex-Nazis as his officials there. Now, however, he seemed to lack his usual determination to do what *he* thought was best. He did not tell the 82nd what to expect. As Colonel Gavin was to record, when on D-Day he spotted a destroyed German armoured scout car, 'I had a peculiar feeling in the hollow of my stomach because no German scout cars were supposed to be in the area and the one I saw might well have been, and I assumed it was, a forerunner of a Panzer Division.' It was.*

The victor of El Alamein had no such compunction or hesitation. Montgomery was a law unto himself. It is not known whether or not Eisenhower ordered him not to tell the 1st Airborne what they might expect when they arrived in Sicily. At all events, if he did, Montgomery disobeyed the order. He told Hopkinson that there were more Germans than 'technicians' on the island; in fact there were two German divisions there, one of them armoured.

The information prompted Chatterton to demand the dispatch of more Horsas from England so that he could transport his six-pounders, plus their jeep-towing vehicles, right on to the landing strips with the first wave of Hicks' gliderborne force. He was not going to have his men landing defenceless against an enemy armoured thrust.

Tragically enough, just over a year later when Montgomery was told that there were two SS Armoured Divisions in the Arnhem area, he refused to take the information seriously. The result was that the 1st Airborne Division was practically wiped out. Now, however, he risked severe censure – for Churchill, like Eisenhower, placed Ultra intelligence at a higher level than many of his senior generals – by informing that ill-fated division what it might expect in Sicily.

Twenty-four hours before take-off Colonel Chatterton walked the beach near the airstrip which would be used by his gliders alone. He had still not made up his mind what height the gliders would start the final assault once the tows had been released, and now he had another worry. Calm weather had been forecast for the invasion, but the waves in the Mediterranean were tipped with white; the wind was beginning to rise.

---

* Two senior US generals narrowly escaped being court-martialled for indiscretions relating to secret signal intelligence. They were General Patch, the future commander of the US 7th Army, and General Cota, commander of the 28th Infantry Division.

It continued to rise throughout the night. Steadily the level on the Beaufort Scale began to rise: force five... force six... force seven. The wind was rapidly approaching gale force.

That night Chatterton did not sleep much as the wind tugged at the flapping canvas of his tent. Doubts and questions without answers followed one another through his racing brain. Surely with the wind at this level the Supreme Commander would order the airborne invasion, even the whole show, postponed? Already the wind was well above the limit for dropping paratroopers. What about the gliders? How would they fare in a wind of this kind and flying by night? Question after question – and no answers.

The next morning, with the wind still blowing across the Sousse plain at almost gale force, the password for the first night of the airborne assault was given to the troops. Montgomery had selected it personally, or so the officers said. It sounded as if he had anyway. It was 'Desert Rats' as the challenge, with 'Kill Wops' as the reply.

Chatterton was not impressed. But now he had other worries, apart from the howling wind. Two hours before take-off a worried officer of the 1st Glider Pilot Regiment asked the Colonel to look at some of the communication wires which were wound around the towrope, which linked the tug and glider. (Visiting a glider squadron, an envious Gertrude Lawrence had been told that the equivalent of 10,000 pairs of nylon stockings went into the making of one tow rope.)

The officer had spotted some black masking tape wound round one of the wires. He and Chatterton unwound the tape to find that the communication wire had been neatly severed. The two men inspected the wires on other gliders and found that the cables had all been cut and covered with the same black masking tape.

Who had carried out the sabotage? What did it mean? Did the Germans know they were coming? Lots of questions – but no answers.

But there was no going back now. Already the gliders were being loaded up. All was controlled chaos, with the men hurrying back and forth under their loads, as the jeeps were driven into the gliders, hauling their 22 hundredweight of six-pounder anti-tank gun behind them, shells already in place on the gun's shield, ready for instant action.

Waiting to take over the controls, one of the US 'volunteers', Flight Officer Bob Wilson, idly watched a covered trailer being manhandled into his Waco. When the Red Devils had gone, Wilson, filled with curiosity, lifted up the canvas and peeked inside the trailer. What he saw there 'really gave me a shock. It was material for marking graves – canvas bags, tags and wooden crosses. Somebody already knew that we wouldn't be coming back!'

General Hopkinson was going in with the first wave of gliders. Left in charge of the rest of the Division was Brigadier Hackett, commander of a parachute brigade. Now Hackett strode over to where Hopkinson was preparing to board his glider. Hopkinson's glider was to be towed by a Texan Lt-Colonel of the US Troop Carrier Command.

Hackett and the American officer had become close friends during their period of training together and Hackett regarded him highly as a towplane pilot. So as Hopkinson, who had only a month to live, donned his helmet, Hackett told the General confidently, 'With Willie here pulling you, whatever happens to anyone else, you'll get there.'

Later Hackett came to the conclusion that these were some of those 'famous last words'. For Willie dumped the Divisional Commander just as hastily as the rest of his comrades ditched the rest of the Air Landing Brigade.

The tugs started their engines and soon all was noise and whirling sand. The C-47s began to roll slowly forward. Behind them the gliders, attached by their nylon ropes, shuddered and bumped down the runway, only half visible in the clouds of sand. As one of the pilots, Sergeant Andy Andrews, recorded afterwards: 'The first part of take-off was in a sandstorm with zero visibility. We were dragged through this dirty yellow wall, mesmerised by the short length of towrope that we could see. It seemed ages before the overloaded glider gained enough speed to stagger up above the cloud and line up with the tug.' Glider after glider followed suit and formed up into their squadrons. The invasion of Sicily was on.

It was six o'clock now. The men of the 1st Air Landing Brigade were relieved to be on their way at last. Some of them had been training for over two years for this. At last they were going into action. Now the black shadows of night started to creep across the floor of the desert below. Before them they had a flight of four hours.

Meanwhile Gavin's men were also assembling on their fields, sheltering from the fierce sun and the wind under the wings of the C-47s. Each man carried two parachutes, two water bottles, a first aid pack, plus 'K' and 'D' rations, the latter containing a bar of solid chocolate known as 'Hitler's secret weapon' on account of the effect it had on the digestive system.

Many of the paratroopers had shaven their hair completely. Others had left a narrow strip down the centre of their skulls and had put war paint on their faces so that they looked like Mohawk Indians on the warpath.

Gavin fretted. The wind was at least ten miles an hour stronger than permitted for a jump back in the States. Would the top brass cancel the drop at the last moment? But nothing came down from divisional headquarters. The jump was still on.

'Load 'em up!' The old familiar cry ran the length of the strip. The heavily laden paratroopers started to shuffle into their planes, each one being handed a personal message from Gavin as they did so. It read:

Soldiers of the 505th Combat Team
Tonight you embark upon a combat mission for which our people and the free people of the world have been waiting for two years.

We will spearhead the landing of an American force upon the island of SICILY. You have been given the means to do the job and you are backed by the largest assemblage of air power in the world's history.

The eyes of the world are upon you. The hopes and prayers of every American go with you.

The term American Parachutist has been synonymous with courage of a high order. Let us carry the fight to the enemy and make American Parachutists feared and respected through all ranks. Attack violently. Destroy him wherever found. I know you will do your job.

Good landings, good fight and good luck.

Colonel Gavin.

It was an uplifting message. But the messages which now followed were less noble and in one case downright alarming. The latter came first. Just after Gavin had settled himself down in his plane, an officer from the weather station came running up. 'Colonel Gavin,' he called, 'I was told to tell you that the wind is going to be thirty-five miles an hour, west to east. They thought you ought to know.'

Gavin certainly did need to know, but there was nothing he could do about it now. Everything lay in the hands of God. He thanked the officer, who left only to be followed by another staggering under the weight of a 'huge barracks bag', which he heaved through the door.

'I was told to give this to you,' he said.

'What the hell is it?' Gavin asked.

'They are prisoner-of-war tags,' the man replied. 'You're supposed to put one on every prisoner you capture, and be sure to fill it out properly.'

Gavin didn't argue. He nodded and accepted the bag. An hour later his personnel officer, Captain Ireland, would throw the lot into the Mediterranean. Gavin and his men had other things on their mind than the administration of POWs. The way the wind was blowing, it seemed most improbable that they'd ever have the chance to take any.

The paratroopers were wedged shoulder to shoulder in their bucket seats — 3,400 men carried in 266 planes, grouped in formations of nine planes. It would take the aerial armada half an hour to pass a given point. As he sat in his C-47, outwardly calm, Colonel Gavin prayed that the moon would last long enough for this great aerial force to jump by its light.

III

SLAUGHTER OVER SICILY

'So come stand by the bar with your glasses
Drink a toast to the men of the sky.
Drink a toast to the men dead already,
THREE CHEERS FOR THE NEXT MAN TO DIE!'

*Wartime airborne song, sung to
the tune of 'The Red River Valley'.*

I

FIRST BLOOD

Colonel Chatterton knew there was no purpose in worrying any more. He had not liked Operation Ladbroke from the first day he had heard about it. There had been too much makeshift planning and too many imponderables. But all that was behind him. The time for action had come.

As he began to strap himself into his seat in the glider in which he would fly the Ist Air Landing Brigade's commander, Brigadier 'Pip' Hicks, into battle, Wing Commander Peter May strolled up. The Wingco, an old friend who commanded the RAF 38th Group, which would help the Americans to tow the gliders into battle, confessed that he had long admired Chatterton's suede chukka boots. It would be a pity if they didn't go to 'a good owner' in the unfortunate event of Chatterton buying it in the coming operation.

Chatterton matched the Wingco's cynicism with his customary sang-froid. 'Of course,' he agreed heartily. 'Just ask my batman. They're yours.'

Now, as the gliders strung out three hundred feet behind their tows, Chatterton looked behind him. He was proud of what he saw. His barely trained pilots, flying unfamiliar gliders, were flying perfectly, hugging the tops of the waves in order to avoid detection by the Italian radar. No glider pilots had ever been asked to undertake such a perilous operation before. His sergeants and staff sergeants, who a couple of years before had never been higher off the ground than they could get on a school playground swing, were flying in formation at wave-top height in the growing darkness.

The plan was for the gliderborne force to fly to Malta, where searchlights would be turned on to guide them. From the Maltese landfall, which Chatterton estimated would take two or three hours depending on the wind, the air armada would turn north to fly the remaining 100 miles to Cape Passero south of the port of Syracuse, Montgomery's primary objective for D-Day.

Now it was beginning to grow dark rapidly. Up front the tugs of Dunn's Troop Carrier Command started to turn on their tiny wing lights. Using these lights and the scarlet flames of the twin-engined planes' exhausts, the glider pilots could judge their own position and keep their distance. More than once in training, glider pilots had overshot their tugs with disastrous results for both glider and tug. But some of the American pilots, either due to fearfulness or forgetfulness, did not turn on the wing lights. In one case an irate major took an axe and chopped a hole in the fuselage of his glider so that he and the pilot could see the tug's exhaust flame and the white star on the Dakota's wings. Thus they steered their way to battle, their eyes watering in the cold wind rushing through the jagged hole, waiting for the first glimpse of Malta.

Down below, unknown to the approaching armada, General Eisenhower was also sweating out their arrival. Later he confessed that at that moment he felt as if his 'stomach was in a clenched fist'. His nerves were stretched to the limit. For he knew the tremendous wind, running at forty knots in Malta, could spell ruin for both the airborne and sea-borne assaults.

Admiral Cunningham, who was with him, tried to calm him, but his customary ear-to-ear smile was conspicuously absent this night. After four years of service in the Mediterranean, Cunningham told Eisenhower, it had been his experience that the velocity of the prevailing wind always decreased after sunset.

Eisenhower said he hoped the Admiral was right. A little appeased, the Supreme Commander, who chain-smoked sixty *Camels* a day to steady his nerves, suggested he and Cunningham should go for a walk on the runway of one of the battered island's airstrips. Suddenly the two men spotted the wing lights of the transports and gliders passing overhead at barely 400 feet. To Cunningham they looked like 'flights of great bats'. But all the time the 'winds of heaven seemed to be roaring and howling round the control tower'. He concluded that, in Eisenhower's present state, 'this was the last place he should have visited'.

Eisenhower rubbed his seven lucky coins for the success of the aerial armada now disappearing into the night when an urgent signal came in. It was from General Marshall in Washington. It asked: '*Is the attack on or off?*' Marshall, famed and feared for his bluntness, was, as usual, pulling no punches. Eisenhower, now cut off from all field commanders, who were already at sea, remarked to Cunningham that he wished he knew. All the same he radioed back that the invasion was still on. But as that long tense evening wore on and the wind velocity stubbornly refused to drop, Eisenhower felt 'there was nothing we could do but pray'.

The anxious glider pilots had no time even for praying. Some ninety-five per cent of the tug-glider combinations had reached Malta. But after turning north for Sicily, the aerial formations became badly disorganized. Some groups split up entirely. Others, trying vainly and desperately to hold formation, were overrun by later formations.

In the half-darkness, it was a tremendously nerve-racking business for both tug and glider pilots. One slight mistake, a single miscalculation, and that would be the end – a collision and the last dive to the Mediterranean below, miles away from the nearest land.

The glider pilots searched the heavens for their tows and for other gliders straggling behind their allotted formation. Planes missed each other by inches. Time and again glider pilots found themselves overtaking their tugs, flying parallel with them, constantly running the danger of fouling the tug's engines with their towropes. The American pilots began to get nervous. Someone in the 51st Group – no one could find out later who it was – made a snap decision. The pilots would rise to 1,800 feet. The Americans reasoned that this would give the gliders two extra miles of free flight once they had been released and allow them to beat the winds. It also meant that the tugs' pilots could release their tows even earlier than had previously been agreed upon!

The first flight of tows released their gliders. Seven gliders severed their links with the C-47s. Silently they came hurtling in, 3000 pounds of men and equipment rushing towards the land. Behind them other flights jostled for positions to be the next. The confusion was growing rapidly. Minutes later the first seven skidded to a bone-shaking stop, tearing up the earth behind them.

Suddenly all hell broke loose. The Italian defenders had finally woken up to the danger. Searchlights stabbed the night sky. Signal flares, red for danger, sailed upwards to explode in a burst of unreal light. Green and white tracer zipped into the darkness. Then the first flak batteries opened up.

To the approaching aerial armada the sudden outbreak of firing looked tremendously frightening and dangerous. But as Wing Commander Peter May was to state at the official enquiry afterwards, the Italian fire was so poor that not one of the American towing planes was seriously damaged. He also pointed out that there was absolutely no anti-aircraft fire within thousands of yards of where the American pilots were supposed to cast off their gliders.

But the flames, the tracer and the generally threatening air of the shoreline confused and, in some cases, panicked Colonel Dunn's pilots. Confusion set in. Some pilots released their gliders at 300 feet so that they passed *through* and not *under* the main body. This added to the chaos as other pilots were suddenly confronted by the silent planes heading straight at them on a collision course. Pilots weaved and turned their unwieldy planes in an attempt to avoid a crash. Some pilots decided they had had enough. They did not even try to unload their tows. Instead they turned about and headed for North Africa again. Others released their gliders miles away from the landing zone and fled for safety. The glider pilots were not without their faults either. In twenty-five per cent of the cases, radio communications between the gliders and their tows had broken — sabotage or accident, no one was ever able to find out. Some glider pilots simply broke the tow without orders long before they arrived at the correct place.

But the main fault, which led to the disaster to come, was that the gliders were released not two miles out to sea, but at twice or even three times that distance. The gliders were sailing in blind. As Chatterton shouted to his co-pilot, 'I can't see a damn thing!' At the same instant he reached for the release lever. He was not alone in his predicament. Over half his fellow glider pilots could not even see the coastline, let alone the landing zone.

Now at last, and at less than 200 feet, Colonel Chatterton saw the shore off Sicily: a cliff face which seemed to be rushing straight at him. Cursing fluently, he pulled the glider up in a climbing turn, hearing the fabric groan and protest under the strain. Then he felt a blow. The whole glider quivered under the impact. Immediately the tip of one of his wings crumpled and fell away. He lost control of the Waco at once. There was no holding it. It started to fall like a stone, straight for the sea. With a tremendous splash, the crippled glider slapped into the waves. At once it began to sink, taking in water at a tremendous rate. There was nothing for it. The staff officers would have to swim for the shore if they were going to save their lives. Chatterton, Hicks and the others dropped into the water and started swimming, tracer zipping over their heads.

Not far away from where Chatterton had just come down, a US 'volunteer', Flight Officer Bob Wilson, was directing his British co-pilot, a sergeant, down. As he did so, he saw for the first time just how far out to sea they had been released. 'It was a terrible sight,' he said after the war, 'because I just knew we wouldn't make it.'

But Wilson tried. He shouted to the Sergeant at the controls, 'Pull the nose up and stall the thing out! Drag the tail and we won't hit hard — at least not in the forward function!'

Desperately the Sergeant tried to follow the Flight Officer's injunctions as they raced towards the sea. But, as Wilson had predicted, they didn't make it. A moment or two later they slammed into the sea, two miles from the shore. The glider started to sink and two men went missing at once. The waves had taken them and threatened to take the rest.

Wilson told them to kick holes in the wing fabric to anchor their feet.

In this way the waves could not sweep them away. 'We got soaking wet when the waves hit us,' he recalled afterwards, 'but at least we didn't have to swim back.' It would take eight interminably long hours before the soaked survivors were rescued by a British cruiser.

Just like Chatterton's, General Hopkinson's glider came down far out at sea. Either the Texan of whom Brigadier Hackett had thought so highly had panicked or he had misjudged the distance to the shore. But Hopkinson, who had personally planned Operation Ladbroke, now suffered the ignominy of having to ditch in the Mediterranean, there to float alone for hours, clutching a piece of wreckage, miserable, angry and plagued with doubts, wondering all the time what had happened to his splendid division. It was several hours before he was rescued. After the war Lord Ashbourne, who in 1943 commanded part of the invasion flotilla with his flag in the destroyer *HMS Keren*, recorded what happened: 'I saw a body floating in the sea almost alongside and evidently alive. I told the captain of the *Keren* to pick him up. A few minutes later a dripping soldier arrived on the bridge. He turned out to be Major-General G. P. Hopkinson, commanding Ist Airborne Division. The last time I had seen him was in 1922 when I had rowed in the same boat with him at Cambridge. We wrung out his clothes, gave him a plate of eggs and bacon and then sent him off to catch up with the rest of his soldiers.'

Breathing fire and furious at what he believed was the cowardice of the US tug pilots, whom he thought had released his gliders much too soon, the little General struggled into the only dry clothes available for a man of his size. Dressed in the second best uniform of one of *Keren*'s Maltese naval stewards, Hopkinson set off to find the rest of his command. He was to be disappointed, for the Ist Air Landing Brigade had disappeared in this first aerial assault on Hitler's 'Fortress Europe'. Of the 147 gliders which had left North Africa, nearly half − sixty-nine in all − crashlanded in the sea, drowning 252 Red Devils − one ninth of the Brigade's strength. Another fifty-nine gliders landed on Sicily, but over an area of some twenty-five square miles. Two were shot down. Several were towed back to North Africa, bringing with them the news of the disaster and the incompetence, or worse, of the American tow-pilots. There was an immediate outcry among those Red Devils still in the camp. Brigadier Hackett, temporarily in charge of the First Airborne Division, ordered that the Division should be confined to their various camps. He feared that his men would take justice into their own hands and lynch the pilots of Colonel Dunn's Air Transport Command.

Two gliders landed on altogether different islands. One landed in Sardinia and the other came to a halt in Malta, though the Red Devils thought they had arrived safely in Sicily. Immediately the young glider lieutenant in charge set about unloading the plane before he came under fire. But not for long. A jeep rolled up, in which were two men, one of whom demanded to know what the hell the Red Devils were up to. The lieutenant answered that he was preparing to go straight into action. Drily, a voice in the darkness answered from the jeep, 'We are sorry to inform you that you are *not* in Sicily, but on the main airstrip at Malta and what's more you're blocking one of the runways and the fighters can't take off. So please take the jeep and pull, not only the trailer, but this bloody glider two hundred yards in that direction!' It took the embarrassed platoon commander many months to live down that unfortunate episode.

Of that great force of planes which had set off, after months of planning, training and back-breaking work to get the Wacos ready for combat, only *twelve* gliders came down in the assigned landing zone, with only *one* of them in visual contact with their target, the Ponte Grande Bridge. Of the Horsa gliders carrying the two companies of the South Staffs who were to capture the bridge in a *coup de main*, six came down in the vicinity. One of these Horsas, piloted by a very popular Glider Pilot Regiment officer, Captain Denholm, hit the river bank at high speed. Viewing the wreckage late next day, Chatterton found that the 'crew and passengers had been blown forward as if down a funnel, but of the pilot there was no sign.' He stood there numb 'looking at the macabre and tragic pile of bodies'.

Now the handful of men who had landed nearest the bridge went into action. Their glider had been piloted by Staff Sergeant Galpin, who had been guided down almost on top of the Ponte Grande Bridge by a helpful Italian searchlight.

Deciding not to wait the allotted fifteen minutes for the rest of the South Staffs to come in and, without benefit of his divisional and brigade commanders to give him advice, young Lieutenant Lawrence Withers and his platoon of South Staffs raced forward through the glowing darkness. As they started off, another glider landed, carrying Major Ballinger of the Royal Engineers and a cargo of Bangalore torpedoes to blow up the wire surrounding the bridge. It was riddled with tracer bullets. The Bangalore torpedoes went up in a great roar. Next instant the glider disintegrated. Bits and pieces of shattered bodies were flung over hundreds of yards. Undeterred, Withers and his men pressed on.

Withers' hastily thought-out plan entailed tackling the bridge from both ends. He would attack from the northern end with half the platoon, and, on a signal from him the rest would assault the bridge from the southern end. Hurriedly briefing his little force, Withers then stole to the river bank. Quietly he and his soldiers slipped into the warm, muddy water of the river and swam across. Time and again Withers cast anxious glances at the dark outline of the bridge, but nothing stirred, despite the fact that the sledge-hammer blows of the anti-aircraft guns on the coast must have alerted the men guarding the bridge.

On the other bank Withers allowed his men a couple of minutes to pour the water out of their boots and check their weapons. Then they were off. Withers, in the lead, could see the bridge quite clearly now, despite the fact that the moon was beginning to wane. Near the little concrete guardhouse he could make out the glowing tip of a cigarette. Typical squaddie, he thought, risking a charge to have a crafty spit-and-a-draw while on duty. Then he concentrated on the task ahead. With a couple of hand signals, he indicated that his men should spread out. Suddenly from the other side of the river a flare hissed into the sky. It was the signal. The rest of his platoon were in position. He hesitated no longer. Whooping and crying like a bunch of drunken Red Indians, his men attacked, firing their sten guns from the hip as they ran.

Erratic rifle fire broke out from the bridge. Somewhere a light machine gun chattered, but the suddenness and violence of this British surprise attack completely unnerved the Italian defenders. Almost instantly they began dropping their weapons and crying, '*Amico, amico, por favore, amico.*'

The Red Devils did not give them a chance to change their mind. Hurriedly they were rounded up and herded into their own guardhouse. The door was locked and a sentry placed outside while Withers and others searched for the charges which were to be used to blow up the bridge in the event of a surprise attack. The Italians in their panic had not attempted to explode them. Now the Red Devils went from charge to charge slashing the wires with their knives and dropping the explosives into the river below. The vital Ponte Grande Bridge was theirs. Just over twenty men had done what two thousand had set out to do.

While Withers flung out a hasty perimeter defence and waited tensely for the inevitable Italian counter-attack, the First Airborne Division's brass were vainly trying to reach the battlefield, as more and more gliders came sailing in to be met by tracer fire and exploding flak shells.

The deputy commander of the Air Landing Brigade, Colonel 'Jonah' Jones, was one such frustrated commander. He, two glider pilots and some of the brigade staff had made a safe landing all right. But when they had time to consult a map, they found they had come down some twelve miles from the LZ and the place seemed to be crawling with Italians. For a few minutes they took refuge in a tumbledown stone farmhouse which had obviously been abandoned years ago; they could hear the rats scampering around everywhere. There they paused to consider what to do next. On the way down they had spotted a well-defended Italian shore battery. It consisted of five guns and the site was surrounded by barbed wire. Jones reasoned that the LZ was too far off for them to help at the moment. He would do more good by attacking the shore battery.

So the bunch of staff officers crept outside to study the lie of the land and the Italians' defences. Hurriedly a plan was worked out and as the first light of the false dawn began to colour the sky to the east, they attacked. Enjoying themselves immensely, pleased to be allowed to see action at last, the chairborne warrriors defeated the Italians in thirty minutes flat. Pulling out the breech blocks of the five field guns and breaking off the firing pins so that the guns were useless, the little party set off with their several score prisoners to find the rest of the Brigade.

At that moment Chatterton and the soaked survivors of the wrecked glider were watching carefully as a small rubber dinghy made its way to shore. There was something strange about the cautious approach of the little craft, and somehow Chatterton knew that the men in it were *not* the enemy. He was soon proved right. The men in the dinghy belonged to the SAS, which in the last few months had made several raids along the coasts of German-held Mediterranean countries. It was their task to clear the cliffs of enemy pillboxes and strongpoints, prior to the landing of Montgomery's assault divisions later that morning.

Chatterton and the others galvanized themselves into action. The prospect of doing something sent the adrenalin coursing through their bodies. Together with the little band of SAS men, the Airborne staff officers began to scale the cliffs, winkling out Italian strongpoints wherever they came across them. By dawn they had succeeded in taking 150 Italian prisoners and felt that nothing could stop them.

Some time during the course of that morning, with the naval guns thundering out to sea and fighter bombers from Malta swooping low over the Italian beach defences to drop their bombs, Chatterton's party bumped into the one commanded by 'Jonah' Jones. The two Colonels had decided to attack a farmhouse which they thought was held by the enemy when a beautiful woman appeared and in perfect English asked them to lunch. By now Jones and Chatterton were decidedly grimy and not a little footsore. 'What about transport?' Jones queried. The woman, who turned out to be an American who had married a wealthy Italian, took them to a barn close by. There to the officers' surprise they found an ancient Italian fire engine, with a six pounder anti-tank gun attached to its rear in place of its tender. How it had come there no one was ever to explain.

Cheerfully the officers and their men clambered aboard and set off in the rickety 1900's vintage fire engine for the American woman's house. There, after posting sentries, who had to be content with bully beef sandwiches, for 'rank hath its privileges', the two Colonels sat down to 'a wonderful lunch', as Chatterton wrote later, 'while all around us there were the sounds of the diminishing battle, the rattle of machine guns and explosives. I don't know how many bottles of Chianti we drank that afternoon or how much spaghetti we ate, but it was a very large and very, very good lunch.'

While the senior officers let their hair down, Lieutenant Withers, still guarding the bridge with his platoon and the stragglers he had collected during the night, was beginning to get worried. At the briefing in North Africa he had been told that the two companies of the South Staffs detailed to take the bridge would be relieved at seven-thirty that morning. It was now eight o'clock, there was no sign of the seaborne troops and the Italians were beginning to mass for the expected counter-attack. Their commanders knew as well as Montgomery how vital the bridge at Ponte Grande was.

About then another twelve stragglers came in to tell their tale and join Withers' force which had now swelled to eight officers and sixty-five other ranks. The latest reinforcements included one of the US 'volunteer' glider-pilots, Flight Officer Samuel Fine, a New Yorker. His Waco, containing a trailer and twelve men, had crashed into a tree on landing. Almost immediately the wrecked glider had come under intense fire. The first man out of the door had been killed at point-blank range and Fine had twice been wounded. Somehow they had fought their way out of the ambush and joined up with the defenders of the vital bridge. 'Just in time,' as Fine recalled afterwards.

Indeed it was just in time. Five minutes later a large staff car, flying an imposing pennant, rolled up. It contained a high-ranking officer, his shoulders heavy with gold-braided epaulettes. Haughtily, as if unaware that the bridge was in British hands, he ordered that the red-and-white striped barrier pole at the approach to the bridge be lifted.

The British reaction was immediate. A hail of fire swept the Italians. The officer went down immediately and his companions flung up their hands in surrender. Hurriedly they were rounded up and sent to the makeshift 'cage' in the blockhouse where they would spend the rest of the coming battle until it was hit by an Italian shell.

Fine, crouched in a hole, watched the front and was one of the first to see the Italians 'creeping down from the north-west' towards the bridge. He clicked the bolt back on the unfamiliar sten gun. He knew what was coming.

It came minutes later. First came the hollow blast of a mortar, followed an instant later by the howl of the falling bomb. It exploded in a burst of flame and a shower of earth, sending red-hot shrapnel scything through the air.

'Stand to!' Withers yelled above the racket, 'Stand to. *They're coming!*'

Under the cover of the mortar barrage, Italian soldiers in their grey-green uniforms were swarming forward in their scores. The battle for the Ponte Grande bridge had begun.

2

DIRTY DANCING

Colonel Gavin's aerial task force had left Malta behind them and were starting the dogleg of their flight to Sicily. Flying low as they were, he could easily see the great invasion fleets below. The sight made him feel uneasy. He knew at once that they were well off course.

The plan had been for the 505th Regimental Combat Team to fly between the great convoys with Patton's Seventh Army to the left and Montgomery's Eighth Army to the right. Now they were flying directly above the great fleets steadily ploughing their way through the mountainous seas towards Sicily. Gavin said a silent prayer that the gunners below wouldn't get trigger happy. If they did, even a one-eyed gunner with the shakes couldn't help but hit the planes flying directly overhead in formation and at such a low height. The thought was too terrible to contemplate.

But Gavin's proverbial luck held and shortly thereafter he could see the faint pink flames and sudden stabs of scarlet on the horizon which indicated that the Allied air forces were softening up their targets on the island. They were almost there. After twenty years in the US Army, he was going to earn his pay in combat for the first time.

Now the C-47s started to climb. To dodge the Italian radar some of the pilots had flown the last dogleg from Malta as low as 200 feet. Later, pilots returning to North Africa would report that they had flown so low that salt spray from the waves had caked their windscreens. Now they had to climb to gain sufficient height for the paratroopers to jump. But the climb brought difficulties. So far their navigation had been visual. Now they were losing sight of the ground below. The haze and the smoke caused by the Allied softening-up of the coastal targets didn't help either. The same sort of confusion which had plagued the British Air Landing Brigade several hours earlier now set in. Pilots, unable to spot the DZ, turned and flew out to sea once more to regroup and make another attempt. Others dropped their paratroopers blind and at too low a height. Some panicked and flew straight back to Africa, as the Italian flak turned its attention on the air fleet. The first plane was hit. Smoke streaming from its port engine, it raced to the ground, carrying its cargo of paratroopers to their death. Minutes later another C-47 was struck and disintegrated in midair. No parachutes fell from the ball of black smoke.

Inside the planes the sweating paratroopers grew fearful. They had seen the flaming torches of the other planes going down. They wanted to be out of the metal coffins before it was their turn. At six hundred feet they were sitting ducks for the Italian gunners below. Sergeant Ross Carter recalled afterwards how 'suddenly long red streaks of flame began to stab and slice the sky into weird patterns of flashes and bursts above, below and around us. Whether by friend or foe, we were being shot at! I felt the urge to kick Toland [his friend] through the door and get into space before our plane became a burning coffin.' Finally his turn to jump came and Carter floated down with 'a double stream of red tracers seemingly going between my legs. Ack-ack shells exploding all around me splattered little puffs of smoke against the moonlight. Some of our planes tumbled out of the sky like burning crosses; others, stopped like a bird shot in flight, crumpled and plummeted. Still others exploded and disintegrated.'

Now everything went wrong. In the confusion and, in some cases, downright panic, pilots scattered their paratroopers over one thousand square miles. Others forced the paratroopers to jump as low as 150 feet. Men hit the ground not to get up again, either unconscious or dead. Broken bones were everywhere.

Major Alexander, one of Gavin's battalion commanders, found himself staring at the red warning light when he knew the plane carrying him and his stick was still over the sea. Further off he could see the glowing tracer sailing up towards the plane. He realized the pilot was panicking. He wanted to be rid of his cargo as soon as possible and flee to the safety of North Africa. Alexander's men did not know that. They wanted to get out of the plane at once. They jostled and pushed and Major Alexander had to cling on for his life, shouting at his soldiers that they weren't yet over land. Finally he succeeded in calming them.

Minutes later Alexander and his battalion jumped into Sicily – right into the middle of an Italian strongpoint, complete with a three-storey concrete bunker. The Battalion Medical Officer, Lieutenant Robert Clee, was one of the first to go down wounded. He fell into a tangle of rusting barbed wire. Desperately he tried to free himself from the prongs which clutched at his flesh and uniform. The Italians didn't give him a chance. Their machine guns centred on the struggling man, outlined in the beam of a searchlight. A burst of fire ripped the doctor's chest apart. He slumped dead into the wire to remain there for the rest of the battle.

Not far away Sergeant Harold Freeman, another member of Alexander's battalion, was similarly trapped in the barbed wire. But he had seen what had happened to the M.O. He feigned death and lay on the wire for five hours while a savage fire-fight raged all around him. It was only when the battle was over that he felt safe enough to make a move.

Captain John Norton, Alexander's executive officer, hit the ground hard, as did most of the battalion. But, unlike most of Alexander's men, he found himself completely alone. So he staggered to a lonely stone house, shrouded in darkness. But the place was occupied, he could tell that, for he could hear the faint hum of voices coming through the thick walls. Pistol in hand, he approached the house and cautiously whispered the password of the day, 'George'.

The answer should have been 'Marshall'. (It had been thought that not even the stupidest paratrooper would forget the name of the head of the US Army, General George Marshall.)

Instead of 'Marshall', however, a voice snarled in a thick Italian accent, 'George – hell!'

At the same instant the Captain ducked. Just in time. A burst of tracer sliced the air where he stood. He had bumped into an Italian command post.

Not far away from the spot where Captain Norton was making a determined effort to sneak away before the Italians became a little too accurate with their light automatic, another member of the same battalion found himself alone and under fire. Unlike his comrades who had shaven their heads in the 'Mohawk look' and had applied war paint to their faces, Sergeant Buffalo Boy Canoe was a real Red Indian, a Sioux to be exact.

Armed with a carbine, which had jammed, and a trench knife, Sergeant Canoe decided that it would be wiser to avoid a confrontation at this stage of the landing. So, in the fashion of his Wild West ancestors, he slithered away into the darkness. A little later he found himself outside a little farmhouse with the sound of the firing dying away behind him. Cautiously he approached the nearest window and peeked in. Three Germans were seated inside drinking from bottles of rough Sicilian red wine.

Canoe had plenty of time – and patience. He stole back to the bushes and waited. He knew at the rate the Germans were consuming the wine that they would have to come outside and get rid of it sooner or later. It was sooner. A drunken German staggered out, his body illuminated by the flickering light of a candle inside. Canoe waited until the German had unbuttoned his flies, then he stole up, knocked the German to the ground and plunged home his knife. Now he waited for the other two. Drunk as they were, they had become suspicious. They came out swaying, holding pistols in their hands. One of them called the missing man's name. Canoe tensed. Slowly he brought out his only grenade. The lever zipped away in the darkness with a sound that he thought must alert the Germans. He counted off the seconds. Then he flung the grenade and ducked. Next moment Canoe was gone, sliding into the night like some silent, predatory animal.

And all the while the transports still kept coming in to drop their cargoes of paratroopers, in some cases abandoning them to their fate, concerned only with their own safety. Captain Robert Kaufmann, for instance, was standing in the door of his C-47, waiting for the green light to flash on. Suddenly the plane ran into flak. It rocked violently as shell fragment rattled the length of its metal skin. Kaufmann was hit in the neck. At the same instant the pilot flashed on the green light; he wanted to be off. Kaufmann fell dying from the plane.

His stick reacted predictably. They had seen the green light and they had seen their officer jump. In rapid succession they followed Kaufmann out of the door. Stick Two followed, then Stick Three – all of them falling to a watery grave in the Mediterranean.

By now General Ridgway, lying off shore waiting to land, knew from preliminary reports from returning aircraft that his 504 Regimental Combat Team had been widely scattered all over Sicily. Though he didn't know the details yet, some of his men had landed in the British zone of operation. Others had been dropped sixty miles away from their objectives. But none had landed in that area from which any counter-attack on Patton's landings would come. Still Ridgway, a product of West Point himself, hoped that at least his regular army officers would heed the old West Point motto and 'march to the sound of the guns'. And indeed that is what most of them did, whether they were products of West Point or young men who a couple of years before had been civilian 'drugstore cowboys', in the parlance of the time. One such was Captain Follmer. He had broken his ankle in three places during the landing and now hobbled on, feeling himself 'the loneliest man in Sicily'. Not for long. He soon found his husky sergeant batman, who promptly put his crippled officer on his broad back and together they set off to find their missing company. Within the hour they had found most of it. But the sergeant was beginning to tire. So a mule was found and for the next three days Captain Follmer directed his own personal battle from the back of a fleabitten old donkey: a member of the most modern branch of the US Army doing battle in the most ancient way imaginable.

For three days Follmer's company blocked some of the roads leading to the beaches, waiting for the infantry of the 'Big Red One', the US 1st Infantry Division, to come up from the beaches to relieve them. In the end he was relieved by no less a personage than his own divisional commander.

Follmer was resting in the shade of some olive trees near his donkey when he felt someone was watching him. He straightened up to look straight into the hawklike face of General Ridgway, who was obviously very displeased by what he saw. 'What are you doing there, sitting on yer ass, Captain?' Ridgway snapped.

Follmer stuttered, 'Sir, I think I broke my ankle and I'm having a hard time getting around. But most of my men are accounted for and they've carried out all of our missions. I've been going to see them at the roadblocks on this old mule.'

Ridgway was appeased. 'Well, keep it up, Captain,' he snapped, and, shouldering the rifle he always carried, Ridgway trudged off, accompanied by two aides, to find the rest of his division. Almost a year later when he dropped into battle in Normandy with the 82nd, the first person that Ridgway would come across in the darkness was Captain Follmer!

Some marched to the guns in a more leisurely fashion, apparently having time enough to enjoy the local cuisine. One such was 1st Lieutenant F. E. Thomas, who was trapped with several men while enjoying the hospitality of some of the friendlier natives over wine, bread and sausage. Suddenly several Germans, armed with automatics, appeared, backed by the guns of three disabled tanks.

Thomas was a quick-thinking young man. Draining his glass, he reasoned with his captors. Allied victory was inevitable, he purred. Why risk their lives like this?

The Germans wavered. They explained that one of their number across the road had been badly wounded. They had heard that the 'Amis', as they called the Americans, had brought with them excellent medical facilities. Thomas agreed. He suggested that in return for their freedom they would see that the wounded German would receive immediate US medical attention.

The Germans put their tanks out of commission and departed, leaving Thomas and his comrades free men with time to enjoy another glass of red wine before they got back in the war.

But it wasn't all beer and skittles. 'Beaver' Thompson, the war correspondent of the *Chicago Tribune*, who had jumped with the first lift, described how one group of lost paratroopers, under the command of Colonel Arthur Gorham, picked as an alternative objective to the one they had been briefed to attack before the fly-in 'a very sturdy, thick-walled farmhouse which had been converted into a military fort held by sixty men with four heavy machine guns and six light ones. It was also well wired with trench defences.'

Colonel Gorham handed the job of tackling the place to Captain Edwin Sayre and twenty-two paratroopers. As 'Beaver' described it: 'Their first attack was launched at 2 o'clock in the morning. They were held up then, but attacked again just before dawn, with rifles, grenades, one 60mm mortar and a bazooka.

'They forced the Italians back out of the trenches and into the house and attacked the house with grenades. Sayre led the assault, carrying one hand grenade in his teeth and another in his left hand, with a carbine in his right hand. A rifle grenade fired at about ten feet blew open the door but the door swung shut again. Sayre walked up, threw open the door and pitched a hand grenade inside.'

The victors found fifteen of the enemy dead and took forty-five prisoners, but soon the house came under fire from one of the dreaded German 88mm cannon and Colonel Gorham ordered a hasty retreat into the hills. It would be two days, fighting all the time, before they finally linked up with the 504th Regimental Combat Team.

Gavin, the commander of that force, determined he would link up with it right from the start, although his staff team seemed to have vanished. All he could find on landing were Captain Al Ireland, his personnel officer, Captain Ben Vandervoort and three paratroopers. Nevertheless he set off cross-country at a half-run, half-walk, collecting another twenty stragglers en route. Then, after twenty years in the service without hearing a shot fired in anger, Gavin came face to face with the enemy.

For some time now the little force had been hearing bursts of small-arms fire and on a couple of occasions they had listened to voices shouting in some foreign tongue which they had been unable to identify. Now the little band stopped as they heard the sounds of steps coming towards them and someone whistling what Gavin took to be '*Sole mio*'.

Gavin whispered to his men to take cover in the shadows cast by a low stone wall which bordered the road. Later, tongue in cheek, he described what happened next. 'It was a lone man, walking down the middle of the road, hands in the pockets of his baggy pants. After twenty years of military service I was about to meet The Enemy face to face.'

Gavin waited till the Italian soldier came level with him, then he stuck his carbine over the wall and commanded in his 'best Italian', '*Alto!*'

The Italian stopped dead in his tracks. In a flash, Captain Vandervoort was over the wall, carbine in one hand, combat knife in the other, crying 'I'll take care of him!'

Gavin wasn't quite sure what that meant. But it was too late now to stop the eager young officer, also going into action for the first time. 'No,' he hissed, 'let's get the hell out of the middle of the road. Let's get over to the shadows. Maybe we can get some information out of him.'

It was no use. The Italian wouldn't – couldn't – respond to Gavin's questions in his fractured Italian. He was quaking with fear, too scared to be able to utter a word. Obviously he had heard the stories the Germans had spread in Sicily. According to the *Tedeschi*, US paratroopers were recruited from the scum of American jails and were murderers to the man.

Vandervoort, who had taken an intelligence course on how to treat prisoners-of-war, now set to work on their first captive. The idea was to remove the prisoner's belt and then slice off his fly buttons so that he would have to hold up his pants and wouldn't be able to escape.

Things went well while Vandervoort removed the Italian's belt, thought the latter kept muttering '*mamma mia*', as if he wondered what the American was about to do to him. But when Vandervoort grabbed at his fly buttons, the Italian had had enough. He thought the *Americano* was about to castrate him.

As Gavin described it afterwards, 'A scream went up that could be heard all the way to Rome. He screamed even louder after grabbing the knife blade with his right hand. The blood ran down his hand as we fell in a kicking, yelling, fighting mass and he got away. I do not know how he did it, but one second he was with us and the next he was gone. I was madder than hell.'

Gavin asked Vandervoort: 'What in the hell did you think you were doing?'

Vandervoort, wisely, thought it better not to answer his CO's question. So they set off again in a brooding silence, feeling that now they must have alerted the enemy for miles around.

They hadn't, but the enemy was already well alerted. Indeed, apart from information he had been receiving from spies in North Africa ever since spring, General Guzzoni, the commander of the Italian Sixth Army, had known the invasion force was heading for Sicily since four thirty on the afternoon of the previous day. It was then that an Italian reconnaissance plane cruising off Malta had spotted five large Allied convoys sailing for Sicily. Two hours and ten minutes later all Italian and German forces on the island had been placed on full scale alert and, as we shall see, reinforcements were heading for Sicily from as far away as Avignon in Southern France.

For a time the 66-year-old Italian General, based at his headquarters in the ancient Sicilian city of Enna, had not expected the Allies to land on the island until the gales off the coast had calmed. But now, with reports of parachutists coming down all over Sicily, he changed his mind. Hours before the Allied ships would start discharging their human cargoes Guzzoni ordered a state of emergency.

He ordered port facilities blown up along the south coast of the island, plus other measures to stop the invaders from discharging the vehicles and other equipment they would need to back up their infantry. More importantly, he ordered the German and Italian air forces to prepare to strike the invaders once it was daylight; also that Italian mobile forces and the German 15th Panzergrenadier Division stationed to the west should proceed eastwards to meet the enemy as soon as possible. Thus, even before Gavin's men could capture the high ground to the front of the Seventh Army's invasion beaches, the Hermann Goering Panzer Division was already alerted for action, while on Montgomery's invasion front Axis mobile forces were hurrying to stop them in their tracks.

For once Ultra was unable to help the Allies to outguess the enemy, for Guzzoni did not use the German Enigma machine to transmit his orders. Instead he used landlines, leaving Ultra blind. Back in Malta the Supreme Commander spent an unpleasant night deprived of news, wondering just how his forces had fared in the gales.

Some time before dawn on D-Day a British signals officer came into his room to report that Montgomery had signalled that his Eighth Army was ashore and everything was proceeding smoothly. Eisenhower nodded his understanding and asked for news of Patton's Seventh and Gavin's 504th. The British captain replied that he had no information on either of those formations.

Eisenhower lit his first *Camel* of the day and then decided to dress. At six o'clock the same British officer came in to report that Patton had been heard of. He was landing successfully on his invasion beaches. So far, as on the British beaches, opposition had been light. But there was still no news of Gavin.

Eisenhower breathed a sigh of relief, though he was still worried about Colonel Gavin and his men. With his staff gathered around him, he turned on the radio to listen to the BBC. Suddenly the programme was interrupted by an announcer who said, 'We interrupt this programme to give you a flash message from General Eisenhower. He reports that the first waves of his landing craft have just landed successfully in Sicily.'

Listening to the same message on the other side of the Mediterranean, Hugh Baillie, President of the United Press Agency, turned to his friend, correspondent Richard Tregaskis, and said sombrely, 'Well, Dick, I guess plenty of our boys have gone to their glory by this time.'

But neither the Supreme Commander nor his two battlefield commanders, Patton and Montgomery, nor even the head of America's premier news service, knew anything of the horror of the battle now being fought by the aerial spearhead of that Allied invasion force, returning to Europe after three years. There a mere handful of men, less than four hundred, British and American, were now involved in combat with elements of two German and one Italian divisions. The slaughter had begun.

3

THE BATTLE OF THE BIAZZA RIDGE

By now the hard-pressed defenders of the Ponte Grande Bridge were very worried. The Italians were attacking in force and their ammunition was running low, yet there was still no sign of the link-up from the coast. The relief force was hours overdue and it looked to a harassed Lieutenant Withers and the surviving handful of men still on their feet that they wouldn't be able to hold the bridge much longer.

What the defenders did not know was that, although the invaders from the sea had easily beaten their way through the static Italian coastline defences, they were being constantly harassed as they pushed inland by mortar and sniper fire. As the leading British brigade, the 17th Infantry, slogged its way up the narrow road inland, boots churning up blinding white dust in the intense July heat, they encountered Italian resistance at every corner.

In vain the commander of the 5th Infantry Division, General Berney-Ficklin, to which the 17th Brigade belonged, urged it to greater effort, for he knew the vital importance of the Ponte Grande Bridge. The Brigade was hampered by the fact that it possessed virtually no transport, at least at the beginning of the relief march. But, as the heat grew more intense, the sweat-lathered infantrymen slogging along the coastal road which led to the bridge commandeered what transport they could find — carts, mules, horses and a few captured Italian army vehicles, anything which would take the weight off their feet.

At the bridge Italian mortar fire was now so accurate that every bomb landed squarely on its target. The Italians had also brought up a small field gun and the gunners, firing over open sights, could not miss. Indeed their first shell shattered the small blockhouse which held the Italian prisoners and killed all of them.

Withers realized that his positions were too exposed on the bridge itself and shouted through parched lips, 'Back to the other side, lads.' His intention was that they should abandon the bridge temporarily, but deny it to the Italians by fighting on from the embankment on the other side of the river.

His men needed no urging. Loosing off quick and accurate bursts from their sten guns and hauling the lightly wounded with them, they backed into the water and began to dog-paddle across, holding their weapons out of the water as best they could. A cheer went up from the Italians. They had the English on the run. A machine gun opened up. Bullets skidded over the surface of the water. Here and there a man screamed with pain and went under, but most of them reached the other side. Nevertheless, out of the original eighty officers and men only fifteen were now unwounded.

Still they fought on all that long afternoon. By now they were down to nineteen men, as Flight Officer Fine remembered after the war, 'We were covered from all sides, with no hope of escape. With the few rounds of ammunition we had left, we foiled an attempt by the enemy to blast us out with hand grenades.'

Far away they could now hear the snap-and-crack of a small arms battle and someone thought he could hear a British Bren gun being fired. The trooper was right. It was a carrier platoon of the Royal Scots Fusiliers overcoming a stubborn Italian defence post. But time was running out for the nineteen. Fine, who had been wounded for the third time, now found that he 'had already used up all the ammunition for the Italian rifle taken from one of the prisoners so I tossed it in the river.'

He was not alone. The defenders had all used up their ammunition. They had two alternatives now — surrender or be shot to death. They chose the former. As Flight Officer Fine put it laconically, 'At 3.15 pm we surrendered.'

Immediately they were surrounded by jubilant Italians, who stripped them of their pens, pencils, watches and other things of value. Then they were herded across the bridge, urged on by the threats and blows of their captors, to start the march towards Syracuse, Montgomery's key objective for this first day of the invasion.

Fine noted how relieved the Italians were now the battle had finished. 'They had had more than enough from the brave little band of fighters,' he wrote afterwards. Still he was very dejected at the prospect of spending a long time in captivity. He had heard enough from his British comrades on how badly the Italians treated their prisoners and he didn't relish the prospect.

Fine's captivity, however, was to be short-lived. Suddenly the prisoners at the head of the weary column started to shout and wave their hands. They had spotted a lone British captain some fifty yards up the road and they were yelling to him to run for it before the Italians captured him. But surprisingly he stood his ground. He dodged behind a tree and, drawing his .38, opened fire. His first bullet hit the leading Italian guard between the eyes. He was dead before he hit the road.

The Englishman's aim was phenomenal. Another Italian fell dead. The guards panicked and blundered into the column of prisoners. Two pushed in front of Fine. Despite his wounds and exhaustion, he reacted instinctively. He knocked the rifles from their hands. One rifle he tossed to a fellow prisoner. The other he kept for himself. The two prisoners fired simultaneously. The running guards dropped to the ground. The re-armed prisoners dropped into a nearby ditch and started potting off their ex-captors. To their surprise, the Italians started to throw up their hands and surrender. New energy flooded into the weary bodies of the survivors. Grabbing as many weapons as possible, they hurried back to the bridge and re-occupied their former positions.

Fifteen minutes later the first Bren gun carrier of the 2nd Royal Scots Fusiliers nosed its way round the bend and immediately joined in the battle. Finally Ponte Grande Bridge was in British hands, with only seventeen survivors still on their feet and fighting. By evening the 2nd Northamptons of the 5th Division's 17th Infantry Brigade, after a fifteen-mile slog down the dusty roads, entered Syracuse. The port had been heavily bombed, but that night it welcomed the first supply ships. As had been planned back in May, 1943, Montgomery had his first port in Europe on D-Day, but the cost to the Ist Airborne had been high.

That evening Sergeant Andy Andrews, one of that brave band of gliders who had flown the Horsas from England, arrived at the bridge in a donkey cart. With him he brought Colonel 'Honker' Henniker and a badly wounded glider pilot. By this time other stragglers had reached the bridge and they started to cross.

As Sergeant Andrews remembered afterwards, 'The march across the bridge started with everyone's morale very high, but the chatter died as the bodies were seen.'

As they reached the crossroads on the other side the men spotted their Divisional Commander, the creator of Operation Ladbroke, General Hopkinson. According to Andrews he was standing there 'rather like a traffic policeman. He appeared small and tired.'

Someone snapped, 'Eyes right!'

As one, the Red Devils straightened their shoulders and clicked their heads to the right, as if they were on the parade ground back in Britain. Wearily Hoppy raised his hand to his cap and Andrews thought, 'as he returned our salute, I couldn't help interpreting the look in his eyes with his own unspoken words: "Thank God, that's over. Not many left, are there?'"

There weren't. Casualties were later assessed as 695 men killed, of whom 326 were presumed drowned; their deaths Hopkinson blamed exclusively on the cowardice and incompetence of Colonel Dunn's pilots. No figure was ever given for the number of the Ist Air Landing Brigade who were captured or reported missing. Those casualties probably doubled the initial figure. Be that as it may, it is clear that Hicks' Air Landing Brigade lost one-third of its effectives killed or drowned in the first two hours of Operation Ladbroke. Later Montgomery would tell the survivors that their sacrifice at Ponte Grande Bridge had shortened the campaign by seven days. His chief-of-staff, Major-General Francis de Guingand, was more realistic. He said that 'the airborne assault had been the only part of the operation that had not been a great success'.

Colonel Frost, Commander of the 2nd Parachute Battalion, was scathingly realistic. He wrote afterwards that the failure of Operation Ladbroke was 'a severe blow to the division. Although the press at that time was complimentary and made out that many wonderful feats of arms had been achieved, *it is doubtful whether this airborne operation had any effect on the success achieved by the initial landings from the sea.*'

While the Red Devils were fighting their battle for the bridge at Ponte Grande, Colonel Gavin was still trudging through the thin light of the new dawn trying to find his command. So far he had managed to find 250 troopers of Colonel Krause's Third Battalion. Gavin did not particularly like or trust Krause who, during training, had made his men carry rifles with the bayonets fixed, even when they went to the mess hall to collect their food and had actually ordered his men to shave their heads before they went into battle. As Gavin related with disgust after the war, now he found Krause 'asleep in a tomato field in the middle of a battle'.

Gavin soon roused him and his men, ejecting them from the foxholes in which they had been asleep. He ordered Krause to take his men and seize some high ground a couple of miles away called the Piano Lupo. Gavin reasoned that, if the Italians did decide to counter-attack the US 45th Infantry Division now coming up from the beaches near Gela, it would be an ideal spot to stop them.

Taking with him a platoon from Krause's battalion and an assorted collection of brass, which included three lieutenant-colonels, several captains and other junior officers, Gavin pushed on once more towards a ridge to his immediate front. True to the old West Point maxim of marching towards the sound of guns, he headed for a height known as Biazza Ridge.

Unknown to Gavin, however, the Biazza Ridge was held not by Italians but by German veterans of the Hermann Goering Panzer Division. Seven hundred panzer grenadiers, backed by a dozen super-heavy Tiger tanks, were on their way to attack the green 45th Division and Gavin with his little force was marching straight towards them.

Gavin's force crossed a railway line and checked out an abandoned railway hut bearing the usual fascist slogan *'vivere pericolosamente'* (live dangerously). The dusty paratroopers had a good laugh when it was translated to them. So far the Italians had not bothered to live up to Mussolini's dictate. Up to now the drop had seemed little different from a somewhat rugged field exercise back in the States. They pushed on and came across a handful of riflemen with the Italian thunderbird shoulder patch of the 45th Division on their sleeves. They were crouching in a ditch at the side of the road and, when they saw Gavin's men, made urgent signals for them to take cover. One of them whispered, 'You'd better be careful, Colonel. There's a bunch of Germans dug in on that high ground up there.' He pointed to the Biazza Ridge. Thus, for the first time Gavin discovered what Eisenhower had ordered Patton to withhold from him in order not to compromise the Ultra secret.

Undaunted, Gavin decided to act. Although he had with him only forty men, several of whom were staff officers sent to Sicily to act as observers, he was determined to attack. He told them what the infantrymen of the 45th had been able to tell him of the German positions on the ridge and assigned each group a particular sector. Then he said quite calmly, 'We'll start our attack just as soon as you can get your men into position.'

Gavin waited until his little team had formed up to left and right of him in a rough skirmish line. When he was satisfied, he jerked his arm up and down three times in the infantry signal for attack.

The paratroopers moved forward, bodies bowed like men slogging through heavy rain. The Germans reacted first. A burst of machine-gun fire swept the lead elements. Three of Gavin's scouts hit the ground, fired and crawled forward to fire again, advancing all the time. It was the same 'march and fire' technique they had learned back in Africa, only this time there was no umpire and the penalty for carelessness was death.

Lieutenant Weschler, the commander of the engineer platoon which Gavin had 'borrowed' from Krause, fell dead, the first officer to be killed that day. But the little force pressed forward, joined now by stragglers from other outfits. Paratroopers, infantrymen from the 45th Division, even two naval officers who had come ashore as artillery observers, all joined in the attack.

Slowly but surely the grenadiers of the Hermann Goering Division began to withdraw. A flight of Messerschmitt 109 fighter-bombers hurtled across the battlefield, flying at tree-top height. The paratroopers stared up at the sinister black and white crosses on the wings, the German pilots' faces clearly visible behind the shiny perspex of their cockpits.

But luck was on the paratroopers' side that morning. The Germans obviously thought the railway hut half a mile to their rear was the attackers' HQ. Swooping down, they shot it up with their cannon and then vanished.

Major Walter Hagen, the executive officer of Krause's 3rd Battalion, came up at the double at the head of some forty men. By midday, with their help, Gavin's little force had clawed its way on to the top of the Ridge. Now came the bloody business of winkling the last-ditch defenders from their foxholes. In the end the last of the Germans withdrew to the other slope of the ridge, leaving the battlefield to the dead. For a while Gavin let his sweat-lathered men rest or loot the German bodies for water. But, as he was to learn in the years of fighting to come, the Germans reacted swiftly. Shells soon started to fall all around his men.

Gavin ordered them to make the German foxholes deeper and to take cover while he reorganized his little force. By now he had been joined by the forward observer for a battery of 155mm guns further to the rear, plus one of the 82nd's own small pack artillery 75mm howitzer. He reckoned that with the aid of this new artillery he ought to be able to keep the Germans on the run; and to keep them on the run was essential. He did not have the ammunition to make a protracted stand on the ridge.

So the little band set off again down the road which the enemy had recently taken. They didn't get far. Rounding a bend in the dusty track, they found themselves faced by six 70-ton monsters, all armed with 88mm cannon. They had bumped into the Hermann Goering's most feared weapon, the Tiger tank, a metal monster that was virtually unstoppable.*

Bravely Gavin's troopers took up the challenge. They knelt in the dust and placed their thin Bazooka rocket dischargers on their shoulders. These were the only anti-tank weapons at Gavin's command. The projectiles hissed through the air. At that range the men couldn't miss. There was the hollow boom of metal striking metal. Shining scars appeared on the Tigers' thick metal hide but the rockets bounced off and the tanks rolled on.

'My God,' Gavin exclaimed to Captain Ireland, his personnel officer, as the Tigers started to mow down the bazookamen before they could reload, 'we were told that there were only a few German technicians on Sicily. Now here's one of Germany's best armoured divisions — and we've

---

* The standard Allied Sherman tank needed to get within 300 yards to have any chance of knocking out a Tiger. The Tiger, however, could easily knock out any known Allied tank at four and five times that range. It is not surprising that there was regular 'Tiger phobia' in many Allied units.

got nothing to fight them with but peashooters.' Major Hagen of his 3rd Battalion hobbled by holding his leg. It had been nearly severed by an 88mm shell from one of the Tigers.

Gavin knew that there would be no more advancing for the time being. His men were falling back everywhere and he could see fear written on their ashen faces.

John Thompson, the *Chicago Tribune*'s war correspondent, who had been the only journalist to jump with the 505th, chanced to make his appearance at the front end just at that moment. Gavin spotted 'The Beaver', as he was known on account of his large beard, coming towards him on hands and knees, with bullets whistling all around.

'Beaver, what in the hell are you doing here? We're about to be overrun.'

'I heard the shooting and came up to see what's going on,' Thompson replied.

'Well, what we don't need,' Gavin shouted above the racket, 'is a dead or captured civilian reporter. Now get your ass back to the rear where it belongs.'

Chastened, 'The Beaver' agreed to go back, but he was close enough to observe what happened next. 'The next hour,' he wrote afterwards, 'was the worst. Everyone expected an attack by the tanks in force and it looked as if there was a good chance that we would be overrun...Then the Colonel [Gavin] called in his last hope and ordered three available howitzers wheeled up for direct fire. I saw one of them come up this hill into position. One trooper rode its barrel while the others muscled the piece up the slope beside a small white house. The tanks began registering hits around the gun almost immediately, but with the coolness of veterans these men placed their gun.'

While the howitzers prepared to meet the challenge of the Tigers, Captain Ireland dropped to the ground next to Gavin. He had to shout to make himself heard: 'It might be a good idea if I went back to the beach and got some help.'

Gavin nodded his head in approval. 'That's the best idea I've heard today. Tell them if they want this ridge held, we're going to have to have more firepower. *And tell them even if we are overrun, we aren't moving off this place!*'

4

SLAUGHTER IN THE SKY

All that day General Patton remained ignorant of what was really happening just off the invasion beaches. Communications were out with the foremost American units of the 1st and 45th Divisions and his main concern was to sort out the seaborne traffic snarl-up and the mass looting by US beach engineers of the personal kit of members of the 45th Division. His other problem was that whatever little air support he received from Malta concentrated, or so it seemed, on bombing their own people rather than the enemy.

All the same Patton did have time to alert General Ridgway that he needed reinforcements immediately. Ridgway should order his second regiment, Colonel Tucker's 504th, to fly across the Mediterranean for a drop on DZs now supposedly captured by its sister regiment, Gavin's 505th. Unknown to both Patton and Ridgway, what was left of the 505th was, at that moment, fighting for its very life.

Ridgway acted swiftly. He sent a signal to 'Bull' Keenens back in Africa in code. The laconic message read, 'Mackall tonight. Wear white pyjamas'. 'Mackall' was the code-name for the operation. 'White pyjamas' meant the 504th would be dropped by parachute. Due to communication difficulties, however, Keenens didn't get the signal till one o'clock the following morning. But as soon as he did he alerted Colonel Reuben Tucker and ordered him to be ready to take off at seven o'clock that evening. Just as had been the case with the 505th, the sister regiment would drop in darkness.

What neither Keenens nor Tucker knew was that all that day the beachheads and the invasion convoys had been under constant aerial attack by Luftwaffe fighter bombers from Sicily, Sardinia and Southern Italy, who seemingly dominated the sky. For the nearest Allied air bases were in Malta and there were only a few of them on the island.

'The enemy's favourite trick', as one of those who underwent that day's bombing told the correspondent of the *Daily Telegraph*, 'seems to be for fighter bombers to sweep down from behind the hills and drop bombs on the shipping, then machine-gun along the line and make off before our fighters can reach them.'

Another eye-witness, Gunner 'Sunny' Hale, noted afterwards, 'The ack-ack from the ships and shore was terrific and the bombs did little damage to the shipping. One ammunition ship was set ablaze, not much else.'

But, despite the flak, the Germans kept up their hit-and-run attacks, urged on by Guzzoni and Marshal Kesselring, the overall head of German troops in Italy. Their plan was to keep the invaders on the beaches until the Axis armour was in a position to drive the troops already on land back into the sea. All day long the gull-winged Stuka dive-bombers kept falling out of the blue July sky like evil black hawks. With sirens howling they came down at 300mph, seemingly intent on self-destruction. Then, at the very last moment, when it appeared they must crash into the sea, their pilots levelled out, bombs dropping from their bellies like deadly black eggs. At the same time the twin-engined Junkers 82s came skimming in over the sea at mast-height, torpedoes flashing from their mounts, while others circled the great fleet below, directing a new secret weapon at the invaders – remote controlled glider-bombs.

As the day wore and the flak grew ever more intense, with the attackers coming in through what appeared to be a network of brown smoke and cherry-red flashes of exploding shells, the Germans sought easier targets.

They found them in the half-dozen hospital ships anchored just off shore, which were already receiving their first loads of casualties. As required by international law, these ships were painted white with huge red crosses on their decks and sides. As dusk began to fall, the ships also lit up stern and bow and the red cross signs on their sides became illuminated. It was quite clear what their role was. That did not deter the pilots of the *Luftwaffe*.

Their first target was the 8,000-ton British hospital ship *Talamba*, anchored two miles off Syracuse, which had already received and treated some hundred wounded men, now being cared for by British Army nurses.

The correspondent of the *Daily Telegraph* watched in horror as the ship received a direct hit and he saw the *Talamba* go under. 'As we twisted and turned, we passed close to the *Talamba*. Between bomb bursts and shells I could hear the shrill calls of women and the hoarse shouts of the men in the water.'

The sinking of the hospital ship marked the end of the day's bombing, but as the exhausted gunners sat down on decks littered with empty shell cases to puff a cigarette or sip a mug of hot cocoa, their mood was understandably vindictive and trigger-happy. They were anxious, too. Out in the shallows the American ammunition ship *Robert Rowan* had sunk after taking a direct hit, but her bow was still exposed and from it poured a thick pall of black smoke. It provided a perfect beacon for the enemy raiders, even in the growing darkness. Now the lookouts searched the sky for a low-flying plane. Below them on the deck the weary gunners knew what their first reaction would be immediately that plane was sighted. They would meet the swine with a solid wall of fire. The enemy wouldn't get within striking distance of the convoy this night!

While the *Luftwaffe* had been sinking the hospital ship Gavin's paratroopers had been desperately trying to hold the tank attack of the Hermann Goering Panzer Division. The pack howitzers succeeded in knocking out two of the German tanks and the infantry huddled behind them had gone to ground. But Gavin, now wounded himself, realized it would not be long before the Germans rallied and attacked again. His only hope was that Ireland would conjure up something from the rear.

Ireland had somehow managed to find General Troy Middleton, the commander of the 45th Division, who was conferring with no less a person than the 2nd Corps Commander, General Bradley, when the dusty, exhausted paratroop captain was brought into his tent. There was no time for military formalities. Hurriedly he explained the mess the remnants of the 504th found itself in on the Biazza Ridge and said, 'We need help, and in a hurry!'

Bradley asked, 'What do you need up there, Captain?'

'Main artillery, but we can use some tanks, too. There are Kraut tanks all over the place.'

Bradley turned to Middleton. 'Give him what he wants,' he ordered.

Minutes later a heavy-set artillery observer for a battery of 155mm guns roared up to Middleton's tent in a jeep. 'Hop in!' he yelled to Ireland as the driver revved his engine. Then they roared off towards the Biazza Ridge. The driver parked the jeep at the foot of the ridge and strapped a big command radio on his back. Together they set off under fire, the artillery observer panting and sweating with the climb.

Although the observer had never been under fire before he showed no nerves. Arriving, panting, at the top of the ridge, he stood bolt upright under German fire and yelled over the radio to the man at the other end, 'To hell with zeroing in! There's so many goddamned targets out there, you can't miss. Fire for effect!'

Seconds later the German line was torn apart. The earth shook like a living thing, as the first 155mm salvoes slammed down. A tank was hit. Its ten-ton turret rose ponderously into the air and slammed down again, but with every man inside dead. Great brown holes appeared everywhere like the work of giant moles. Bodies were thrown into the air. Suddenly the Americans' luck had changed. The Germans were beginning to pull back.

Half an hour later it was all over. The Messerschmitts, which had been prowling overhead looking for targets of opportunity, vanished, and the Germans, all spirit knocked out of them for this day, pulled back to another ridgeline. They would live to fight another day – thirty more in most cases before they fled to the mainland of Italy, while the victorious allies watched in frustrated impotency, but for now they had had enough.

Gavin, his wound patched up, decided it was time to get his house in order before he pushed on. He ordered that the wounded be treated first, then the dead collected for burial. In the meantime he had a chore of his own to carry out.

Proud as he was of his little command in their first battle, he was also angry at some of the defects of his officers, in particular Colonel 'Cannonball' Krause. He hadn't been overly pleased to find the Colonel sleeping in that tomato patch when he had first stumbled across him and his battalion. Later he had ordered Krause to bring up the second half of his battalion to help in the fight for the Biazza Ridge. As he stated later, 'Here was a chance to take his battalion into combat against the toughest opposition we could find.'

But Krause could not be found. To his astonishment, Gavin found out later that Krause 'had gone back to 45 Division headquarters to tell them what was going on. I just couldn't believe it.'

Then, in the middle of the battle Krause had made a surprising appearance. He counselled retreat. As Gavin noted afterwards, 'I was furious'. But Krause maintained 'that all my battalion was killed, wounded or pinned down and ineffective'.

Gavin told Krause that 'we were going to stay at the top of the hill with what we had and fight the German infantry that came with the tanks. He said we didn't have a chance, that we'd be finished if we tried to stay there. He went to the rear.'

Later, in self-justification, Colonel Krause stated that he had gone to the rear to have a small wound treated, but as most of the force which held the Biazza Ridge, including Gavin himself, had been wounded, the excuse did not carry much weight.

So Gavin went looking for Krause in the growing darkness. As one senior airborne officer related afterwards, Gavin came across the missing Colonel 'sitting on a roadside curb, head down and sobbing. Krause said, in essence, his troopers would never be as brave again as they had been that day.'

Two years later, during the Battle of the Hurtgen Forest, Gavin would come across many company, even one regimental, commanders who had broken under the strain of the terrible fighting in those rugged pine woods of the German border country.* By then he had matured; he could understand that men, even tough ones like 'Cannonball' Krause, could stand up to only so much pressure in combat. But on this day Gavin was simply an angry man who believed he had been let down by one of his senior officers. Krause was relieved on the spot and sent home in ignominy to wonder about his one and only day of combat for the rest of his life.

Now Colonel Gavin had only one other task to perform before he would order the advance to continue. All evening the survivors of the Battle of Biazza Ridge had been carrying the dead to the collecting point in the rear. By now the survivors knew that, although they had turned back one of the assault units of the Hermann Goering Division, it had been the men of the 'Big Red One's' 16th Infantry Regiment, aided by stragglers from the 82nd Airborne, who had really borne the brunt of the German counter-attack, just as at the Ponte Grande Bridge over in the British sector, it had been the seaborne forces who had actually saved the invasion. Perhaps their comrades had died in vain.

But it did not prevent those who had survived and who would live to fight another day from respecting the supreme sacrifice of their young comrades who had died before they had really begun to live. Tenderly they lay the dead in their shallow graves. Rough wooden crosses were fashioned from K-ration boxes or from the stocks of shattered rifle butts. Helmets were hung aslant these crosses, as the regimental chaplain, clad in khaki uniform like the rest of the paratroopers, held a simple service. Then there was a moment of silent prayer.

Standing there with his head bowed, Captain Ireland risked a quick peep at Colonel Gavin. There were tears in his eyes. He was weeping for the dead.

But the killing was not yet over on this night of Sunday, 11 July, 1943. That morning, concerned that the land-and-sea-based anti-aircraft gunners might fire at Tucker's 504th Regiment as it flew in to reinforce Patton's Seventh Army, Ridgway had called Browning, seeking reassurance that the fleet wouldn't open fire at the lumbering air transports. Browning had answered that the Navy could 'make no such promise'.

The answer hadn't pleased Ridgway. He had driven forthwith to 7th Army Headquarters and had told the staff there that 'Unless you give some assurance that the Navy won't open fire on my men I'm going to officially protest this follow-up drop.'

The threat appeared to work. Seventh Army *seemed* to obtain an

---

* See C. Whiting: *The Battle of the Hurtgen Forest*, Leo Cooper Ltd, for further details.

assurance from the Navy that the guns wouldn't open up as long as the transports kept to the designated air routes. A little appeased, Ridgway had driven out to make a personal check on the land-based anti-aircraft batteries. That night Tucker's planes would fly 35 miles along the coastline of Sicily, now packed with the invasion forces. Could he rely on the army's gunners not to open fire after a day of heavy German bombing? Five of the battery commanders to whom he spoke said they knew of the aerial over-flight. One confessed he didn't. So the artillery liaison officer who accompanied Ridgway said a briefing would be given that afternoon for *all* battery commanders. At this briefing the officers would again be warned that the planes they would hear and perhaps see were American; there must be no firing. With that Ridgway had to be satisfied.

Back in North Africa, Colonel Tucker, the commander of the 504th Parachute Regiment, was convinced that it would be, in the parlance of the Air Force, 'a milk run'. The weather was excellent. There was no wind to speak of and they were to drop at a DZ already secured by Gavin's men. Confident and eager for action, Tucker went from plane to plane shouting above the roar of the C-47s' engines, 'Let's give the bastards hell men! You know what to do!'

'Bull' Keenens, who had not yet qualified to jump and who had been ordered by Ridgway not to accompany Tucker, decided he would disobey that order. He would go along with the 504th as an observer. Then he would return and supervise the shipping of the rest of the division to Sicily. This disregard for orders was typical of the Assistant Divisional Commander. He had waited many years for that first general's star. Now he was going to enjoy the privileges that it gave him. He'd tag along with Tucker, despite Ridgway's order. But this would be the last order that General 'Bull' Keenens would ever disregard.

So they set off, plane after plane, with one of the paratroopers in Colonel Tucker's C-47 scribbling in his illegal diary (personal documents were not allowed to be taken into combat), 'Glad to be going. The tension of waiting is over. The colonel, a human dynamo, is raring to go.' Everything was going well.

Two hours later the first serials started to approach Malta. Down below the seachlights snapped on and guided the planes forward as they changed course to start the last dog leg to Sicily. Half an hour later the first serial spotted the coast of Sicily. In formation they continued their flight through the darkness, broken only by the flicker of Mount Etna to their right and to the front the faint red smudge of the burning ammunition ship.

For five minutes they flew the length of the invasion beaches. Then the red warning lights changed to green. Immediately the paratroopers started to shuffle forward, laden down with two parachutes, packs and weapons.

Seconds later they were falling out of the planes, floating down to the waiting reception at Farello Airfield DZ. Not a single man was injured in that drop. They had suffered worse drops back in training at Fort Bragg. It had been easy.

It was now twenty to eleven at night. The time had come for the mass drop of the rest of the 504th Regiment. The planes were coming in at seven hundred feet, the paratroopers already standing up in their sticks ready to jump. The tension was almost over. They were there and they were safe. Now all they had to face, dropping on a DZ guarded by their own comrades of the 505th, was a twisted ankle and a ricked back if they landed badly.

Suddenly a lone machine gun started to fire at the transport. Tracer began to hurtle through the sky. Almost immediately it was joined by another, either on shore or on one of the ships just off the coast — no one would ever find out. The fire of those two machine guns seemed to act as a signal. Guns opened up everywhere. Abruptly, the night sky was full of exploding shells. Signal flares spurted from the transport planes. Down below the gunners took no notice of the recognition flares. They wanted vengeance for the attacks of the day. Later the gunners stated that they thought the troop-carriers were German bombers. Others said they took them for German planes dropping their own paras on the invasion beaches.

In a matter of minutes hundreds of guns and machine guns had joined in the barrage. At that low altitude it was difficult to miss. Slugs and shrapnel ripped through the metal fabric of the planes slaughtering the tightly packed sticks of paratroopers as they readied to jump.

Sergeant Ross Carter of the 504th was waiting for orders to jump when 'suddenly long red streaks of flame began to slice the sky into weird patterns of flashes and bursts. We were being shot at!'

Suddenly someone punched him and out he went. Carter looked up and reckoned he was one of the lucky ones. All around him planes were being shot out of the sky.

Down below, Ridgway and General Patton, who had come up specifically to watch the paradrop, looked on in horror as the slaughter continued. Patton kept muttering over and over again, 'Oh, my God! Oh, my God!' Ridgway could not stop the tears that welled up in his eyes. His crack regiment, which he had trained so long and hard, was being slaughtered before his eyes.

Still the killing went on. Planes were coming down all over the beach. Others plummeted straight into the sea, taking their cargo of young men to their deaths. For days to come the corpses of those young paratroopers would be washed ashore. Within thirty minutes after the first serial had successfully parachuted down, twenty-three planes of the original 144 had been shot down and another sixty were so badly damaged that they would require extensive repairs before they could fly again. 318 paratroopers were killed or wounded, twenty per cent of the total force, with still more casualties to come.

Colonel Tucker's own plane came in with the third serial. Zooming low over the sector held by the 'Big Red One', it was met by a tremendous hail of fire. But Tucker kept calm. He ordered the pilot to fly the length of the beach until he found the DZ, despite the fact that the fuselage was being systematically ripped apart. Later back in North Africa the astonished Air Force mechanics found that the plane had been hit one thousand times!

Grimly the pilot carried out the orders as, inside the debris-littered plane, paratroopers cried out in pain or slipped bleeding to the metal floor as they were hit by shrapnel. At last the pilot spotted the flares marking the DZ. Tucker didn't hesitate. He was out of the door in a flash. His officers followed. One of them was hit in the throat as he came down. But Tucker had no time to help him. He had to ensure the safety of the last serial. Red-faced with anger, he released his chute and ran to where the turret gunners of a bunch of Sherman tanks were blazing away at the paratroopers floating down in their chutes. He nearly blasted them away from their machine guns with his curses. But the killing continued.

Now with paratroopers floating down everywhere, the naval gunners, seemingly convinced that they were German, indulged in what they called a 'turkey shoot'. Contrary to international law, they started killing them as they came down slowly and helplessly on their chutes.

As one shocked but articulate seaman, Machinist Mate Herbert Blair, told the correspondent of the Army magazine *Yank* afterwards, 'Why did I have to go on deck? Hit after hit we score until ship after ship bursts into flame or falls spiralling into the sea. But something is wrong. From the wounded ships parachutes come fluttering down, some in flames, others to billow out in a slow descent. Then some trigger-happy gunner aboard another ship decides to pick off the supposedly helpless Jerries. Soon every gunner is firing away at the troopers who dangle beneath the umbrellas of their chutes.

'*Cease firing! Cease firing!* Stand by to pick up survivors! Stand by to pick up survivors!

'Only then does the dreadful realization descend like a sledgehammer upon us. We have wantonly, though inadvertently, slaughtered our own gallant buddies. I feel sick in body and mind.'

That night, as one pilot said grimly, 'Evidently the only safe place for us over Sicily tonight is over enemy territory!'

Hurriedly, as the firing finally ceased and the slaughter was over, a message was flashed to Colonel Harry Lewis's 325 Glider Infantry Regiment. It was to stay in North Africa 'in view of the unfortunate incident'. Later Ridgway signalled that he had 'no formal element of Combat Team 505 under my control', adding that some elements of 504 were 'dribbling in'.

Back in Africa, the 82nd Airborne's artillery commander, General Maxwell Taylor, was now in charge of what was left of the division. After Tucker's men had departed, he had fallen into an exhausted sleep, reasoning that 'Bull' would soon be back to take over control once more. At one o'clock that morning he was awakened by a frantic messenger who told the General that many of Tucker's planes were limping home badly shot up and filled with dead and wounded paratroopers.

Taylor, a wise and controlled man, who would rise to the highest command in the US Army, took the news calmly. He guessed that the young officer was exaggerating: airborne operations always seemed a muddle at first. All the same he got dressed and drove to the nearest landing strip. What he saw there horrified him. There were flak-ridden C-47s slewed at angles all over the field, some with their canopies cracked and splintered, others with smoking engines being doused by mechanics wielding fire extinguishers; still others with flattened tyres and smashed undercarriages. Ambulances, sirens howling, rushed back and forth, bearing away the wounded. In one plane a shocked Taylor saw a whole stick of young paratroopers dead in their seats, their chutes neatly strapped on their bullet-riddled chests. Now he knew that a tragedy really had occurred on the other side of the Meditteranean.

As Monday dawned, Colonel Tucker could assemble only one artillery battery and one rifle company on the DZ, a mere 550 of the 2,000-odd men who had flown from Africa on the previous evening. Effectively the 505 Parachute Infantry Regiment did not exist any more.

Gavin, for his part, could muster only 1,200 men out of the 3,000-odd who had flown in with him in the reinforced 504 Parachute Infantry Regimental Team. Out of the 5,307 paratroopers flown into action a mere 2,000 were fit for combat that morning. In the end 3,883 paratroopers were finally accounted for, leaving 1,200 dead or missing, an effective casualty rate of some 27 per cent, and for what?

Back in Malta, an infuriated Eisenhower was not concerned, for the time being, by what the 82nd and their comrades of the 1st British Airborne Division had actually achieved in Sicily. His concern was why there had been such a tremendous slaughter for so little gain. Suspending all further airborne operations by the 82nd (though not for the 1st Airborne – tragically), he signalled Patton for an immediate report on the 'Sicilian disaster'.

Patton replied immediately and Eisenhower signalled: 'If the cited report is true, the incident could have been occasioned only by inexcusable carelessness and negligence on the part of someone. You will institute within our command an immediate and exhaustive investigation into the allegation with a view to finding responsibility. Report of pertinent facts is desired and if the persons found responsible are serving in your command, I want a statement of the disciplinary action taken by you. *This will be expedited*!'

Eisenhower's demand was couched in the worst form of US Army jargon, but its intent was clear. There had been a scandal and Eisenhower, fighting his first battle as Supreme Commander, was not going to be held responsible. Just in case the scandal of the airborne landings ever came out, Patton would have to have a scapegoat ready to throw to the Great American Public.

But for the time being both Eisenhower and Patton had other, more pressing, problems on their hands than the slaughter of the paratroopers. Over in England the 'boffins of Bletchley' were working flat out deciphering a whole series of Enigma messages that were coming in from Hitler's headquarters in the East and from Kesselring's in Italy.

The Allied landing in Sicily had now caused Hitler to break off the great battle of Kursk, 'Operation Citadel', which he had hoped would break the back of the Red Army at least for 1943. Now the Führer turned his attention to the potentially disastrous situation in Sicily.

Kesselring advised, rightly as it turned out, that the Axis forces, in particular the German ones, should make a fighting withdrawal from the island and make a stand higher up the boot of Italy. Hitler had other, more political considerations in mind, though he realized the military wisdom of Kesslring's strategy. 'Smiling Albert', as Kesselring was always called by his soldiers on account of his unwavering optimism and broad smile, did not want the *Wehrmacht* to suffer yet another mass surrender, as it already had twice this year − at Stalingrad and in North Africa.

Hitler, however, was worried about the fate of Mussolini if Sicily fell. He knew from his spies in Italy that the Duce's position was already very shaky. If Sicily went, would Mussolini go with it? What would be the position of Italy then? Where would the Italian Army stand? Where the Italian Fleet? Where the whole country with its land border with the Reich? If Hitler didn't act decisively, the whole of his southern flank in Europe might be endangered.

As always he acted swiftly while his generals dithered. He decided that Sicily *had* to be fought for in order to bolster up Mussolini's prestige. Contacting the Duce, who was receiving hourly signals from the island that his men were surrendering en masse to the Allies, he arranged to meet him in Northern Italy to discuss the Sicilian situation. At the same time he ordered the reinforcement of the toe of Italy by German troops, and fresh *Wehrmacht* units to be sent to the island itself to bolster up the 15th Panzergrenadier and the Hermann Goering Divisions.

In particular, he contacted General Student, commander of his parachute troops. Back in the great days of 1940, Student's paratroopers had virtually conquered Holland single-handed. A year later they had taken Crete against determined opposition, but with such great loss to themselves that Hitler had told Student there would be no more mass airborne operations. In July, 1943, there was under Student's command a new elite reserve based in France, consisting of two parachute divisions, *Fliegerkorps XI*. These 30,000 experienced parachutists were Hitler's most effective mobile reserve. Student, glad to think he was back in favour after the slaughter of his *Fallschirmjager* in Crete, made one of his usual bold proposals to the Führer. He suggested his whole Corps should drop immediately into the Allied assault area while the invaders were at their most vulnerable. Hitler turned Student's suggestion down; it was too dangerous, he said. But the Führer did order Student to send the commander of his 1st Parachute Division, General Richard Heidrich, to Rome to report to Kesselring for orders. Heidrich's division was to be sent to Sicily immediately.

Even before he went to see Kesselring, Heidrich alerted his 3rd Parachute Regiment for rapid deployment. Of all his senior commanders, Heidrich knew that Lt-Colonel Ludwig Heilmann, the 3rd Parachute Regiment's commander, was the most aggressive. He was also a man who would carry out *any* order without question. Heilmann had been a soldier for 22 years, joining the old *Reichwehr*, aged 18, in 1921. He had fought with the *Fallschirmjager* in Poland, France, Crete and most recently in the Siege of Leningrad. 'Koenig Ludwig', as he was known behind his back, was the ideal man for the fighting which the 1st Division's commander suspected would soon come.

At midnight on 11 July Heidrich called Heilmann on the phone. The General came straight to the point. Heilmann's Third was to spearhead the 1st Division's immediate move to Sicily as reinforcement for the hard-pressed German divisions there. 'You will personally reconnoitre the landing zone. The Field-Marshal [Kesselring] will provide you with a swift combat aircraft. Start at zero five hundred hours in the morning. Conduct yourself according to the situation. We ourselves don't know what is going on over there. *Hals und Beinbruch*'.*

That Monday morning Colonel Heilmann and two staff officers took off

---

* Literally 'break your neck and legs', ie. Happy Landings.

from Orange Air Field outside the old Papal seat of Avignon. It was a beautiful morning and the pilot made good time in the 6,000-kilometre non-stop flight over France and Southern Italy to Catania where they were supposed to land. But Heilmann could see that the city and airfield were under attack. Plumes of smoke were rising on all sides. But the pilot went in, weaving like an infantryman, advancing through heavy small arms fire. Later Heilmann described the landing as 'a work of art, as was the take-off'.

While one of his two staff officers rushed off to organize the transport for his regiment − it was to join the hard-pressed 'Battle Group Schmalz' (named after its commander) of the Hermann Goering Division − Heilmann and the other staff officer set off to search the area south of Catania for a suitable DZ for the 3rd Parachute Regiment.

It didn't take them long. Fighting their way through crowds of terrified Italian soldiers who had thrown away their weapons and were fleeing before the advancing British, and keeping a wary lookout for Allied fighter bombers, they motored down Highway 114 till they reached an area of flat ground. Heilmann made a quick assessment of the terrain lying between the Gornalunga and Simeto Rivers and decided it would do in an emergency such as this. Knowing that every minute counted if the rot in Sicily was to be stopped, he telephoned back the co-ordinates of the DZ. Behind him as he spoke were three well-defined hilly features which overlooked the planned DZ. The features did not particularly interest the Colonel, who had too many other things on his mind, but they should have. For while his *Fallschirmjager* back at Orange Field waited for their orders to fly out, in North Africa other paras wearing the red beret of the Red Devils were taking a last look at their objectives for that night. In a few hours' time the men of Colonel Frost's 2nd Parachute Battalion, as part of Brigadier Lathbury's 1st Parachute Brigade, would drop and seize those three features, exactly two hundred and fifty metres south of Heilmann's planned DZ. 'The Green Devils'* and the Red Devils were on a collision course.

---

* The name the 1st German Parachute Division gave to itself after the small green devil unit insignia which they had painted on their vehicles.

IV

END RUN

'During the planning it had been thought that, having taken, held and handed over the Primosole Bridge, we of the 1st Parachute Brigade would advance on Catania as part of the 8th Army. Now we, like the 1st Airlanding Brigade, were to be shipped back to Africa useless and unused for the remainder of the campaign. It was yet another humiliating disaster for the airborne forces and almost enough to destroy even the most ardent believer's faith.'

Colonel Frost, 2nd Parachute Battalion

1

'A BRIDGE TOO FAR'

The Red Devils of Lathbury's 1st Parachute Brigade had been waiting for three long days. Encamped in their tents in the blistering July heat near the airstrips, the 2,000 men of the Brigade waited hourly for the call to action. By now they knew the disaster which had befallen their comrades of the 1st Air Landing Brigade. They had seen the American planes which had towed their gliders to Sicily return, limping and trailing smoke, their fuselages ripped and holed by machine-gun fire.

On the second day of their wait they had been trucked out to the airstrips, laden with weapons and kit, and had stood by the planes waiting for embarkation orders. They had waited for two hours before being told they were returning to camp; the operation had been cancelled for twenty-four hours. Dejected and feeling let down, they had driven back to their tents.

But there was some relief. Many of the men who would soon drop over Sicily were fresh from England. They had been hurriedly flown to North Africa to fill the gaps in the ranks of the 1st Parachute Brigade which had recently seen six months of very hard fighting in North Africa. These men were going into battle for the first time. That day the new boys heard that the intended drop of their sister brigade, the 2nd Parachute Brigade, had been cancelled altogether. Would that be the fate of their own operation?

By now they all knew what their objective was. It was to drop, capture and hold the ugly iron bridge at Primosole, which Montgomery needed urgently if he were to advance on to the plain of Catania. This bridge they would hold until, in theory at least, they were relieved by Montgomery's 50th Infantry Division the following morning.

The plan envisaged two platoons of Alastair Pearson's 1st Parachute Battalion, plus a Sapper platoon commanded by Major Murray, dropping as close as possible to the bridge and capturing it by a *coup de main* in typical Red Devil fashion. Five minutes later two platoons of Colonel

Yeldham's 3rd Battalion would drop and capture a four-gun artillery battery manned by Italians nearby.

Within the next half hour it was planned that the rest of the 1st Battalion would organize the defence of the bridge, while the 3rd Battalion established itself on a loop of the River Simeto about 1,000 yards north of the bridge. Below the bridge Colonel Frost's 2nd Battalion would capture and hold the three features known in code as 'Johnny I, II and III'. Thus there would be defence in depth with the Brigade prepared for enemy counter-attacks from both north and south until relief arrived.

For Colonel Frost, 'Brigadier Lathbury's orders had been crystal clear and I felt, therefore, that there was no doubt in everyone's mind as to what had to be done.' Frost, who had been critical of Hopkinson's flawed plan for 'Ladbroke' right from the start, was pleased with Lathbury's plan for 'Operation Fustian', as the drop was code-named. He felt that this would be no second Ponte Grande fiasco. Besides, this time the opposition would be different. For the three colonels under Lathbury had been warned by the Brigadier to expect not only Italians, but also Germans, equipped with armour. How Lathbury knew that particular piece of information Frost would not find out till years afterwards. But at the time it was 'damned useful'.

Now, on Tuesday 13 July, eighteen hours after the cancellation of the 1st Parachute Brigade's drop, Lathbury was relaxing in his tent when his Brigade Major, David Hunter, came through the flap 'full of suppressed excitement'. He saluted and said, 'Marston tonight, sir'. It was the code-word for the drop on the Primosole Bridge.

Lathbury called his three battalion commanders to his tent. The last briefing was concise and to the point. Between them the four veteran officers had won six DSOs and two MCs. They weren't the kind to waste time on idle chatter. They all knew what to do and were determined to do it. The conference over, Lathbury shook each one of them by the hand.

By five that afternoon the trucks bearing the 2,000 men of the Brigade were arriving at the dusty landing strips. The Americans who were to fly them to Sicily were already waiting for them. The Yanks sorted the paratroopers into serials and allotted them to their planes, according to the C-47's number which had already been chalked on the truck in question. It all seemed quick and efficient.

Lieutenant Peter Stainforth, however, was not too impressed when he moved closer to the C-47 which was going to convey his serial to Sicily. He winced when he saw the state of the plane, which the crew had named 'Miss Carriage'. 'The fuselage had been peppered with flak and the holes had only recently been hastily patched. Black marks smeared the underside of the wing behind the exhaust manifold. Her paint was chipped and dingy from long service in the African theatre.'

But the plane's cigar-smoking crew chief was full of confidence. He smiled at the pained look on Stainforth's face and said, 'Yeah, we've seen plenty of service in this crate. And this little business won't worry us any. Don't get this baby wrong. I guess she could fly you there and back by herself.'

The troops started to clamber aboard. They were laden down with weapons, grenades, spare rations, clips of ammunition and odd bits and pieces. The 3rd Battalion was also lumbered with the new kitbag weapon-container devised by Frost. Yeldham's men had had little time to try out the device. For some of them this lack of experience would prove fatal.

They took off as the sun started to go down in the west. Slowly the formations joined up and started to head for the coast. On the other side of the Mediterranean another airborne force — German this time — was also flying out to sea. They were the last elements of Heilmann's 3rd Parachute Brigade, on their way to join their 1,400 comrades who had jumped into Sicily the previous day. The men in the planes, men like 24-year-old Leutnant Martin Poeppel, were mostly veterans. They had fought in Poland, the Netherlands, Crete and of late in Russia as ordinary infantry. They were tough and young, not convinced Nazis on the whole, but still full of their own *Fallschirmjager* creed, which made them believe they were the cream of the German *Wehrmacht*, superior even to the Armed SS. And in truth they were. In the years to come, when even the SS turned and ran away, the Allies regarded the German paras as their most formidable foes, the last to surrender, the first to die.

Poeppel spotted the airfield at Catania. It appeared to be in total confusion, planes of all types scattered everywhere, some of them wrecked, some of them smouldering and burning. 'Two of our planes are ablaze on the airfield,' he recorded afterwards. 'Has there been a raid? If so, our tired old crate [which had lagged behind the rest of the formation] brought us luck after all. We haven't even stopped rolling when a lorry shoots out and orders us to be quick. British fighters have attacked two of our planes during landing and set them on fire.'

Hurriedly the paras dumped their gear in the truck and set off to report to Poeppel's commander, Major Schmidt, who led the 3rd Regiment's heavy machine-gun company. Swiftly 'the latter gives them their orders as the roar of four-engined bombers drown his words: the "Tommies" are coming in again to bomb the airfield.'

An hour later Poeppel's squad was camped in a grove of olive trees, cleaning their weapons, eating 'Old Man' (canned meat reputed to be made of the bodies of old men from Berlin's workhouses), washing the stew down with 'nigger sweat' (black ersatz coffee) and waiting for the 'Tommies' to come.

While Poeppel's outfit rested, Major Schmidt ordered his second-in-command, Captain Laun, to move the battalion south towards the Primosole Bridge. Schmidt motored to 'King Ludwig's' HQ, where Heilmann told him, 'Something's bound to happen tonight. The enemy will try to sneak through to the Catania plain and, to do so, he'll send in more troops — either by sea or by air. If he manages to land them in our rear and to dig in, then we're cut off for sure. So your battalion will remain south of Catania. Hold the bridge over the Simeto and put one company between there and the sea.'

Heilmann's appreciation of the developing situation on the Catania front was exactly right. Not only was a parachute landing planned by Montgomery for that night, but a seaborne one as well. All that day Montgomery's 50th Division, the Tyne-Tees, had been battling towards the town of Lentini and the plain of Catania beyond. There they had bumped head-on into *Kampfgruppe* Schmalz, now reinforced by Heilmann's paras. Progress had begun to slow down for the Division was not only exhausted by the battle for Sicily but worn down by two years of fighting in North Africa.

Montgomery felt frustrated. He turned the heat on General Kirkman who commanded the 50th Division. Kirkman drove up to his leading brigade to ginger them up and to his surprise found the men digging in and brewing up after a hard battle the night before. Kirkman went over to the brigadier in charge and told him, 'You're not going to sit down and rest. You go on now, until you drop if necessary, occupying the ground which you'll have to fight for tomorrow. Get 'em all on the move. Now's the time to go on!'

Kirkman returned to his vehicle to be greeted with the news that he had to return to his headquarters immediately; no less a person than the Army Commander himself wanted to speak to him.

Kirkman sped back to his HQ to be confronted by Montgomery, who, for some reason that he could not fathom, was wearing the green beret of the Commandos. Montgomery let Kirkman into the secret. The 1st Parachute Brigade was to be dropped that night and he, Kirkman, had to get his weary division as far forward as possible and at the greatest speed to relieve them. Montgomery didn't want another fiasco like that of the Ponte Grande bridge. He ended his instructions with: 'Go on at all possible speed'. Then he was gone.

Kirkman began to realize the urgency of the matter. Why else would an army commander come so far up front to give orders to a humble divisional commander? That was normally the role of a corps commander. Kirkman set off for the front once more, the dull drumroll of the guns to his front indicating that his lead brigade had hit the enemy again.

Montgomery has often been accused of being narrow-minded and opinionated, but he didn't wear blinkers and he was an exceedingly good judge of men. He had seen that Kirkman's men were tired. They had been fighting for three days and they lacked transport — a lot of their transport had been sunk at sea by the German bombing. They needed all the help they could get if they were to reach the paratroopers in time.

As soon as he reached his new HQ in the port of Syracuse Montgomery summoned the commander of the 3rd Commando Regiment from his base ship the *Prince Albert* to meet himself, General Dempsey, the commander of the corps to which 50th Division belonged, and Admiral McGrigor, the Scottish commander of Naval Force 'B'.

Colonel Durnford-Slater, the Commando, found all three high-ranking officers in good spirits. For a change General Dempsey was allowed to do most of the talking. He told the Commando leader, who had been with the green berets almost from the start, 'We've got a new operation for you tonight. It's an ambitious one, but I think you'll like it.' In fact, it would turn out to be one of the most perilous engagements ever to be undertaken by the commandos in the whole of the war.

They were to be put ashore that night from their base ship behind enemy lines at the Bay of Agnone. From there the 1st Commando was to push inland for five miles and seize the Ponte dei Malati, the highway bridge across the River Lentini, one and a half miles north of Lentini. The importance of the bridge lay in the fact that it was on Highway 114, the route along which the 50th Division was currently struggling in its attempt to capture Lentini and link up with the paratroopers soon to drop at Ponte de Primosole.

Durnford-Slater, whose men were tired by earlier operations during and after the initial landings, nevertheless accepted the task with alacrity, especially when he was informed that the bridge was held only by Italians. All the same he was cautious, for, as he said of himself, 'I have an instinct for danger and... that bridge was the only road linking the German and Italian armies with their bases in the Messina area. It seemed likely to me that Jerry would want to make sure it was guarded.'

But Durnford-Slater, who had a hot temper — at the end of the war he was so annoyed by the behaviour of Field-Marshal Milch, the *Luftwaffe* general responsible for the bombing of London, that he hit him over the head with his own marshal's baton — kept tight control over himself as Montgomery said to him, 'Everybody's on the move now. The enemy's nicely on the move. We want to keep him that way. You can help us to do it. Good luck, Slater.'

Dempsey was not so optimistic. Just before he left, he whispered to Slater, 'If, by any chance, 50 Division, who will be our leading troops, don't get through to you by first light tomorrow morning, take off and hide up for the day.'

Durnford-Slater had just three hours to plan the landing. He decided it should be done in two flights. The first would secure the beach. Through them the second flight would head for the Ponte dei Malati bridge, while two patrols would be sent out, one to the north to link up with the paratroops at Primosole Bridge, the other to the south to meet the infantry of Kirkman's 50th Division.

Briefed at speed, the men prepared for the landing, discarding their helmets and all unnecessary gear; they would go into action wearing only pullovers and carrying iron rations, which consisted of a metal box filled with bitter chocolate. All in all it was going to be a shoestring operation which depended upon the 50th Division linking up with the 1st Commando before it ran out of ammunition.

At seven that evening the *Prince Albert* weighed anchor and they set off. It was not long before they ran into trouble. It was still light when suddenly a lean grey shape came surging towards them.

'*E-boat!*' a lookout yelled, as the guns started to chatter and a hail of tracer sailed towards the German torpedo boat. Cannon shells stitched the air, the E-boat weaving from side to side as it jockeyed for position. In a minute she would loose off her torpedoes and be off at 40 knots before the Allied fighter-bombers circling off the coast found her.

'*One!*' the lookout cried as the first torpedo splashed into the sea and hissed towards the *Prince Albert*, the bubbles clearly visible beneath the surface.

'*Two!*' Another hit the water.

On the bridge, Commander Peate, the *Prince Albert*'s skipper, yelled out an order to the helmsman. Just in time the sailor hurled the ship to port. The first torpedo hissed harmlessly by. Again Peate cried out. Again the helmsman sang out the new course and again the big ship heeled under the strain as he swung her in a different direction. Again the torpedo swished past the troop carrier without damage.

Now the danger was over. Dark spots had appeared on the horizon. Allied planes, the skipper of the E-boat must have thought. He swung her round and the next moment he was heading for home at top speed; the tense commandos could relax.

Slowly the *Prince Albert* began to approach the coast. To the right the commandos lining the rails could see the tracer bullets and Very lights soaring into the sky above Catania, with now and then flak shells exploding as Allied bombers came in for another attack. To their front, however, no light broke the darkness. All seemed to confirm the news they'd heard since they had sailed. It was that the Italian general commanding that section of the coast had surrendered. Indeed one of their number, Colonel Tom Churchill, a cousin of the great man himself, who went into action wielding a broadsword, had actually seen the general in question that same afternoon sitting 'under a tree assiduously polishing his boots with a handkerchief'. All seemed well; the enemy was on the move, just as Monty had said they were.

Then the waiting green berets spotted two planes trailing flame and smoke behind them hurtling into the sea, followed a moment later by the roar of main engines, punctuated here and there by the eerie swishing sound of a glider. They raised their heads as one. An airborne fleet was passing overhead. It was the 1st Parachute Brigade coming in for its drop at the Primosole Bridge.

But there was no time to concern themselves with what might happen to their comrades of the 1st Para. Their own hour had come. The loudspeaker broke into life, summoning the various troops to their stations. They were going in.

As always Colonel Durnford-Slater led his men into the attack. He was first ashore where he found himself alone; a weapon had jammed the ram of the landing barge, leaving him standing on the wet shingle in the bright moonlight in full view of four pillboxes which were pouring fire at him.

Not for long, however. His commandos erupted from the assault craft, firing from the hip. Others still in their barges were using a newly developed technique for raking the beach with fire while they were still running in. In an instant all was chaos. The attack lost cohesion. As one of the attackers recorded afterwards, 'The assault craft seemed to lose all momentum and crawled towards the beach in a huddled group.' But soon tested leaders like Captain Peter Young, who had taken part in virtually every commando raid of the war up to now, rallied the men 'with a few well-seasoned words' and they started to move inland. But they knew by now they were not facing the Italians but the veterans of Heilmann's 3rd Parachute Brigade.

So on that Tuesday night of 13 July, 1943, they advanced upon each other; Lathbury's 1st Parachute Brigade soon about to drop; Major Schmidt's Machine-Gun Battalion advancing into the unknown, but well aware of Heilmann's words, 'will send in more troops — either by sea or by air. If he manages to land them in our rear, then we're cut off for sure'; the 1st Commando Regiment trying gamely to make the vital Ponte dei Malati; and somewhere to the rear Kirkman's weary veterans of the 50th Division. The actors were in place, the scene had been set, the action could begin.

2

'HAPPY BIRTHDAY'

Colonel Alastair Pearson, commanding the 1st Parachute Battalion, awoke with a start. The transport had suddenly given a great lurch which sent his stomach sliding off into the unknown. He blinked and everything came into focus. Puffs of drifting smoke went by the ports and by craning his neck he could see great blobs of flame below. Later he would learn that the Germans had fired the haystacks so that they could see their targets better. But at that moment Pearson thought the fires might be those of burning Allied aircraft.

Obviously their American pilots thought the same. Suddenly the main pilot swung the transport round in a tight circle and started to head back the way they had come. Pearson ripped off his parachute and edged his way to the front of the plane and into the narrow cockpit. The co-pilot was clutching his head in both hands. The other pilot was hunched in his seat, gaze fixed hypnotically on the coast.

'What the hell do you two think you're playing at?' Pearson demanded.

Through gritted teeth, the pilot said, ' I'm not prepared to go in.'

Pearson let rip. 'And I'm not prepared to go back.'

'You'll have to go back, Mac. *I'm* not committing suicide.'

That did it. Pearson pulled out his revolver and pointed it at the co-pilot. 'Well, I'd better start by shooting you,' he declared. 'Then perhaps it will encourage him.' He turned the muzzle on to the main pilot. 'And I'll shoot you if necessary because I've got a perfectly good pilot sitting in the back.'

And he had, too. The soldier was an ex-RAF pilot who had been court-martialled years before on a charge of dangerous low-level flying.

The threat worked. The two Americans could see that the Scots colonel meant every word that he said. He *would* shoot them if they did not do as he commanded. Reluctantly they agreed to turn round and head for the DZ.

Minutes later the green light began to wink. It was time to jump. One after another the first stick fell out of the plane, tracer zipping through the air and flak shells exploding in great bursts of red and black. The paratroopers hadn't a chance. As Pearson spotted the loop of the River Simeto and the Primosole Bridge, his men slumped dead in their shroud lines on all sides. Then the last man of the stick came hurtling down in a 'Roman candle'; the terrified pilot had dropped him so low that his parachute had not had time to open.

The survivors of the 1st Battalion drop picked themselves up and started to head through the darkness towards the Primosole Bridge.

Colonel Yeldham's 3rd Battalion fared even worse than Pearson's. As the Battalion's War Diary recorded: '*Plane fired on by our flak ships... Run into heavy flak, this time the enemy's... Red light, green light — we float down into a world of searchlights, tracer bullets and burning corn stalks... 3rd Battalion consists of CO and Batman, RSM and Batman, intell.sgt and one pte... Realize we are dropped on wrong DZ.*' And finally the awful realization: '*No sign of remainder of Bn.*'

The sixteen gliders attached to the force were no luckier than the 3rd Battalion. Four of them went down just off the coast, more victims of 'friendly fire'. Others managed to survive Allied guns, only to run into those of the enemy. One glider, piloted by Sergeants Moore and Garrett, carrying twelve soldiers of the South Staffordshire Regiment, managed to dodge the flak and coning by Italian searchlights. But then the pilots' luck ran out. The two thousand pounds of men and equipment came racing in at an impossible speed. Up loomed a rough field littered with boulders. There was no holding the glider. It slammed into a large stone and whirled round in a flurry of dust and soil, just in front of an Italian pillbox. Moore's ankle was broken and he was pinned down in his seat. Garrett, unhurt, kicked his way out through the side of the cockpit just as the Italians in the pillbox started lobbing grenades at the wrecked glider and the trapped infantrymen. Within seconds the glider started to burn fiercely. Through the burning ribs of the wrecked glider he could see half a dozen dead South Staffs reduced to the size of pygmies by the heat. He darted forward to help one infantryman who had managed to crawl out, but stopped when he felt a blow on his left elbow. A piece of shrapnel had torn away most of the joint.

Meanwhile Moore was struggling frantically to free his leg, the sweat pouring down his brow as the flames got closer. He gave one last tug and heard a dry snap. He was free but had broken his leg in the process.

The two sergeants crawled to the shelter of some rocks. Just in time. The glider was rocked by a tremendous explosion as the Bangalore torpedo it contained exploded. Debris rained down on them as they crouched there, knowing that they had failed even before they had started.*

Lieutenant Peter Stainforth of the Royal Engineers had survived his first flak. Now the green light flashed and his batman hit him on the thigh – the signal to jump. He went out at a rush. 'After the inferno of flak and the pandemonium inside the aircraft, I was overwhelmed by the unexpected stillness. My parachute had pulled me up with a jerk and now there was no sound expect for the wind rustling in the dark, silken shadow above my head. I felt afraid my floating body might provide an individual target for the enemy gunners.'

But luck was on his side. No one took a shot at him and he managed to dodge the burning haystacks which were turning night into day. But 'before I was fully conscious of what was happening I landed heavily on my back in a gully ten feet deep, having struck its wall with a force that knocked all the breath out of my body and left me gasping among the reeds. For some seconds I lay and sobbed for air, incapable of unravelling myself from the silken cords.'

Then 'Something warm was pouring down my leg and my fingers encountered a wet patch. I must have been hit, I thought.' But his beginner's luck held and he found 'that the water bottle beneath my smock had burst and been flattened by the impact.'

He grabbed his sten and set off to look for the battle.

Colonel Frost was luckier than most of his comrades. 'Our flight went exactly according to plan. Later I learned that some of the other squadrons had flown over the Navy and had been fired upon... We, however, saw none of this... Our aircraft flew steadily on. The gum-chewing crew-chief ordered us to our various states of readiness, the aircraft throttled back to the recognized best parachuting speed and despite all the distractions from the ground we were all duly dispatched to our duties below.'

Frost hit the ground hard, falling into a ditch and badly injuring the ligament of his left leg. Still he managed to crawl out, find a stick and, ignoring the pain, set off to find the rest of his battalion. He was disappointed with what he found. Apart from most of his 'A' Company, he could discover only 'odd bits and pieces of the Battalion'. He concluded that, 'There could be no doubt that few of the other squadrons had flown in as staunchly as ours had done. In fact we saw no other aircraft flying in formations anywhere.'

Again the poorly trained ex-civilian US airline pilots had failed the paratroopers, both British and American. By the time the fleet of Dakotas and sixteen gliders had reached the Sicilian coast they had been well and truly broken up by enemy and friendly fire. As a result and in the panic

---

* Both survived. Garrett's arm was amputated and he was invalided out of the service. Moore went on, however, to take part in the equally abortive attack at Arnhem the following year.

that followed the planes scattered in many different directions. Some paratroopers were dropped in the mountains of Southern Italy to die there lonely and forgotten. Others fell into the sea and drowned. One group landed on Mount Etna. In the end less than 20 per cent of the 1st Parachute Brigade dropped in the target area according to plan. Thirty per cent were returned to Africa through no fault of their own and never heard a shot fired in anger in the coming battle. Brigadier Lathbury, soon to be a casualty himself, had exactly twelve officers and 283 other ranks out of a total of 1,856 men to fight both armoured elements of the Hermann Goering's *Kampfgruppe Schmalz* and Heilmann's Third Parachute Regiment.

Leutnant Martin Poeppel, of Major Schmidt's Machine-Gun Battalion of the 3rd Parachute Regiment, was already in action against Lathbury's paras. At ten o'clock that night he and his men had been alerted by sentries shouting 'German paratroopers!' Poeppel sprang out of his blankets in the olive grove. He knew more reinforcements were coming in from the 1st Parachute Division in France, but 'when the signal flares light up the eerie darkness we can see yellow and red parachutes. In an instant we all realize what's going on. British airborne forces overhead!'

Poeppel and his men attacked the confused British paras. 'Great volleys of fire, a fantastic performance from our men behind their guns. More and more aircraft are arriving, gliders coasting down to earth. Our fellows behind the machine guns are firing like supermen. Four big American transport planes, Douglas type, crash to the ground in flames and three gliders are set on fire. Wounded men, mostly Tommies, are brought in. Here and there I can hear the deep voices of British NCOs... Other men come in with serious wounds, but still want to get out there again. These are absolutely fantastic men. Prisoners are arriving constantly.'

In the break after the initial reaction, while the *Fallschirmjager* established a firm line against the intruders from the sky, Poeppel had a chance to talk to his prisoners of the 1st Parachute Brigade. He wasn't impressed by them or their equipment.

'They're certainly not eager to fight and their equipment looks fairly pathetic. Their footwear is generally old and worn out.'

[So it should have been. The men of the 1st Parachute Brigade had marched all over North Africa for the last nine months.]

'There guns look pathetic, reminding us of Russian weapons. Simply knocked together, the muzzle sights consisting of just an emergency sighting bar. Their parachute rations aren't what we remembered from Crete either, and in no way comparable with ours.

'Physically these are medium-sized, good-looking fellows, some of whom have already fought in Africa, while others are direct from Britain.

In my opinion, their spirit is none too good. They tend to surrender as soon as they face the slightest resistance in a way that none of our men would have done. They reckon Mr Churchill is a good man, but not a model or example to follow. And they're not as sure of victory as they were on Crete in 1941. All in all I get the impression that these troops are somewhat different to the ones we faced in 1941. They have deteriorated in every respect.'

But the young paratroop officer's opinion was to change radically by the time the last of Heilmann's Regiment had been chased off Sicily.

While Lathbury's 1st Parachute Brigade was having its first brush with the Germans, the commandos were working their way steadily towards the vital Ponte dei Malati. They had to fight for every yard of ground, against snipers, last-ditch machine-gun posts and, here and there, Italian-held pillboxes. But by three o'clock that morning the leading elements of the 1st Commando had reached the bridge itself. Under the command of Captain Young, they rushed the surprised defenders. There was the sharp snap-and-crackle of a small arms battle as the Italian defenders rallied, but the skirmish didn't last long. After a quarter of an hour the Italians had either fled or surrendered to the jubilant commandos.

Durnford-Slater ordered Young to consolidate the bridge's defences, while other troops were sent over to the other side of the river to form a bridgehead. But the troop soon ran into trouble. In the lead Lieutenant Herbert, who had been wounded during the landing, but who had refused to be evacuated, crawled up the opposite bank and peered over the top. The orchard beyond seemed full of enemy transport and soldiers and he spotted at least one Tiger tank hidden among some trees. Hurriedly he sent back a report to Durnford-Slater on what he had seen, but unfortunately nothing was done to make the bridgehead on the other side more secure in case of a German counter-attack. Instead, the commandos had, as Durnford-Slater put it, 'a perfectly marvellous time shooting up everything that came and causing complete confusion.'

A Piat team brought their cumbersome anti-tank projector into action on the bridge itself and knocked out a giant German truck containing ammunition. The ammo continued to explode for a long time, illuminating the countryside and outlining the many Germans trying to flee north across the bridge. While this was going on, other commandos climbed under the bridge to rip out the demolition charges and throw the explosives into the river.

Dawn found the wounded and dying commandos stretched out in a hollow as Durnford-Slater surveyed his position. It wasn't too good. The bridge was his, admittedly, but there was little cover to protect the defenders and already a Tiger was rumbling forward to begin shelling the commando positions.

He conferred with Peter Young and explained that there was no sign of the relief from the 50th Division yet and there was no hope of stalking the Tiger tank advancing upon them; the ground was too open for the Piat team. As they were talking there came the howl of a mortar being fired, followed by the shriek of a falling bomb. It was clear that the Germans were hotting up their attack on the bridge. How long was it going to take the 50th Division to reach them?

Captain Rann of Pearson's 1st Battalion wondered the same. A little earlier he and fifty men had rushed the Primosole Bridge and captured it easily from its Italian defenders. Fifty Italians had been captured; the rest had fled. Now as Colonel Pearson limped up, his left trouser leg flapping about his ankle and his revolver stuck gangster-style in his waistband, the defenders of the bridge could see the Germans approaching.

There were some 2,000 of them packed into trucks as the convoy advanced cautiously on the bridge, now held by 120 lightly armed paratroopers. Behind them came the heavy armour, tanks and field guns. Already the first Messerschmitts were beginning to take off from Catania Air Field. The defenders were obviously going to have a bitter battle on their hands soon.

About then Brigadier Lathbury came hobbling up, together with Peter Stainforth, responsible for clearing demolition charges from the newly captured bridge. The Brigadier had been wounded in the backside by an Italian who had thrown a grenade at him and fled. Stainforth had come across him with his trousers about his ankles, while 'his batman applied field dressings to splinter wounds in his back and thighs'.

Wounded as he was, Lathbury still intended to carry on. He asked Stainforth, 'How long will it take you to get all this stuff off the bridge?'

'Only a quarter of an hour, I think sir.'

'Ok; so get a move on. It must be finished by daylight. How long would it take the Boche to put it back?'

Stainforth told him four hours. Brigadier Lathbury reasoned, as he put Pearson in charge of the bridge's defences, that if the tiny defence force could hold on until midday at least, before giving up the bridge, it would be almost dark before the Germans could rig it for demolition again. By then the advance elements would surely have reached them.

Unwittingly Brigadier Lathbury was beginning to rehearse the tragic events of that 'Bridge Too Far' in a year's time which would see him and all the other officers who would survive this day either dead, wounded, on the run or in enemy captivity.

But now he concentrated on putting his tiny force into position, covering the extended defences as best he could with only one-tenth of the men he had expected to have available.

Frost wished Lathbury 'Happy Birthday', which it happened to be, then hobbled off to capture 'Johnny I' and by dawn it was in his hands. Now he had 140 men in position, poised for all-round defence, but with no heavy weapons or communications.

At six that morning the enemy, as Frost put it later, 'opened the proceedings'. From the direction of 'Johnny II' enemy machine guns opened up on the 2nd Battalion's positions. Half an hour later enemy mortars joined in and Frost's little force had nothing with which to counter the German heavy weapons. All they could do was to cower in their holes, hastily scraped in the sun-baked earth, and take it. Casualties started to mount.

On the bridge itself Pearson heard the sound of firing in his rear and knew that Frost was in trouble. It wouldn't be long before he was in a similar situation. He issued an order, his only one of that long day. It read simply: 'Fight the barbarians off as long as possible.'

But for the time being luck was on his side. Somehow, as the German *Fallschirmjager,* supported by mortars and heavy machine guns from Poeppel's section, came running in for their first attack on the bridge, a forward observation officer, Captain Vere Hodge, appeared. Immediately he set up contact with the British 6-inch cruiser HMS *Mauritius,* lying somewhere off the coast.

The hard-pressed Red Devils didn't have long to wait for the cruiser to open fire. With a tremendous roar the first salvo of 6-inch shells howled down with devastating effect. The shells ripped great gaps in the ranks of the advancing Germans. Men went flying into the air. The attack came to an abrupt halt.

But the infantry were followed almost immediately by Messerschmitt 109s. Flying at tree-top level, they came hurtling down the valleys, machine guns blazing, seeking out the men in their foxholes. Casualties were beginning to mount. It was time the 50th Division arrived.

The lead elements of the Tyne-Tees Division, northerners for the most part, East Yorks, Green Howards, Durham Light Infantry, small hardy men who had weathered the Depression on the dole on a diet of fish-and-chips and tea sweetened with condensed milk, tried to reach the bridges, But they had been marching continuously for four days. They were exhausted, short of water and racked by the 'runs'. Mile after mile they battled their way northwards, marching through the rising white dust like silent ghosts, their faces brick-red and dripping with sweat. The temperature was already 35° centigrade in the shade and all the time the

Germans, retreating as they were, kept up their dogged defence. The road to the bridges was littered with the bodies of the men of the 50th Division, their arms bearing the crossed T's of their divisional sign.

On the first bridge they had to reach if they were going to relieve the Red Devils time was running out rapidly. Most of the commandos on the bridge were wounded and there were dead commandos everywhere as the Tigers pounded the bridge area relentlessly with their 88mm cannon. Durnford-Slater ordered an attempt to be made to capture a tumbledown farm in order to take the Germans under flank fire. But the attack stalled almost immediately as the Germans brought down a hail of artillery fire on the attackers.

Colonel Durnford-Slater made a hard decision when he heard the bad news. Remembering General Dempsey's last words, and with still no sign of the relief force, he ordered a move into the low hills to the east. There what was left of the Commando would lie up till the men of the 50th Division came in sight. If they didn't appear by nightfall, then he was determined to take his Commando out through the German lines. They'd go in small parties, each commanded by an officer or an NCO, and make their way back to the beaches.

Durnford-Slater was depressed at his own decision, but he didn't let his survivors see that. They needed all the encouragement they could get. So, in little groups, they disengaged themselves from the battle and slipped away, leaving Durnford-Slater and Young to bring up the rearguard behind the walking wounded.

Most of them managed to get through, to be told by General Dempsey that the 'Men of No 3 [Commando] are the finest body of soldiers I have ever seen anywhere'. But the price had been high. One hundred and sixty officers and men had been killed, wounded or captured in the day's action, nearly half the force.*

But the loss of the bridge hindered the progress of the men of the 50th Division even more and now the Primosole Bridge was under heavy and constant attack by Heilmann's paras and the tanks of the Hermann Goering Division. All that afternoon the Germans attacked and retreated a few hundred yards to allow their artillery to plaster the defenders, then attacked again, while snipers, seemingly hidden behind every tree, systematically picked off Pearson's men.

By mid-afternoon Pearson had lost twenty men killed and about fifty wounded, but he kept warding off every German attack. The canny knack that he had picked up in North Africa of knowing exactly where the enemy

---

* Afterwards Montgomery ordered the Ponte dei Malati to be renamed 'No. 3 Commando Bridge' in their honour.

would attack next had not deserted him and he was ready to switch his few men around the bridge to deal with any new threat.

But the strain was telling on the survivors. Wandering around his shrinking perimeter that afternoon, with the slugs pinging off the girders of the bridge and tracer sweeping the water below, Colonel Pearson came across a para, his rifle flung aside, clutching his head in his foxhole.

'What's wrong?' Pearson asked, kneeling beside him.

'I've got a sore head,' the man answered. 'The noise is driving me mad. I canna go on.'

Pearson straightened up, face flushed. His boot flashed and he grunted, 'And now you've got a sore backside as well. Get on with your job.'

The would-be victim of 'combat fatigue' was cured immediately. Grinning sheepishly, while his mates in the other foxholes roared with laughter at the C.O.'s remark, he picked up his rifle and began firing again.

But Pearson knew he couldn't hold out much longer. Although stragglers had been arriving at the bridge all through the afternoon, casualties had reduced his holding force to exactly sixty men — and his ammunition was running low. *Where was the 50th Division?*

3

THE POOR BLOODY INFANTRY

By late afternoon the former Italian pillboxes on the bridge itself were under direct fire from German anti-tank guns. White blobs of metal, solid-shot shells used for penetrating the armour of tanks, were being fired at the concrete structures. In one of the two pillboxes guarding the southern end of the bridge, Captain Gammon watched as the left-hand pillbox, which was empty, came under fire. 'To this day,' he said afterwards, 'I swear as each round of solid shot struck it it heeled over and bounced up again. Perhaps it was the heat haze of the dust or my fevered imagination – it was made of reinforced concrete – but I swear it did!'

Then Captain Gammon realized that 'each pillbox in turn was to take its punishment and that mine was next. Suddenly there was a crash, fumes, dust and something hit me in the chest. I could hardly see. Where's the door? Had it collapsed? A shaft of light and I groped my way out into the blinding sunshine.'

At the same time that the pillboxes came under fire Heilmann's *Fallschirmjager* had crept forward as close as they dared, using the cover of the stunted trees which grew near the river and set fire to the reeds on the river's edge in several places. Their plan was to smoke the defenders out. Flames started to lick through the vegetation and Brigadier Lathbury, who had been wounded again, realized he couldn't hold the southern bank. He ordered his men to withdraw, while those on the bridge gave them as much covering fire as they could with their limited ammunition.

Now, as his survivors scrambled through the muddy water, with German bullets pursuing them, Lathbury knew he couldn't hold Primosole Bridge much longer. He had stuck it out for fifteen hours against vastly superior odds. If he was going to get his few survivors out, he would have to do so tonight under cover of darkness. Sadly he made his decision.

Young Stainforth was manning a captured Italian Breda when its ammunition ran out. He felt impotent and useless. As he recalled afterwards, 'Our ammunition was now virtually finished and our guns had fallen silent one by one as their limited stock ran out. Rifle ammunition had gone to feed the Brens and very few of the men had any left. Our own Vickers was down to its last belt and only occasionally rattled out a round or two.'

Just then, as the sun was beginning to go down, Stainforth was startled by a rustling in the ditch behind him. He spun round, but it was not a German. It was that same Brigade Major who, in what now seemed another age, had informed Lathbury that 'Marston' was on.

He told Stainforth, 'The Brigadier has given the order to abandon the bridge. Collect as many men as you can and make your way back to our own forces over the hills to the south. Our tanks can't be far away now. Clear out of here and go like hell before the enemy comes through.'

Stainforth and his survivors needed no urging. The Vickers gunner fired one last burst. Then, flinging the gun, tripod and all, into the bushes, he and the rest fled. 'Without looking back, we squirmed through the undergrowth, down the embankment and went like the wind.'

Now Pearson moved off with the handful of survivors, leaving only the seriously wounded behind. They had held the bridge for sixteen hours and Pearson felt the defeat at Primosole keenly. The intention was to head for Frost's battalion on 'Johnny I', which was expecting an imminent attack (it didn't come). But once he had cleared the area Pearson had no intention of leaving his hiding place above the bridge.

Here, together with his Provost Sergeant, a veteran of North Africa nicknamed 'Panzer' Manser, and his batman, Jock Clements, Pearson watched and listened as the German paras tried to salvage the explosive charges from the water below. But after one attempt to blow the bridge, they withdrew for the night and, as Pearson grumbled afterwards, 'Not a soul came near it all night!'

But if the Germans didn't press any further, the British did. At seven-thirty that night, as Pearson's men scrambled for cover on 'Johnny I', a troop of Sherman tanks came rumbling up to Frost's HQ. They were followed a little later by a company of the 6th Battalion, the Durham Light Infantry. The 50th Division had arrived at last.

The DLI had marched twenty-five miles that blazing hot day and, as tough as they were, they were in no position to attack immediately; they were whacked. They dropped to the ground and fell asleep at once.

But their weary officers had no time for sleep. A group of them approached the bridge, littered with shot-up vehicles and German and British dead in their camouflaged smocks, and surveyed it in silence. Although the bridge was clearly visible in the fading light, nothing could be seen of the *Fallschirmjagers'* positions north of the river. For all the DLI party knew, a whole division of German paras could be hidden over there.

They turned their binoculars and night glasses on the bridge itself. It was 400 feet long, built of girders and was about eight feet above the river, the banks of which were bordered by thick reeds, which still smouldered from the fires started by the Germans. North of the bridge, on either side, there were two farms. No smoke came from their chimneys and nothing moved outside, but even the most inexperienced subaltern among them knew that the Germans had probably turned them into strongpoints. With their thick white walls and narrow windows barred with oaken shutters, they would make ideal strongpoints. They crept back and started to plan an attack for the morrow.

The CO didn't like the hurriedly-drawn-up plan of attack for six o'clock the next morning, but the infantry colonel had his divisional commander, General Kirkman, breathing down his neck. He, in his turn, was being harried by Montgomery to achieve even greater speed and break through the Primosole Bridge and on to Catania. So the plan, bad as it was, had to be put into operation.

Early next morning, the two surviving paratroop colonels, Frost and Pearson, had a grandstand view of the infantry attack, supported by tanks and artillery. As Frost wrote after the war, a little tongue in cheek, 'We had never taken part in such an operation and having seen this were determined never to do so.'

There was massive expenditure of ammunition on suspected enemy positions. Medium machine guns kept up continuous pressure and tanks were interspersed with the infantry. There was a smokescreen to cover the last and most dangerous stretch. The infantry plodded remorselessly on with bayonets fixed for the final assault across the river. The Germans held their fire until the Durhams were within fifty yards, more or less point-blank range, then mowed the leading platoons down. Then they engaged the follow-up platoons. They fired burst after burst of machine-gun fire at the tanks, which had the effect of forcing them to remain closed down and therefore unable to identify enemy targets. The enemy anti-tank fire appeared nevertheless to be ineffective. But without protection the infantry faded away and then the Durhams and the tanks came back.

The first attempt to recapture the bridge had failed miserably.

But the failed attack had an effect on the Germans. The arrogant young para-lieutenant Martin Poeppel now 'felt as sick as a dog, aching limbs, headache, dry throat, the whole works'. As stragglers started to flood through the 3rd Parachute Regiment's lines after the abortive attack, he came to the conclusion that these men 'seem thoroughly weary and lacking in fighting spirit'. The spirit of the Green Devils was waning as well, for that evening his CO decided they should withdraw to a new position five hundred metres away and then Peoppel decided he was too weak to continue. A few hours later he found himself in an Italian armoured car travelling at high speed to the military hospital at Catania. His part in the battle for the Primosole Bridge was over.

Now the DLI planned to attack once more. This time the task was given to the 6th Battalion's sister organization, the 8th Battalion, commanded by Lt-Colonel Lidwell. Lidwell didn't like the plan one bit. As the Regimental History of the DLI records, 'The prospects looked gloomy indeed for the 8th Battalion.' But as Lidwell outlined his plan in the presence of Brigadier Lathbury, Brigadier Currie of the 4th Armoured Brigade and the two Parachute Colonels, he did not reveal his doubts.

Ninety minutes before the DLI attacked, the gunners of the 50th Division would put down an artillery concentration on the bridge, moving it slowly to about 500 yards to the left of the Primosole Bridge. Then, for the last ten minutes before the DLI went in, the gunners would swing their fire back and plaster the bridge itself. As soon as the barrage had lifted, the 8th DLI would ford the river − it would be full moon then − and go for the Primosole from the far bank.

It was a bad plan and Lidwell knew it. A frontal attack of this kind looked to him to be suicidal. Hadn't the 6th DLI's attack proved that? But the bridge was holding up the advance of the whole of the 8th Army and Montgomery wanted it captured, cost what it may.

It was then that Alastair Pearson butted in. According to the chronicler of the Durham Light Infantry, 'He was unshaven, his khaki shirt and trousers were covered in stains and grime and he looked dog-tired.' But the dour Scot could not contain his anger at the stupidity of the infantry any longer. In a loud voice, as if to himself, he exclaimed, 'Well, if you want to lose another bloody battalion, that's the right way to do it.'

The two Brigadiers took his interruption in good part and said, 'All right, Alastair, how would you do it?'

Pearson explained that when he had withdrawn the previous night he had crossed at a ford about a mile downstream from the bridge. He said that it was impossible for the German paras to cover the whole opposite bank. Most likely they'd concentrate their strength near the bridge itself. So why not make a left hook out wide and catch them by surprise? 'I will take you across the river,' he went on, 'and put you on the bridge. But after that you're on your own. I will cross that bridge and I'll be up that road as hard as I can bloody well go.'

The infantryman laughed a little nervously, wondering whether they should take him seriously. But in the end they agreed to his offer. Then he made his only condition. He wanted three miles of white tape from the engineers. Pearson knew his ordinary P.B.I. Infantrymen had a nice habit of getting lost at night and he was having none of that. He was going to mark out the route for them with the white tape, normally used by engineers to show gaps through minefields.

They set off at midnight. There was little sound save for the rumble of the permanent barrage in the distance. Here and there signal flares shot into the air and the long column of men froze in tense apprehension. But the flares weren't meant for them and they went on. In front of the battalion was Pearson's batman, Jock Clements, who knew the way best. He was followed by 'Panzer' Manser unrolling the white tape. Then came Colonel Lidwell, his three company commanders and Pearson, 'all the eggs in one basket', as one of the former joked nervously. Later Pearson commented, 'They were very distressed, as they had never been so near to the front in their lives.'

On the other side nothing stirred. It seemed as if the front had gone to sleep, something for which a very weary Pearson was grateful. Now he turned to his batman. 'Away across yon river,' he snapped.

Jock Clements looked at his CO incredulously, '*Me,* sir? he asked.

'Ay, you,' Pearson answered. 'You know the way, don't ye?'

Reluctantly Clements waded into the muddy water and crossed, stealing cautiously up the opposite bank. There he squatted and waved a shaded torch to the infantry waiting to cross.

As loud as he dared, Pearson called to his batman, 'Don't just wiggle that torch about,' he ordered. 'Away on and have a look around.'

Clements set off to search the area, returning some five minutes later to signal that all was clear; the Durhams could cross. Pearson crossed with them and then, his job done, he turned to Colonel Lidwell, saying, 'Now for heaven's sake get your men out to the edge of the scrub because they'll [the Germans] be here in the morning. You can guarantee that. Remember what happened to the other battalion.' With that he wished Lidwell and his company commanders luck and set off back the way he had come. Now it was up to the poor bloody infantry to retake the Primosole Bridge where so many of Pearson's men had died.

The Durhams went in with elan. Under the cover of light automatic fire, the infantry dashed for the bridge. A few *Fallschirmjager* were encountered, but 'to the accompaniment of shouts and cheers,' as the Regimental History of the DLI has it, 'these were speedily disposed of with bayonets, grenades or Tommy guns'.

Lidwell's radio communications had broken down and he was unable to contact his rear HQ. He needed the rest of the battalion up at the bridge quickly to meet the anticipated German counter-attack. Just then a cyclist appeared out the darkness. Luckily for him the Durhams were not trigger-happy, for the lone cyclist was, of all things, a War Office observer out from London. He was told the problem and he set off, pedalling for all his worth, to bring up the rest of the 8th DLI.

It was already daylight when 'B' and 'C' Companies appeared, marching in single file. As they approached, a wag from the battalion poked his head out of a shattered farmhouse window and yelled, 'Bash on, 'C' Company. There's only a few Eyeties up in front.'

The vicious burst of MG 42 fire, loosing off 1,000 rounds per minute, soon told the reinforcements that they were not dealing with the Eyeties. These were Heilmann's paras and they had bumped right into them!

The DLI scrambled for cover to both sides of the road, while Lieutenant Jackson and his platoon rushed the German machine gun. They were cut down before they had gone a dozen paces. But now the DLI were up and advancing once more. A lethal game of hide-and-seek began in the thick vineyards on both sides of the bridge road. As the Regimental History says: 'It was very difficult to distinguish friend from foe in the shadows and it meant every man for himself with no quarter asked or given on either side.'

Some Durhams were shot at pointblank range as paras popped up from their hiding places. Others stalked the Germans silently and bayoneted them to death in their hiding places. But there seemed to be ever more of them in their camouflaged smocks and rimless helmets. Men fired at trees thinking they were the enemy. Others flung grenades into the tangled undergrowth, though they often caused more damage to their own side than the enemy.

In those first twenty minutes, the hardest of the whole war for the 8th DLI, both sides fought to a standstill. The DLI's 'B' Company and the German paras opposing them, for instance, had 100 per cent casualties. The vineyards were full of dead and dying soldiers of both sides. Then as if by some strange form of mental telepathy, both sides broke off the action and withdrew.

A few minutes later the German paras rallied. They counter-attacked, yelling their hoarse battlecry and firing machine pistols from the hip. They overran a platoon commanded by Sergeant Mitchison. He slammed to earth and feigned dead. A para kicked him in the ribs. Mitchison stifled his cry of pain. The German muttered '*Tod*' and passed on. He didn't get far. The sergeant counted ten, sprang to his feet and ripped the German's back apart with a burst from his tommy gun.

Not far away Sergeant-Major Brannigan seized a bren gun. In full view of the enemy, standing bolt upright, he blazed away with the automatic, swinging it from side to side. The Germans reeled back. But one of them took a careful, aimed shot. Brannigan fell dead.

Colonel Lidwell's positions were now under attack everywhere and his losses were mounting steadily. That afternoon his mortar section fired over 600 bombs, as the paras rushed the DLI positions time and again. Lidwell radioed for help and heard that General Kirkman was sending in the rest of the brigade, the sister regiments of the 6th and 9th DLIs.

Lidwell, in his shattered farmhouse HQ, its walls pierced with shell holes, waited for their arrival. He knew that any large-scale attack would throw him off the hard-won bridge. The two new battalions had to come soon, for he sensed that the German paras were massing for a night attack.

Just then he heard the rumble of tank tracks. He and his officers rushed outside. They thought it might be from Brigadier Currie's armoured brigade, come to help them. Orders were given not to fire, for it certainly appeared to be a British Sherman. The dust which rose in clouds along the bridge road made it hard to see, but the DLI could just make out a man in the turret waving his arms excitedly. They held their fire until the tank was some two hundred yards away when the man ducked inside the turret and the Sherman's 75mm cannon roared into action, joined a second later by the tank's machine gun which sprayed the Durhams' positions with lead. Then, as suddenly as it had appeared, the tank swung round and rattled away as fast at it could go, leaving the Durhams gasping in surprise. Later they learned that the Sherman had only been captured hours before and hurriedly pressed into German service. As the history of the DLI records: 'The paratroopers did not miss a single opportunity of inflicting casualties. They were first-class fighting troops and fanatics to a man.'

At one thirty the following morning the two fresh battalions went over to the attack. But the paras were waiting for them; they were determined to stop the Tommies at the Primosole Bridge. They fought back savagely in the vineyards. Indeed they fought, as one eye-witness put it, 'until they either shot down their enemies or were shot down themselves'.

The Durhams rushed up their six-pounder anti-tank guns. Then they started winkling out the paras individually. Still the *Fallschirmjager* held on. Alarmed at the steeply rising casualties, the infantry COs asked for tank support. Currie's Shermans rumbled up and plunged into the confused mess of the vineyards, spraying the undergrowth with their turret machine guns, their big guns blasting away all the time. The slaughter was tremendous and no quarter was given or expected.

Suddenly German resistance began to crumble. A captured soldier of the 8th DLI appeared carrying a dirty white handkerchief. Behind him a few rimless steel helmets popped out of the vines. The Durhams were cautious. They knew about the *Fallschirmjagers'* little tricks by now. But the Germans had had enough and were surrendering. All along the line held by the 3rd Parachute Regiment handkerchiefs and bits of white cloth tied on twigs started to be raised. The *Fallschirmjager* came streaming in, hands above their heads, urged on by the bow-legged little men from the north, prodding at their prisoners with their bayonets. It was all over. The bridge at Primosole was secure at last.

At last the victors had time to view the road and it was a horrifying sight. Everywhere there were broken rifles, abandoned machine guns, a litter of blood-stained uniforms, empty ammunition boxes, a shattered six-pounder anti-tank gun, the shell of a burnt-out Sherman tank – and the dead. Bodies were everywhere, German and British paratroopers, Italians, and those of the Durham Light Infantry.

As the history of the DLI stated, 'Men who had experienced the fiercest fighting of the North African campaign at Alamein and Mareth said they had never seen so much slaughter in such a small area.' In all, the three DLI battalions had lost 500 men, killed, wounded or missing, while 360 German dead were found and 160 were taken prisoner.

That afternoon, just before the captured battalion commander of the *Fallschirmjager* was led away to the cage, to spend the rest of the war in a POW camp, Colonel Clarke, the CO of the 9th DLI, stopped him and his escort for a moment. The Colonel stretched out his hand towards the puzzled German Major, as he stood bare-headed in the sun. Then he realized that Colonel Clarke wanted to shake the hand of a very brave man.

That afternoon Pearson and the survivors of his battalion were riding back to Syracuse when their convoy was stopped by two immaculate redcaps on motorbikes. The Commander-in-Chief was coming up to inspect the bridge in person. And there was Monty in his three-badge black beret riding in his camouflaged staff car. He spotted the battered red berets of the paratroopers as Pearson snapped to attention and saluted. Montgomery recognized him and said, 'Ah, Pearson, I'm delighted to see you. You've made a big difference to my campaign.'

He went on to inspect the men, staff officers following him, busily handing out packets of cheap 'Victory' cigarettes to the paratroopers. Then Monty was off in his staff car, leaving Pearson to wonder whether all the blood and sweat had really been worthwhile. But he revealed nothing to his men. Assembling them for the last time – soon he would be leaving them for good – he said, 'We were represented when the Primosole Bridge fell. I don't think we have to admit defeat yet.'

He faced them, pipe gripped in his lips. Then the pipe started to shake. His whole body was trembling. Sicily had finished the man who had won four DSOs and one MC in little more than a year. He had caught malaria. His time with the 1st Airborne Division was over.

4

THE RECKONING

Now the survivors of the 1st Airborne Division started to return to their bases in Tunisia. Old friends were reunited. Tall tales were told. One officer explained how he had landed on the lava slopes of Mount Etna itself. Another had dropped inside the crater but had somehow survived and made his way back, dodging the Germans and living off apples. Most were happy that they had survived, not given to reasoning why their high hopes of the previous week had been dashed so cruelly. They had survived; that was the main thing.

Some, who knew more of what had happened and what was happening now, were bitter. Frost learned that, after all the self-sacrifice and effort at the Primosole Bridge, Montgomery had now decided that he would try and outflank Catania and changed the direction of the whole 8th Army attack inland. At the British 71st General Hospital at Sousse a very sick Pearson, who would soon be invalided home, came across a very badly wounded DLI officer. He told the Colonel, 'I was there when you told my Commanding Officer not to stay where he was, but to push out to the edge of the scrub. But as soon as you disappeared, he changed everything. And by Christ, we suffered!'

All of them, however, were angry with the American pilots who had either towed them to battle or dropped them over Sicily. Hopkinson, who had only a month to live before he was killed in action in Italy, was particularly outspoken, calling the Americans cowards. Even those US 'volunteer' glider pilots who had flown the ill-fated 1st Air Landing Brigade into battle felt the same. In the end someone high up decided that what Chatterton called a 'fiasco' caused by 'sheer ignorance' could only be smoothed over by a party. So the 1st Air Landing Brigade invited all the pilots and ground crews of the 51st Troop Transport Command to a massive binge at their Tunisian base, complete with flowers in empty ammunition cases and as much black market red wine as they could drink.

While their soldiers boozed and became friends with the Yanks once more, the senior officers of the 1st Airborne Division discussed their future and that of the Division over whisky provided by Hoppy. Despite the 'utter failure of the Air Landing Brigade's operations in Sicily,' as Frost maintained, the General liked to call conferences of his brigade commanders and their battalion commanders after dinner in the tented mess. Here Hoppy would try to convince them that in all future operations each brigade should consist of parachute and gliderborne elements. As Frost wrote after the war, 'Nothing was ever decided but I was reproached by Gerald Lathbury when he came back... for he almost snarled at me, "I hear that you have been conniving at the break-up of the 1st Parachute Brigade!" '

Frost 'forbore to comment', but, unknown to all of them, even the most senior, the whole concept of large-scale use of airborne troops was under consideration in both London and Washington, for already Eisenhower, who on 15 July clamped an embargo on all future airborne operations, American or British, had already written to General Marshall in Washington, 'I do not believe in the airborne division'.

Still in Sicily, Ridgway was vaguely aware that something was going on behind the scenes, for he had already been asked to make a report on the 82nd Airborne Division's operation in Sicily. Patton had told him, 'Despite the original miscarriage, Colonel Gavin's initial parachute assault speeded our ground advance by forty-eight hours.' Yet suddenly Patton was no longer talking about a new airborne operation in the region of Naples. His division was, in his opinion, being wasted as ordinary infantry slogging their way through Sicily in what someone compared to 'an extended road march', with more casualties resulting from heat exhaustion and 'Montezuma's revenge' than from the fleeing enemy. What was going on?

On 22 July the 82nd Airborne was taken out of the line and Colonel Gavin, depressed by the loss of life on the initial drop, wrote to his daughter Barbara, 'When this war ends, I think I would like to be a curate in an out-of-the-way pastorate with nothing to do but care for the flowers and meditate on the wickedness of the world. I have had more than enough excitement and danger to do for a lifetime.' Little did Gavin know that his days of excitement and danger were not over by a long chalk. Being the realistic officer he was, Gavin set about organizing a regimental brothel for his outfit. He wasn't having his men coming down with VD.

What Gavin didn't know as he set about establishing the 504th's bordello was that on the same day that the Primosole Bridge was taken for good General Eisenhower had ordered that all future operations planned for both the 82nd Airborne and the 1st British should be suspended.

Eisenhower's prime concern was the scandal of 'friendly fire'. He was intent on hushing up the losses caused by his own anti-aircraft gunners and the inexperience of the American pilots on both the 1st Air Landing Brigade and Colonel Tucker's 505th Parachute Regiment. But he also wanted to cover himself in case the story ever came out. Basically it didn't till long afterwards (just as the Patton slapping scandal didn't).

On the 13th he received a report from Brigadier-General Paul Williams of the troop carrier command, responsible for taking the allied airborne forces in to Sicily. Williams had placed the responsibility fairly and squarely on the ground and naval anti-aircraft gunners, a view which was endorsed by General Spaatz, the head of the USAAF in the Mediterranean. The latter stated that heavy flak from both land and sea had been the root cause of the massacre in the sky. In Williams' and Spaatz's opinions there had been a definite lack of coordination between air, navy and ground. Either that or the communications between the half-dozen higher headquarters involved, spread over Sicily, Malta, Egypt and Tunisia, were at fault.

General Williams did not specify who had opened fire first. Instead he said that both ground and naval forces had fired upon his unfortunate pilots. Another airman, Eisenhower's deputy supreme commander, Air Marshal Tedder, concurred. The British airman went even further. No friend of Montgomery, who had had a big hand in planning the airborne operation, he maintained that the airborne missions had been unsound because in the latter cases the planes carrying the paratroopers to battle required Williams' planes to fly over thirty-five miles of land where two armies were locked in battle.

'Even if it is physically possible for all the troops and ships to be duly warned,' Tedder wrote, 'which is doubtful, any fire opened up either by mistake or against enemy aircraft would almost certainly be supported by all troops within range. AA firing at night is infectious and control almost impossible.'

Cunningham wasn't having that. The old salt went to the defence of his ships' crews, both American and British. The lack of anti-aircraft discipline was not the problem. He maintained that 'no question of indiscipline can arise. All ships fire at once at any aeroplane, particularly low-flying ones which approach them.' In his opinion, the major cause of the disaster was bad routing and bad navigation on the part of the pilots.

Thus Cunningham passed the buck. It was the army's and air force's fault. Browning was not going to have the army planners blamed, including naturally himself. It was, in his view, the fault of the pilots. 'The navigation by the troop carrier aircrews was bad... It is essential both from the operational and morale point of view that energetic steps are taken to improve greatly on the aircrews' performance up to date.'

Montgomery thought the same, though for once he did not voice his opinion publicly. Instead he wrote in his diary that 'the glider operation on D-Day failed badly'. The parachute operation on the Primosole Bridge 'also failed'. These failures were due to the fact that 'the pilots of the aircraft were completely untrained in navigation and were frightened off their job by the flak'. 'The big lesson,' he wrote, 'is that we must not be dependent on American Transport aircraft, with pilots that are inexperienced in operational flying. Our airborne troops are too good and too scarce to be wasted.' He ordered all further British airborne operations cancelled. Later, when he heard that Browning was trying to convince Eisenhower to relax *his* ban on airborne ops, he sent a 'furious signal' to Field-Marshal Alexander, demanding that Browning 'cease and desist'.

Patton, as always, took the matter personally (he believed in airborne troops, incidentally). He wrote in his diary, 'As far as I can see if anyone is blameable, it must be myself, but personally I feel immune to censorship... Perhaps Ike is looking for an excuse to relieve me.'

In the end nothing came of the inquiry into who was responsible for the ill-fated airborne assaults and the battering the planes and gliders took through 'friendly fire'. General Ridgway summed it up in a letter he wrote to HQ on 2 August, 1943. Desperately trying to secure the future of his division, he said that he had tried again and again to obtain naval cooperation to ensure that his planes were not fired upon, but he had failed. He maintained that 'the lessons now learned could have been driven home in no other way, and these lessons provide a sound basis for the belief that recurrence can be avoided. The losses are part of the inevitable price of war in human life.' Maybe so, but that conclusion was little comfort to the families of the many hundreds of young men who had been killed by their own comrades, dead before they had fired a shot at the enemy.

But now there were bigger issues at stake than who was to blame for the fiasco. The whole future of large-scale airborne forces lay in the balance. Eisenhower's 'eyes-and-ears' in Sicily, the somewhat elderly General John P. Lucas, submitted a report to the Supreme Commander in which he stated that 'the organization of Airborne Troops into units as large as divisions is unsound'. In his opinion it 'was impossible to land an airborne division in an area where a divisional HQ could keep it under control. By the nature of things the division would be too scattered.'

There was a great deal of truth in what Lucas had to say. The lack of control in nearly all large-scale airborne operations after 1943 would prove the elderly General right − and Eisenhower saw this. He wrote to Marshall in Washington, 'I do not believe in the airborne division. I believe that airborne troops should be organized in self-contained units, comprising infantry, artillery and special services, all of about the strength of a regimental combat team.'

This recommendation, based on the Lucas report and Eisenhower's own feeling that the airborne losses in Sicily had been 'inexcusably high', meant that a decision had now to be made in Washington, not only about the 82nd Airborne, but also the 11th and 101st Airborne Divisions and the two others planned, the 13th and 17th.

As Gavin wrote after the war when he learned what had been going on behind the scenes in the US Department of War: 'Apparently Eisenhower wanted to use small packets of paratroopers for special missions. I was puzzled by the fact that no senior officers from higher headquarters came to Sicily during or after our operation. Certainly no high-ranking officer ever discussed the mission with us afterwards.' So the negative views reaching Washington were impressions gained from Eisenhower's headquarters hundreds of miles from the action. Obviously the future General Gavin did not know of the Lucas mission.

But the fat was now in the fire and there were several influential generals in Washington eager to take up the issue. Just as in the British War Office there were senior officers who did not like the idea of 'private armies', such as the SAS, Airborne and Commandos, which drew off the best men from the regiments of the line, there were those in the Department of War who objected strongly to these special forces. They were simply a costly drain on manpower and equipment, with their planes, gliders and specially designed airborne weapons and equipment.

In particular, the influential General Lesley McNair, the Army's Commander of Ground Forces, who ironically enough would be killed himself by 'friendly fire' in Normandy in a year's time, took up the issue. He was ready to pare the airborne outfits to an even smaller size.

After Sicily, he wrote, 'My staff and I had become convinced of the impracticality of handling large airborne units.' He was prepared to 'recommend to the War Department that airborne divisions be abandoned... and that the airborne effort be restricted to parachute units of battalion size or smaller.'

General Marshall, that austere figure whom even President Roosevelt dared not call by his first name, hesitated. There was talk of turning the airborne divisions into air landing ones, brought to battle in transports which would land on airfields rather than drop by parachute. Someone else suggested 'light divisions', highly mobile and lightly armed units that could be rushed to any trouble spot at high speed. But again these 'light divisions' would not drop into action.

In the end General Marshall invited the commander of the 11th Airborne Division to establish a board of inquiry into the future of the airborne arm. It was named after that commander as the 'Swing Board'. Thus while the 82nd Airborne and the 1st British Airborne Divisions continued to be used as ordinary infantry in the battle for the toe of Italy until they were sent back to Britain for the Normandy invasion, the Swing Board deliberated upon the future of the airborne arm. They came up with some very practical ideas, such as the use of a specialized parachute pathfinder unit which would jump before the main body of a para-attack and would guide the transports' pilots to the DZ with beacons, radios and the like. They also made suggestions for the improved training of transport pilots and their ability to navigate accurately, but all the time the Swing Board knew that the days of large-scale parachute operations could well be numbered.

Then, on the other side of the world, a US general more dashing, flamboyant and arrogant than ten Pattons took a hand in the game and changed the balance in favour of large-scale airborne operations once more. The general was possessed by a paranoia that was almost certifiable. Although he was immensely proud of his Scots heritage and was praised by Churchill, Montgomery and Sir Alan Brooke − 'the greatest general and the best strategist the war has produced' − he hated the British as he did all Europeans. He was tremendously brave, winning 22 medals for bravery and risking death on the battlefield in Korea when he was seventy, yet his troops called him 'Dugout Dug'. A mother's boy, who was scared of his mother even when he was a five-star general, he kept a beautiful Eurasian mistress for years between his two marriages. As someone said of this flamboyant general-politician, you 'either admire him or dislike him. You are never neutral on the subject'.

The general in question was General Douglas MacArthur, now the Allied Supreme Commander in the Pacific, where, from his base in Australia, he was now beginning to 'island hop', striking back at the circle of islands which the Japanese had captured at the start of the Pacific war. By holding these islands the Japanese hoped to wear the Americans and their Australian allies down and prevent the war, especially the aerial war, ever reaching the Japanese homeland.

Now, in early September, 1943, he wanted to retake airstrips in the captured Australian possession of New Guinea. From here MacArthur reasoned, he could base his bombers and fighters to speed up the next stage of his drive to Japan. MacArthur planned to drop 1,700 American parachutists in the Markham Valley near to the town of Lae. The valley was one of the few spots in Northern New Guinea where airstrips could be built quickly and easily. But speed was of the essence if MacArthur was going capture it before the Japanese counter-attacked in strength. To ensure that his men had the kind of heavy artillery support that Ridgway's paratroopers had lacked in Sicily, MacArthur recruited a troop of the 2/4 Australian Field Artillery Regiment.

These men were trained as parachutists within forty-eight hours, while means were devised to carry their stripped-down 25-pounder guns underneath the transports, a new technique which would be adopted by all airborne forces over the next few years.

The airborne attack on the remote, rain-sodden Pacific island would not have excited any comment and certainly would not have swayed US official opinion in favour of retaining large-scale airborne forces save for one thing: *the Supreme Commander suddenly decided to go along with the paratroopers*! It was as if Eisenhower had accompanied Gavin's men to Sicily or Montgomery had gone along with the gliderforce bound for the Ponte Grande bridge.

On the evening before the drop General Kenney, MacArthur's chief of the air force, told his superior that he was going to fly out with the paratroopers. 'They are my kids,' he said, 'and I want to see them do their stuff.'

MacArthur thought for a few moments then he said, 'You're right, George. *We'll both go.*'

George Kenney nearly had a heart attack. The Supreme Commander in the Pacific, the man who was virtually the dictator of all Allied forces in the area, was going to risk his neck over enemy territory during a combat drop. It was unthinkable.

Kenney told him that it would be foolish to risk the life of the Commander-in-Chief, 'having some five-dollar-a-month Jap aviator shoot a hole through you'.

MacArthur was adamant. He shook his head and said, 'I'm not worried about getting shot. Honestly, the only thing that disturbs me is the possibility that when we hit rough air over the mountains my stomach might get upset. I'd hate to throw up and disgrace myself in front of the kids.'

MacArthur continued that it would be the first taste of combat for the paratroopers and he said he wanted to 'give them such comfort as my presence might mean to them'.

So it was done. MacArthur joined the paratroopers for the first mass US combat jump against the Japanese. As the men fell in to board the transports, Kenney remembered MacArthur, wearing sunglasses and puffing his corncob pipe, his trademarks just as much as Montgomery's black beret, 'walking along the line, stopping occasionally to chat with some of them and wish them luck. They all seemed glad to see him and somehow had found out that he would be watching the jump.'

Minutes later MacArthur, the most important Allied officer in the whole of the Pacific, took off on the long journey from Australia to New Guinea in the lead Flying Fortress. He didn't throw up. Neither did he allow the worried pilot to turn back when one of his engines failed. 'Carry on,' he ordered. 'I've been with General Kenney when engines quit and I know the B-17 flies almost as well on three engines as it does on four.'

In due course the airborne regiment landed safely directly on the DZ and set about capturing their objectives. Highly pleased with himself, MacArthur returned to his Headquarters and wired his young wife Jean, 'It was a honey'.

MacArthur disliked, even distrusted, the Press. Correspondents' dispatches were censored if they were thought to be unfavourable to the person of the Supreme Commander. But he made quite sure that the 'folks back home' knew that the man the troops called 'Dugout Dug' had actually flown into action with the paratroopers. As always he had a keen eye for publicity. So the gentlemen of the Press were given detailed information of the heroic exploits of the Supreme Commander, while in New Guinea the paratroopers in their foxholes under Japanese fire were singing to the tune of 'The Battle Hymn of the Republic',

'Mine eyes have seen MacArthur with a Bible on his knee.
He is pounding out communiqués for guys like you and me.

Ending with:

'And while possibly a rumor now,
Some day 'twill be a fact
That the Lord will hear a deep voice say
Move over, God, it's Mac.'

But nobody in the States had any inkling of their boys' attitude to Douglas MacArthur, whose communiqués, with few exceptions, were always about MacArthur. What they learned from the Press was that the Supreme Commander had actually flown a mission with his troops. Ninety-six transports had dropped 1,700 paratroops, *successfully*, with few casualties, against a surprised Japanese opposition. Within twenty-four hours the engineers they had brought with them were busy building the first of the fighter strips ready for the next action against the Japs.*

---

* A year later, when the same regiment dropped on an island just off the coast of New Guinea, the drop became another Sicily. The navigators of the transports panicked when they came under fire at Noemfoor Island. They dropped their troops too low, causing many casualties and, just as was the case in Sicily, the third wave of paratroopers was dropped into the sea.

The publicity given to the successful drop in the Markham Valley, New Guinea, swung the balance in favour of retaining divisional-size airborne forces. The 'Swing Board' proposed a few more reforms in the practice of large-scale drops and then quietly wound itself up.

The bitter cost of the airborne assault on Sicily was swiftly forgotten. In due course the two divisions which had suffered so greatly in the second week of July, 1943, were sent back to Britain to prepare for further large-scale parachute operations, three in all, over a period of nine months. In time there would be whole airborne corps, both in the British and American armies. Eighteen months after the disaster in Sicily, General Ridgway, now commander of the US XVII Corps, would have four whole parachute divisions under his command, his old 82nd, plus the 101st, 13th and 17th Parachute Divisions.

In the future there would be mass drops such as the three-divisional one in Normandy, with perhaps thirty per cent casualties, or the two-divisional one over the Rhine, that would result in thirty-five per cent casualties. And, of course, there would be that much more celebrated 'Bridge Too Far' at Arnhem, where those brave officers and men who had succeeded in saving themselves at the Primosole Bridge finally succumbed to the SS.

There a whole airborne division, the 1st Airborne, was decimated. Perhaps only one in ten of the young men in red berets who had set out so bravely nine days before returned beaten to their own lines. The lessons of Sicily the year before had remained unlearnt, and the Red Devils, cheerful, defiant, brave to the very last, paid the butcher's bill. They always did.

V

ENVOI

Soldier, rest! thy warfare o'er,
  Sleep the sleep that knows no breaking,
Dream of battled fields no more,
  Days of danger, nights of waking.
                              Sir Walter Scott

Today there is little to be seen in Sicily for the devotion and self-sacrifice of those young men of fifty years ago. Mount Etna broods over the two British cemeteries containing the dead of Montgomery's Eighth Army, and on a small hillside near Agira there is the Canadian cemetery. But the American dead are long gone. All 2,440 who died on the island were transferred to an American war cemetery on the Gulf of Salerno four decades ago.

The invasion beaches, such as Licata and Gela, have been transformed into holiday complexes for sun-starved North Europeans, and barefoot kids who once accosted Allied soldiers for *caramelli* and 'cigarettes for Papa' are now middle-aged prosperous hoteliers and store-owners. The *autostrada* runs through what was once a bloody battlefield and those bridges, which for a week or so seemed the most important in the world, have vanished. All that remains to remind the curious visitor that once young men fought and died here are the old, abandoned farmhouses, the shrapnel marks pocking their stone walls, and that bold slogan which made Gavin's young men laugh: '*Live Dangerously*'.

Like all the other conquerors who had come to Sicily over the centuries – Greeks, Romans, Arabs, Crusaders, Normans, Germans – the Anglo-American victors came, stayed a few years and then departed, leaving the native Sicilians, as always, iron-willed, insular, and mistrustful of anyone but their own kind. With one exception.

Today there is one legacy of the American invaders of 1943 which has flourished, gained in strength and prospered mightily over the years. It is a sombre, enduring part of the native Sicilian's life. Those smiling shopkeepers in Palermo who sing snatches of Puccini as they hand over the groceries; the little kids who offer 'to look after your car, mister'; the youths on the motor scooters with their 'shades' and brilliant smiles and gold neckchains are all part and parcel of the Matia and Mafia-linked crimes.*

Back in 1943 we Anglo-Americans came to Sicily to bring the islanders freedom. What we really brought was a new fascism, that of the Mafia. That is what, ironically enough, the Red Berets, the All-Americans and all the rest of those brave young men died for.

* On the day this was written, February 28/29, 1992, a Mafia bomb destroyed a new police station at Tortoeici, near Messina, while in a town nearby a fire burnt the shop of an ironmonger who refused to pay protection. In 24 hours there were five Mafia killings.

SOURCES

I. *The War in the Shadows*
Obituaries —*Daily Telegraph* and *The Times*, November, 1991.
C. Whiting: *Canaris*, Ballantine, New York, 1974.
A. Cave-Brown: *Bodyguard of Lies*, Comet, London, 1987.
Edited: *After the Battle*, No. 16.
C. D'Este: *Bitter Victory*, Fontana, London, 1988.
J. Wolf and J DiMona: *Frank Costello*, Hodder & Stoughton, London, 1974.
D. Mure: *The Phantom Army*, Sphere, London, 1977.
R. Campbell: *The Luciano Project*, McGraw-Hill, New York, 1977.
T. Waldron and J. Gleeson: *The Frogmen*, Evans Bros., London, 1954.
D. Strutton and M. Pearson: *The Secret Invaders*, Hodder & Stoughton, London, 1958.
The Denver Post, 13 October, 1991.
John Kennedy and the Nazi Spy, Home Video, New York, 1991.

II. *THE GREAT PLAN*
L. Thompson: *The All Americans*, David and Charles, Newton Abbott, 1976.
G. Devlin: *Paratrooper*, St Martin's Press, New York, 1979.
'Rags' Lathouwers: *A Fighting Heart*, Ted Davis, Fayetteville, N. Carolina, 1949.
82nd Airborne Division in Sicily, and Italy, After Action Report, 1945.
P. Stainforth: *Kings of the Wild*, Grafton, London, 1988.
E. Hoyt: *Airborne*, Stein and Day, New York, 1979.
C. Blair: *Ridgway's Paratroopers*, Dial Press, Garden City, New York, 1985.
W. Breuer: *Geronimo*, St Martin's Press, New York, 1989.
B. Biggs: *Gavin*, Archon Books, New York, 1980.

M. Dank: *The Glider Gang*, Lippincott, Philadelphia, 1977.

J. Frost: *A Drop Too Many,* Buchan & Enright, London, 1982.

J. Gavin, *On To Berlin*, Bantam, New York, 1978.

J. James: *A Fierce Quality*, Leo Cooper, London, 1990.

III. *SLAUGHTER OVER SICILY*

W. Breuer: *Drop Zone Sicily*, Jove, New York, 1985.

M. Poeppel: *Heaven and Hell*, Spellmount, Tunbridge Wells, 1988.

M. Blumenson: *Sicily: Whose Victory?* Ballantine Illustrated War History, Pan, London, 1969.

R. Carter: *Those Devils in Baggy Pants*, Signet, New York, 1951.

C. Whiting: *Hunters From the Sky*, Leo Cooper, London, 1975.

J. Mrazek: *The Glider War*, Hale, London, 1975.

M. Ridgway: *Soldier*, Harper, New York, 1956.

IV. *END RUN*

Hilary St George Saunders: *The Green Beret*, Four Square, London, 1949.

W. Manchester: *American Caesar*, Hutchinson, London, 1979.

Daily Telegraph, July 1943.

N. Hamilton: *Montgomery*, Coronet, London, 1983.

Garland and Smyth: *Mediterranean Theater of Operations*, Department of the Army, Washington, 1963.

S. E. Morison: *Sicily — Salerno — Anzio*, Little Brown, Boston.

A. B. Cunningham: *A Sailor's Odyssey*, Hutchinson, London, 1960.

INDEX

Adonis, Joe, 39, 40
Agnone, Bay of, 141
Alden, Surgeon D. Carlos, 85
Alexander, General Sir Harold, 43, 63, 165
Alexander, Major, 108
Alfieri, Lt. Paul, 41
Allenby, General Sir Edmund, 25
Anapo Canal, 79
Andrews, Sgt. Andy, 91, 118
Antonopolous, Sgt, 77-9
Ashbourne, Lord, 101
Atwood, Sgt. Percy, 75

Baillie, Hugh, 114
Ballinger, Major, RE, 102
Bellstedt, Oberleutnant, 47
Berney-Ficklin, General, 116
Biazza Ridge, 119, 120, 125-9
Blair, Machinist Mate Hubert, 130
Bradley, General Omar, 61, 125
Brand, Seaman, 14-16
Brittain, Cdr. T.B., 50
Brooke, General Sir Alan, 21, 22, 35
Brown, Sgt. Nigel, 75, 77
Browning, Brigadier 'Boy', 56, 61; arrogance, 68; refuses to reassure Ridgway, 127; 164-5
Bryant, Cdr. Ben, 13, 14
Burbridge, Capt., 12, 13
Buzzard, Operation, 73-82

Canaris, Admiral, 34, 44
Canoe, Sergeant Buffalo Boy, 109
Carter, Sgt. Ross, 108, 129
Cartland, Barbara, 58
Casablanca Conference, 19-23
Castellammare, Gulf of, 14
Chatterton, Colonel George: and founding of Glider Pilot Regiment, 57; briefed by Hopkinson, 65-66; asks for U.S. aid, 69-70; and Operation Buzzard, 74; recce over Sicily, 79; misgivings over plans, 80, 89, 90; leaves for Sicily, 97; lands, 100; post mortem, 162
Chenfalls, Alfred, 46-8
Chicago Tribune, 111, 122

Cholmondeley, Sqn. Ldr. Sir Archibald, 27n, 29
Churchill, Colonel Tom, 143
Churchill, Winston: at Casablanca, 19; in Gibraltar, 45-7
Clark, Colonel Hal, 83
Clarke, Colonel, 161
Clarke, Brigadier Dudley, 48
Clee, Major Robert, 108
Clements, Jock, 155, 158
Colossus, Operation, 54
Conway, Major, 77
Cooper, Lt., 9, 10, 13
Cooper, Major Alisdair, 75, 76
Costello, Frank, 39
Cota, General, 89
Crusade in Europe, 72
Cunningham, Admiral A.B., 30, 71, 98, 164
Currie, Brigadier, 160

Daily Telegraph, 124
Daly, Lt., 56
Dansey, Captain Claude, 24
Deane-Drummond, Lt. Anthony, 54-6
de Guingand, Major-General Francis, 119
Dempsey, General Sir Miles, 141, 142, 153
Denholm, Captain, 102
Dewey, Thomas, 38, 40
Doenitz, Admiral, 36, 43
Dunn, Colonel Ray, 69, 79, 83, 86, 98, 99, 119
Durham Light Infantry, 151, 155, 156, 157, 158, 159
Durnford-Slater, Colonel John, 141-3, 149, 152

East Yorkshire Regiment, 151
Eden, Anthony, 44; visits Gavin, 62
Eisenhower, General Dwight: at Casablanca, 23; and Anglo-American relations, 68; and Ultra, 87; with Cunningham in Malta, 98; 114; suspends airborne operations, 164

Fejos, Inga, 36
Fine, Flight Officer Samuel, 105, 117, 118
Flynn, Sgt. Harry, 75

Foggia, 53
Follmer, Captain, 110
Freeman, Sgt. Harold, 109
Freyberg, General Bernard, 82
Frost, Colonel John; commands 2nd Para Bn,
    86; plans flight to Sicily, 138; landing, 147;
    takes 'Johnny 1', 151; 156; post mortem,
    163
Fustian, Operation, 138

Gairdner, Maj-General Charles, 23
Galpin, Staff Sgt, 102
Gammon, Capt, 154
Garrett, Sgt, 146
Gavin, Colonel James: background, 59-60;
    commands 505th Para Regt, 61; sacks
    Gray, 81; 83,91; message to troops, 92;
    flight to Sicily, 107; encounters enemy,
    112; and Colonel Krause, 119; at Biazza
    Ridge, 119-22; wounded, 125; post
    mortem, 163
Gela, 64,73,83,87,88,119
Goebbels, Josef, 49
Gorham, Colonel Arthur, 111,112
Gornalunga River, 134
Gray, Colonel James, 81
Green Howards, 151
Guzzoni, General Alfredo, 49,113,114,124

Hackett, Brigadier 'Shan', 91,101
Haffenden, Lt-Cdr Charles, 37,39
Hagen, Major Walter, 121-2
Hale, Gunner 'Sunny', 124
Hall, Sergeant, 77
Heidrich, General Richard, 133
Heilmann, Lt-Col Ludwig, 133-4
Henniker, Colonel Mark, 118
Herbert, Lt, 149
Hewitt, Admiral Kent, 72
Hicks, Brigadier 'Pip': commands 1st Air
    Landing Brigade, 65; 70,83,89,97,119
Hoare, Sir Samuel, 33
Hodge, Captain Vere, 151
Hopkinson, General 'Hoppy': commands 1st
    Airborne Div., 58,64; briefs Chatterton,
    65; 83; ditches, 101; post mortem, 163
Howard, Leslie, 47-8
Hunter, Major David, 138
Husky, Operation, 23,63

Ireland, Captain Al, 92,121,122,125,127
Irvine, Seaman, 13

Jackson, Colonel C.I.A., 53
Jenks, Staff Sergeant Gordon, 73-6

Jewell, Cdr. N.L., 31
Jones, Colonel 'Jonah', 103,104

Kairouan, 77,83,85
Kaufmann, Captain Robert, 110
Keenens, Brigadier 'Bull', 66,81,84,123,128
Kennedy, Lt John F., 37
Kenney, General George, 168-9
Keren, HMS, 101
Kesselring, Field-Marshal Albert, 49,124,131
King, Admiral, 20,36
Kirkman, General, 140,144,156,160
Koch, Colonel, 88
Krause, Colonel, 119

Ladbroke, Operation, 65,83,97,119
Lansky, 'Little Man', 39
Lanza, Joseph 'Socks', 37,39
Lathbury, Brigadier Gerald: commands 1st
    Para Bde, 84; leaves for Sicily, 138; 148;
    wounded, 150
Laun, Captain, 140
Lee, Major William, 59-60
Lentini, 140,141
Lewis, Colonel Harry, 66-8,131
Lidwell, Colonel, 158,160
Lord, RSM John, 84
Lucas, General John P., 165,166
Luciano, Charles 'Lucky', 38

MacArthur, General Douglas, 167-8
MacFall, Captain, 40
MacFarlane, General Mason, 27n,46
McGrigor, Admiral, 141
McIntyre, Admiral, 19
Macmillan, Harold, 20
McNair, General Lesley, 166
Manser, 'Panzer', 153,158
Marshall, General: at Casablanca, 20,22; and
    Ultra, 87; signal to Eisenhower, 98; 166,167
Martin, Major, 30-4
Mauritius, HMS, 151
May, Wing Cdr Peter, 97,99
Meinertzhagen, Colonel, 25-6
Menzies, General Stewart, 35
Messina, 84
Middleton, General Troy, 125
Mincemeat, Operation, 27-34
Mitchison, Sgt, 159
Monrovia, 55,50,88
Montagu, Lt-Cdr Ewen, 27-31
Montgomery, General Sir Bernard: at
    Casablanca, 23; rejects plans for Husky,
    63; in Sicily, 161; post mortem, 165
Moore, Sgt, 146

Moran, Lord, 19
Moreno-Fernandez, Salvador, 33
Mountbatten, Lord Louis, 30-1
Murray, Major, 137

Normandie, 36
Northamptonshire Regt, 2nd Bn, 118
Norton, Captain John, 109
Nye, General Sir Archibald, 43

Parsons, Capt Edward, 13
Passero, Cape, 97
Patch, General, 89
Patton, General George S.: at Casablanca,
    23; on *Monrovia*, 50; attitude to
    Montgomery, 63; organizes
    reinforcements, 123; witnesses 'friendly
    fire', 129; 163
Pearson, Colonel Alastair: commands 1st
    Para Bn, 86; 137; at Primosole,
    145,152-3,155; plan to capture bridge,
    157-8; invalided, 161
Peate, Commander, 142
Piano Lupo, 119
Poeppell, Lt Martin, 139,148,156
Ponte dei Malati, 141,149
Ponte Grande, 65,103,105,116,127
Primosole Bridge,
    84,135,137,140,146,160,161
Prince Albert, 141,142
Pritchard, Major T.A.G., 55-6
Punta de Umbria, 32
Purchase, Bentley, 28-9
Pye, Admiral William, 24

Quayle, Anthony, 45

Rann, Captain, 150
Ridgway, General Matt, 61,66; disciplined
    by Eisenhower, 68-9; falls out with
    Cunningham, 70-1; in Sicily, 110-11;
    organizes reinforcements, 123; seeks
    reassurance from Browning, 127-8;
    witnesses 'friendly fire', 129; post mortem,
    165
Robert Rowan, 125
Rommel, General Erwin, 45
Roosevelt, President F.D.: at Casablanca,
    19,20; 166
Royal Scots Fusiliers, 2nd Bn, 118
Ruff, Colonel, 67

Safari, HMS, 12,14

Salé, 74,76,77
Sayre, Captain Edwin, 112
Schmidt, Major, 139-140
Sciacca, 13
Sele, River, 55
Seraph, HMS, 31-3
Shaker, Lt Kenneth, 85
Shirer, William, 45
Simeto River, 134,138,146
Smith, Lt Bob, 14,16
Smith, General Walter Bedell, 64
South Staffordshire Regt., 79,102,105,146
Spaatz, General Carl, 164
Spilsbury, Sir Bernard, 27-8
Stainforth, Lt Peter, 87,138,147,150,154-5
Stevens, Capt John, 14
Student, General Kurt, 82,133
Swing Board, 167,169
Syracuse, 97,117

Talamba, 124
Taylor, General Maxwell, 131
Teacher, Lt-Cdr, 9,11
Tedder, ACM Lord, 23,164
Thayer, Cdr Robert, 41
Thomas, 1st Lt F.E., 111
Thompson, 'Beaver', 111,122
Tito, Marshal, 49
Tragino, R., 53
Tregaskis, Richard, 114
Tucker, Col. Reuben,
    62,67,71,80,83,123,131

Unbending, HMS, 10,13
United, HMS, 12,15
Unrivalled, HMS, 12,14
Unruffled, HMS, 14

Vandervoort, Captain Ben, 112,113
Vizzini, Don Calogero, 40,41

Wedemeyer, General Albert, 22-3
Weschler, Lt, 120
Wilkinson, Squadron Leader, 74
Williams, Brigadier-General Paul, 164
Willmott, Lt-Cdr, 11
Wilson, Flight Officer Bob, 70,90,100
Withers, Lt Lawrence, 102,105,116

Yank, 130
Yardley, Colonel Doyle, 68
Yeldham, Colonel, 138,139,146
Young, Captain Peter, 143,149,150